English Renaissance Drama

ESSAYS IN HONOR OF

Madeleine Doran & Mark Eccles

EDITED BY STANDISH HENNING, ROBERT KIMBROUGH, RICHARD KNOWLES

Southern Illinois University Press : Carbondale and Edwardsville

Feffer & Simons, Inc. : London and Amsterdam

Library of Congress Cataloging in Publication Data

Main entry under title:

English Renaissance drama.

"A selected bibliography of works by Madeleine
Doran": p.
"A selected bibliography of works by Mark Eccles": p.
Bibliography: p.
Includes index.
CONTENTS: Harbage, A. Copper into gold.—Hunter,
G. K. Were there act-pauses on Shakespeare's stage?—
Beckerman, B. Shakespeare and the life of the scene.
[etc.]
1. English drama—17th century—History and criticism
—Addresses, essays, lectures. 2. English drama—Early
modern and Elizabethan, 1500–1600—History and
criticism—Addresses, essays, lectures. 3. Doran,
Madeleine, 1905– 4. Eccles, Mark.
PR653.E69 1976   822'.3'09   76–18907

ISBN 0–8093–0777–4

Contents

Preface

Madeleine Doran and Mark Eccles came to the University of Wisconsin within one year of each other in the early 1930s and retired from the classroom within one year of each other, in 1975 and 1976. For some forty years they have enhanced a department uncommonly rich in Renaissance scholars, and though they now no longer lecture daily in Madison, they will continue to teach us as only they can.

In more ways than one this collection illustrates the Elizabethan "figure of quick conceite," by letting the part stand for the whole. The authors of these essays are only a few of the many who must count themselves the students of Professor Doran and Professor Eccles; everyone studying the English Renaissance drama in the middle of the twentieth century has learned and profited from their indispensable work. Moreover, though the range of subjects treated here is wide, it represents only a few of the literary interests of these two scholars whose published work embraces textual studies, editing, linguistics, stylistics and imagery study, iconography, critical theory, literary history, biography, and purely dramatic criticism— to say nothing of original poems and familiar essays, reviews, and surveys of scholarship.

The essays which follow have been arranged in roughly chronological order: Harbage sets the immediate pre-Shakespearean scene, and Hunter, Beckerman, and Ackrigg discuss ideas which range through Shakespeare; Leech, Webber, Whitaker, and Bullough are concerned with separate Shakespeare plays; and, Charney providing a transition through Shakespeare, Ornstein, Barish, and Waith move on to Jacobean drama.

The late Robert K. Presson, Professor of English in this University from 1949 to 1974, did most of the earliest planning for this book. It would have pleased him, as it does his collaborators, to present it as an envoy of the respect, gratitude, and affection felt for Madeleine Doran and Mark Eccles here and in the wide community of minds wherever English Renaissance drama is studied and enjoyed.

S. H.
R. K.
R. K.

Madison, Wisconsin
December 1975

List of Contributors

G. P. V. Akrigg is Professor of English at the University of British Columbia.

Jonas A. Barish is Professor of English at the University of California-Berkeley.

Bernard Beckerman is Professor of Dramatic Arts at Columbia University.

Geoffrey Bullough is Emeritus Professor of English Language and Literature at the University of London.

Maurice M. Charney is Distinguished Professor of English at Rutgers University.

Alfred B. Harbage is Cabot Professor Emeritus of English at Harvard University.

George K. Hunter is Professor of English at the University of Warwick.

Clifford Leech, formerly Professor of English at the University of Toronto.

Robert Ornstein is Professor of English at Case-Western Reserve University.

Eugene M. Waith is Professor of English at Yale University.

Joan Webber is Professor of English at the University of Washington.

Virgil Keeble Whitaker is Sadie Dernham Patek Professor Emeritus of Humanities (English) at Stanford University.

English Renaissance Drama

ALFRED HARBAGE

Copper into Gold

*T*HE SUN which touched literature to gold in
the last decades of the sixteenth century distributed its rays capriciously,
and the drama might well have remained an occluded area. Sidney was
gloomy, not without cause, as he viewed the piebald dawn, "our Tragedies
and Comedies . . . observing rules neyther of honest civilitie nor of skilfull
Poetrie." Then emerged the tragedies and comedies, histories and pastorals,
and tragical-comical-historical-pastorals which, like the actors performing
them, were "the best in the world." Since the change in the quality of plays
resembles a transmutation, an alchemy-metaphor serves better than a
solar-metaphor to suggest the means by which it was, in part, effected. The
present essay will treat an economic phenomenon which occurred in the
1570s, the decade preceding the golden age of English drama. An
alternative title, cunningly alliterative, would be "Pennies into Poetry."

What the drama needed when Elizabeth ascended the throne was not the
observance of old "rules" but the enlistment of new talents. This was the
case with literature generally. Spenser's Cuddie, "the perfecte paterne of a
Poete," laments that he "little good hath got, and much less gayne."
Incentive to becoming an author was minimal when authorship seldom
offered even a bare subsistence. There were three groups to which writers
could look for monetary reward: patrons, stationers, actors. When Sidney
and Spenser voiced their complaints, 1579–81, the actors had just moved
from the tail to the head of the list; that is, they had just established the
means for rewarding authorship on a more substantial scale than prevailed
among publishers and patrons. In the following decades the actors paid
more to persons with literary talent than did others, and—witness the
preeminence of drama in the literary accomplishment of the age—they
received more in return.

To supply a reasonably lucrative market for playscripts (not disinter-
estedly to be sure), the actors had first to win prolonged access to large

numbers of paying spectators. They had to establish themselves in a center of population like London, where they could extend the number of playing days a week and the number of playing weeks a year, encouraging in the process investment in stage-*cum*-auditorium facilities. During the first decade of Elizabeth's reign London was only another stop on the tours of the strollers. So far as we can discern, no company of adult actors was based in or near the metropolis. The band of court interluders inherited from the preceding reign was perishing of senescence. The surviving members continued to receive their stipends, and to organize a few provincial tours, but they performed no play at Court after 1559 and could have made no more than sporadic London appearances. Only one member was still alive in 1569. The companies playing at Court provide, until the very end of the era, the best index of the companies playing other than transiently in London; and Court performances in the sixties were mainly by the chapel and grammar school boys of St. Paul's, Whitehall, Windsor, and Westminster.

There is neither space nor need here for discussion of the amateur and semiprofessional groups presided over by chapelmasters and schoolmasters. They were in a sense resident companies, since they sometimes performed before paying spectators in halls in or near the city. However, they never attracted a general public, or stabilized themselves financially. The history of those which went most thoroughly "professional" is a history of economic failure. Obviously they never acquired the resources to offer an open and active market to playwrights. As to their repertory, the one surviving early sample of it, Richard Edwards's *Damon and Pythias* (1565), together with the titles of lost plays, indicate a leaning to classical subject matter, and aspiration to consideration as art. The latest and best samples, the plays of John Lyly, are far from contemptible, but they are also far from suggesting endless possibilities of future development. Shakespeare took instruction from them, as from much else, but Lyly had better be considered a successor of Edwards than a predecessor of Shakespeare; his plays terminate rather than initiate a trend. The most interesting thing about chorister drama in the present context is its dominance of Court entertainment in the sixties, its waning in the seventies and eighties, and its complete absence in the nineties. What happened at Court recapitulates what happened in London: the men forced the boys to bow out.

Although the offerings of the men in the sixties seem to have been deemed old-fashioned and infra-literary, associated in the minds of the cultivated with balladry and wayside gymnastics, this homely fare, casually purveyed, was available to any who relished it. Dozens of acting troupes were on the road, with as many as eight a year visiting towns like Coventry, only a fraction the size of London. London with its suburbs already sheltered over a hundred and twenty-five thousand souls, seven times as many as its closest rivals, York, Bristol, and Norwich. Moreover, it was the most accessible of all cities by river and road, and was surrounded by the area most finely crisscrossed by the tracks of the strollers. A cordon of pickets could not have kept them out of it. There were, in fact, no laws in the sixties, including the series of acts in restraint of rogues, vagabonds, and loitering people, which would exclude a troupe, providing one of its members bore a certificate, however old and tattered, affirming that he was the retainer of some lord, knight, or gentleman. Except in time of plague, the strollers had the same right to seek hospitality and to exercise their mystery in a private London dwelling as in any manor house in the shires, and the civic authorities at their most hostile never contested this right. Acting publicly was a different matter since in London, as elsewhere, the time and place of performance were at the discretion of the authorities. However, it was hard to tell where London began and ended.

As representatives of the livery companies, the mayor and aldermen exercised a kind of rule over the whole area, but their firm jurisdiction failed to embrace certain intramural "liberties," as well as Westminster and the suburbs and adjacent hamlets in Middlesex and Surrey. Even in their own indisputable territory rulings were hard to enforce in the absence of a regular police force. There would always be a scolding Dogberry, but the apprentices would rarely raise the cry of clubs against anything so peaceful in intent as a troupe of players. It might make purely local arrangements, say by contributing part of its take to the rates for the deserving poor, or to a parish officer deserving and poor in his own right, and then move on before serious questions could be put from above. Or it might post its bills, and sound drum and trumpet in the city proper, but stage its plays at a carrier inn on one of the arterial highways outside the gates. Authority if sought would be obtained from a county justice.

An amorphous "theatre" was available in London before any structure so-called existed. Its nature is defined by a city precept of 1569 forbidding summer playing in any "mansion howse, yarde, court, garden, orchard, or other place or places whatsoeuer, within this Cittye of London, the liberties or suburbes of the same," including the premises of "Inkepers, Tablekepers, Tauernours, hall-kepers, or bruers." [1] In the conywarren of tenements and enclosures were many places, indoors and out, where plank stages could be set up and entrance-pennies collected. The Saracen's Head Inn at Islington and the Boar's Head Inn without Aldgate were in use for plays before Elizabeth's accession. In the sixties the "hall-keper" of St. Botolph's Church without Aldgate was renting its Trinity Hall to the players for a shilling a performance, about fourteen times a year.[2] It was small, but well-located, just beyond the city gate near Whitechapel Road. A mile further east at Stepney the Red Lion Inn was fitted with scaffolds for playgoers in 1567. Just past the western city line on Fleet Street, the Bel Savage Inn was in use by players in the seventies, and had been for some time. The same is true of the Cross Keys, the Bull, and the Bell inns, ideally located along Gracechurch-Bishopsgate Street, which bisected the city in crossing from Shoreditch to London Bridge. A mile south of the Bridge at Newington a playing place existed in 1580. The pitch was probably traditional. We run small risk in hypothesizing such places on the great northern road through Shoreditch before the first "regular" theaters were built there.

With no lack of visiting troupes, or of *ad hoc* facilities for their performances, the question must rise of why civic opposition to the players did not become energetic and vocal in the sixties instead of the seventies. The answer must be that it was not until the seventies that their activity seemed formidable. Before then the strollers were truly strollers, their home base elsewhere if anywhere, their raids brief if numerous, and their audiences fairly small. The typical troupe would have been content with small gains. Provincial towns regularly limited the number of performances lest too much money be taken out of the community, and so long as only a few performances could be offered at each pitch, only a few plays would suffice for a repertory. To become a fixture in London was beyond the resources and hopes of the troupes through the sixties. The attitude of the authorities grew from annoyance to consternation when the exploitation of London ceased to be disorganized and diffuse.

The conquest was effected by troupes which were exceptionally able and vigorous. Their spearhead was one which claimed as its patron Robert Dudley, Earl of Leicester. Dudley's players had figured among the few adult troupes appearing at Court during the dominance of the choristers. For three consecutive Christmas seasons, from 1560 to 1562–63, they had been chosen along with the Paul's and the Chapel boys to present plays to the Queen. Since this was the warmest season in the long period of Elizabeth's affection for Dudley, their election is not surprising; however, if *Cambises* was actually theirs, played as "Huff, Suff, and Ruff" at Court, they had a true claim to favor. This "Lamentable Tragedie mixed full of pleasant mirth" would seem quaint by 1597 when Falstaff offered to grieve in its vein, and it seems primitive indeed to us now, but it was phenomenal in 1560, effecting a break with the didactic and farcical interludes which had prevailed in the popular repertories. Ten years later most of the plays shown at Court and in London by the adult companies would be similarly filled with arresting deeds and strong passions. The rifling of history and pseudohistory, of romances and novellas, had begun. What was needed were poets who could supply language adequate to the deeds and passions.

In 1572 the right to tour with plays was denied to all but the household servants of barons of the realm and persons of "greater Degree." [3] The effect if not intention of the statute was to strengthen the actors, since it forced them to regroup into fewer and better companies. Leicester's Men promptly wrote to their patron, requesting him that he would now retain them as his "daylie wayters"—

not that we meane to crave any further stipend or benefite at your Lordshippes hands but our lyveries as we have had, and also your honors License to certifye that we are your houshold Servaunts when we shall have occasion to travayle amongst our frendes as we do usuallye once a yere.[4]

The wording is amusingly deferential to certain proprieties: their yearly "occasion to travayle" could stretch into months, and their "frendes" were any group of people willing to drop pennies in the gatherer's box. Their lord supplied no "stipend." The petition was signed by the six members of the company, including James Burbage, father of Richard and first builder of the kind of theater in which Richard would star, and also Robert Wilson, famous for his "quick extemporall wit" and destined to be one of the hardiest perennials of the actor-playwright species. There is a concluding blessing:

> Long may your Lordshippe live in peace,
> A pere of noblest peres:
> In helth welth and prosperitie
> Redoubling Nestor's yeres.

This was the ballad measure of *Cambises* and much of the rest of the popular drama. Probably Wilson was not the only one in the group who could turn it out; the old "fourteeners," as Dr. Johnson would one day aver, practically wrote themselves.

Leicester's Men appeared at Court three times in 1572–73 and three times in 1573–74, receiving beside the standard fee of £6 13s. 4d. for each performance a bonus of £10 "for a more rewarde by hir Ma^tes owne comaundem^t" and another of ten marks "by waye of speciall rewarde for theyre chardges cunyng and skill." [5] Clearly they were in favor. In May 1574, they received letters patent from the Queen authorizing them to perform "aswell for the recreacion of oure loving subiects, as for oure solace and pleasure when we shall thincke good to see them." Why the patent was issued when the company already held the enabling certificate of Leicester is indicated by one of its specific provisions—that it might play "aswell within oure Citie of London and liberties of the same" as in other parts of "oure Realme of England." [6] It was a shield against civic opposition. In this year the company had appeared at Court not only in the Christmas season but two months later at Shrovetide. The inference is that they had been playing in London in the interim, just as they must have been doing for some weeks prior to Christmas so that their plays would be ready for the trials conducted by the Office of the Revels. This means a London season for this company of three months at the least in 1573–74—by no means a touring visit.

The expansion of the Elizabethan theatrical "season" seems to have provoked among historians no explicit discussion, but it was of crucial importance in the proliferation of playscripts. The prime time for plays, the only proper time in the mind of the conservative, was the twelve days of Christmas from St. Stephen's Night to Twelfth Night. This focal period expanded forward and backward until it stretched from Allhallows to the pre-Lenten festivities of Shrovetide, with a renewal during the post-Lenten festivities of Eastertide. Thus the "normal" season became the six months from the beginning of November until the end of April, with an intermission in Lent. It was the time of year when assemblies of people were least apt to spread the infection of the ever-endemic plague. The playing at Court and in the chorister or "private" theaters pretty consistently confined itself to this season until the end. However, October and May seemed pleasant months for playing in innyards and open arenas, as did even September and June, until ultimately the adult professionals might play almost throughout the year, and even prove careless about observing Lent. Within seasons the number of playing days increased. Sunday performances were at first common, but the mounting number of spectators, wooed away from divine service, underlined the impropriety and additional weekday ones were substituted, until at least some companies were playing six afternoons a week. Holiday performances, scheduled so as not to conflict with the hours of common prayer, were banner occasions.

Leicester's was not the only company extending its London seasons and increasing its weekly number of playing days after 1572. Soon drawing abreast of it in the number of Court performances, including ones both at Christmas and Shrovetide suggesting prolonged London stands, were the companies of Warwick and Sussex. The identity of the patrons is instructive. Ambrose Dudley, Earl of Warwick, was Robert's elder brother and, like him, a member of the inner circle of the Queen's Privy Council. Thomas Radcliffe, third Earl of Sussex, was another such member and Lord

Chamberlain. It would seem that having a Privy Council member as patron was useful to any company aspiring to a stable existence in the metropolis. In April 1582 a letter requesting the removal of certain restrictions upon playing was sent to "our very Louing frende the Lord maior of the Citie of London." [7] Of the six members of the Privy Council who signed the letter five were the patrons of troupes, with one of them destined to become the patron of Shakespeare's in 1594. The patent of 1574 giving Leicester's Men royal sanction to play "within our Citie of London" would have conferred like privilege upon the players of the other Privy Council members, *de facto* if not *de jure.* All were touchy about their prerogatives, viewing a slight to their livery as a slight to themselves. When a fencer wearing the badge of Warwick was denied the right to perform for a prize in London, the Earl wrote a letter to the Lord Mayor, not as a Council member but as a sorrowing individual, the Mayor's "very louing frende." [8] The tone of that official's reply reminds us of the wary "love" of Mayor Astley for the Earl of Lincoln in Dekker's *Shoemakers' Holiday.*

The small group of men, usually under ten, who met in executive sessions to transact the business of the realm spent little time at their country estates; they were in constant attendance upon the Queen when not on missions in her service. The troupes wearing their badges were only theoretically based at their manors, just as they were only theoretically their "daylie wayters" and "houshold Servaunts." (Even the Queen's Men, organized in 1582, received no stipends.) Rather they were self-managed, self-financed, and usually self-organized London trading companies with Court credentials. The "lyveries" (dress uniforms) they received from their lords, and even the cash fees they received for Court performances, constituted only a fraction of their income. If we reckon with the income of the Master of the Revels, head of one of the departments under the Lord Chamberlain, we confront the startling fact that the Court took in more hard cash than it paid out, in consequence of the playacting of its "Servaunts." The master received fees for licensing all new plays and each week of performance in playhouses, so that his take finally rose to about £400 a year, that is four times the annual stipend of the Queen's elegant Gentlemen of the Privy Chamber. He was worth his cost to the players since the more plays the better from his point of view. When London officials sought the counsel of Archbishop Whitgift in 1592 on how the city might rid itself of players, he cannily advised them to provide an annuity for the Master of the Revels. The idea was canvassed but rejected, because of the cost, not because of moral scruples about bribery. After all, the players were bribing the Master with benefit performances.

To be sure, this Court official was not originally given his licensing power as a monetary plum. The Court simply lost patience with the delaying tactics of the City, which was inclined to use licensing power as a means of extirpating the drama rather than regulating it. When we ask, why the conflict in the first place, why the Court was *for* the players and the City *against* them, we find the cause a little more complex than Cavalier gaiety pitted against Puritan gloom. It is true that the Privy Council in its communications to the city fathers argued that plays contributed to Her Majesty's "solace" and players needed a chance to perfect themselves by practicing in public. It is also true that noblemen as a class were not antagonistic toward amusement, and the particular noblemen of the Council were not averse to having men in their liveries please the Queen and the public.

On the other hand they were not, as the more frivolous courtiers could have testified, fun-loving idlers. They were sober and hardworking politicians, coping daily with large problems of national security and small ones of social welfare, some of the latter so trifling that they would now be delegated to a clerk in a minor government agency. The fact is that their sponsorship of the players was in line with their general economic policy. They were well-disposed to new enterprise and inclined to support it with patents and grants of monopoly. We are so accustomed to thinking of the abuses of monopolies that we are apt to forget that the original intention in granting them was to combat stagnation by insuring rewards to persons with new ideas and a readiness to take risks. Although Leicester's company was not granted a monopoly in its patent of 1574, the gesture was in that direction. Two letters from the Privy Council to the Lord Mayor and the Surrey and Middlesex justices, dated in December 1578, require them to "suffer . . . to exercise playeng within the Cittie" this winter the Paul's and Chapel boys, and Leicester's, Warwick's, Sussex's, and Essex's men and *"no companies els."* [9] The Council members were not for a carnival community, far from it, but they were able to recognize that entertaining could be a legitimate business and that money in circulation could be a sign of wealth, not waste. It would be pleasant to think that they were interested in plays as art, but there is small indication of this, although some of them, including the Dudleys, were interested in promoting the graver forms of literature.

The civic opposition to the players also had an economic basis. It is true that it was colored by another kind of opposition, not specifically "Puritan" as usually alleged, but generally religious. What the Brownists, the most easily identifiable of the early Puritans, thought about the drama no one seems to care; probably they seldom thought about it at all. It was the establishment clergy, headed by Grindal, then Whitgift, who thought about it considerably and did not like its mounting vogue. It was a worldly thing, and beginning to make audiences outnumber congregations. We can pardon their failure to stress the fact that churchgoing was compulsory, at least in theory, and playgoing was not. We can even sympathize with their point of view: the neighborhood of St. Paul's might some day become as attractive to players as to stationers, and the Cathedral itself, after pupating as a bookstore, might spread the bright Satanic wings of a playhouse. The attacks by the preachers, White, Stockwood, Field, and by the pamphleteers, Fenton, Northbrooke, Gosson, Munday, Stubbes, were moralistic and religious in tone; but if we notice the moment at which they appeared during the London theatrical expansion of the seventies, and if we read between the lines, we must recognize that they were largely the verbal artillery of the municipal forces which viewed the playacting enterprise as an economic threat.

The opposition to the players was centered in the upper echelon of the burgess hierarchy, those members of the livery companies who had been most successful and who held the largest stake in civil order and a "stable" economy. These could not be expected to take the broad view of the national government. Although tradesmen themselves, they could not understand trading in anything so intangible as dramatic poetry. As audiences grew in size from hundreds to thousands, they were appalled by the inroad upon working hours. Commercialized amusement for the masses was not then taken for granted, and never before had purveyors of delight operated on such a scale or at such a profit. The phenomenon caused a deep conservative tremor among leading citizens. Lesser ones were less disturbed, were in fact supplying the audiences. An order of April 1582 from the Lord Mayor to the freemen of the livery companies bidding them to keep their families, servants, apprentices, and presumably themselves away from plays proved to be a signal failure.

John Stockwood was especially incensed by "the gorgeous Playing place erected in the fieldes . . . as they please to haue it called, a Theatre." [10] The building by James Burbage in 1576 of the first "regular" theater is the most spectacular single event of the decade so far as stage history is concerned, but certain common assumptions about the event are open to question. Probably the site in Shoreditch was not chosen solely, or even mainly, in order to escape the jurisdiction of the London authorities, but because space was available there; the inns along Gracechurch-Bishopsgate Street remained in use for play performance for another eighteen years. Certainly it was not, as always stated, built for Leicester's Men. It was built for whoever could use it to the profit of the owners, despite the fact that James Burbage was still listed as one of Leicester's Men in the patent of 1574. No one company in 1576 would have had the backlog of plays, or the capacity for feeding new ones into the repertory, such as let the Admiral's Men in the nineties command exclusive use of the Rose. Burbage would certainly have welcomed Warwick's, Sussex's, or any other thriving company as well as Leicester's, possibly with different ones alternating on successive days. There was no reason why he should not. The Theatre as well as the Curtain was used by a variety of companies in the eighties even though Leicester's was still active. And finally the building of the Theatre was not the cause of the London boom in playing, although it must have accelerated it; rather it was an effect. Aware of what was happening during the earlier years of the decade, Burbage saw an opportunity and seized it.

Nothing illustrates more vividly the new financial status achieved by the playacting enterprise than the amount of money invested in the building of the Theatre. In 1567 about £8 10s. was invested in fitting the Red Lion Inn at Stepney with scaffolds for playgoers. Just nine years later, about £666 was invested in building the Theatre. The same man, John Brayne, grocer of Bucklersbury, was the capitalist in both instances, earning for himself the title of first known investor in metropolitan-area theatrical property by his first venture, and the most victimized by his second. The story of the Burbage-Brayne partnership is familiar in type. Burbage had an idea, and Brayne, his brother-in-law, had money. The combination seemed ideal at first, but less so later, when the Burbages seemed to think that the Braynes should be content with getting their money back, without too much consideration of profits due for the risking of it. James Burbage truly made a great contribution. As a Leicester's company member, or former member, he had both influence and a knowledge of what actors needed in the way of a playhouse, and as a former joiner he had some knowledge of architectural design. But we should spare a moment of reverent consideration to the contribution of John Brayne. It was also in 1576 that Martin Frobisher embarked on the first of his voyages to seek a Northwest Passage. The total cost of his fleet, the *Gabriel*, the *Michael*, and their pinnace, was £444, just a third less than that of the Theatre. Sir Thomas Gresham, the great financier, risked £100 in backing Frobisher's venture. It is a sobering thought that a Bucklersbury grocer risked more on a better route to the land of golden poetry than the Queen's banker risked on a better route to the golden Indies. If the aristocracy supplied protection and a trace of luster to the new activity which bred the glory of English dramatic literature, the lower middle class supplied its financial sinews—as well as most of the literature.

In 1577 a second regular theater was built in Shoreditch. How much venture capital was needed remains unknown, but even if the Curtain cost only half as much as the Theatre, £1000 was invested in playhouse facilities in 1576–77. Hope alone would not have worked this wonder; the investors must have been reasonably sure that these costly edifices would pay. An exploding clientele for plays is indicated by the existence of four leading companies at the end of the decade: Leicester's, Warwick's, Sussex's, Essex's. The actor-sharers in these were all making a living—a shockingly good one in the eyes of the envious—even though half their take went as rental to theater owners and a fair portion of the rest for costumes, playscripts, licensing fees, and so on. Leicester's Men received more in the way of fees for Court performances than any other company, but these averaged only £17 a year from 1572 to 1582. The bulk of the income of this and the other companies came from the London populace in the form of pennies. These must have been falling in a virtual Danaë's shower.

Here then are abundant players, playing-places, spectators. We are bound to ask, where are the plays? Not a single text assigned to a particular company survives from the 1570s. Only two texts assignable to adult companies survive at all: *Sir Clyamon and Sir Clamydes* and *Common Conditions.* The titles of about thirty lost and anonymous plays belonging to particular companies are preserved in Court records. Most of these must have been heroical and peripatetic romances, on the order of the two unassignable texts which survive; however, some of the titles suggest other kinds of subject matter, including notorious English crimes. An indication of the variousness of the plays being offered is provided by the pamphlets of Stephen Gosson. He says that "baudie Comedies in Latine, French, Italian, and Spanish, haue beene throughly ransackt." [11] He describes some of his own plays: *The Comedy of Captain Mario*, "a cast of Italian deuises"; *Praise at Parting*, "a Moral";[12] *Catiline's Conspiracies*, "vsually brought in to the Theater" and showing "the rewarde of traytors in Catilin, and the necessary gouernment of learned men, in the person of Cicero." [13] He mentions "twooe prose bookes plaied at the Belsauage," and *The Jew* and *Ptolome* "showne at the Bull, the one representing the greedinesse of worldly chusers, and bloody mindes of usurers: the other very liuely descrying how seditious estates, with their owne deuises, false friends, with their owne swoordes, and rebellious commons in their owne snares are ower-throwne." [14] Obviously the plays mentioned in Court records (none of those described by Gosson) represent only the tip of the iceberg; and heroical romances and moral interludes do not fully represent the nature of repertories in the seventies. Gosson's description of *The Jew* suggests that the pound-of-flesh and choice-of-caskets story was already on the stage; indeed other evidence indicates that the Romeo and Juliet story had been staged as early as *Cambises.* The Belsavage and Bull inns were still serving the players along with the Theatre and the Curtain.

The enterprise of the actors had created a vacuum and new talents were being drawn in. The crying need was for scripts. The creation of a new company, such as the Queen's in 1582, does not mean the spontaneous generation of a new repertory. Authors had to be found. Tarlton could not have supplied a modicum of what the Queen's company needed after 1582 anymore than Wilson could have supplied a modicum of what Leicester's company needed after 1572. Who were the new playwrights? The case of Gosson provides a clue. We think of him now as pamphleteer and preacher, but he was first a "university wit," following a career at Oxford by becoming a playwright in London and then turning against his employers. Gosson was an earlier Robert Greene, and his recruitment by the players may well have resembled Greene's. When Roberto met the Player, who no longer carried his "Fardle a footeback" but was able to build a "Windmill" (theater) at his own cost and to value his share of playing apparel at £200, the indigent scholar asks how he may be employed: "Why sir, in making playes, said the other, for which you shall be well paied, if you will take the paines." [15] Greene was exaggerating when he made the Player say that men of his profession "get by schollers their whole liuing," [16] but they had in actual fact put themselves in a position to employ university graduates by the time the first "regular" theater was built. Gabriel Harvey was far too lofty in spirit to write for them, but at least the thought occurred to him. In 1578 he wrote jestingly to Spenser:

I suppose thou wilt go nighe hande shortelye to sende my lorde of Lycesters or my lorde of Warwickes, Vawsis [Lord Vaux's], or my lord Ritches players, or sum other freshe starteupp comedanties unto me for sum newe devised interlude, or sum maltconceivid comedye fitt for the Theater, or sum other paintid stage whereat thou and thy lively copesmates in London maye lawghe ther mouthes and bellyes full of pence or twoepence apeece.[17]

Gosson's fellow "university wits" of the seventies may have been men like Thomas Watson and Mathew Royden, who we know wrote plays, although we have no inkling what plays. Or they may have been men whose later work we have. Too often, as in the case of Shakespeare, we assume that a playwright's career began with the first surviving mention of it or with his first surviving play, but the records are so fragmentary and the early plays so often lost that the assumption is rarely justified. John Lyly's *Campaspe* need not have been his first play, and one cannot help thinking of those "twooe prose bookes plaied at the Belsauage" before 1579. His mysterious *Woman in the Moon*, a "poet's dreame,/The first he had in Phoebus holy bowre," [18] could conceivably be a versified rendition of one of these. George Peele's *Endymion* need not have been a first play either, but a deviation, in his case momentary, to the more precious mode of chorister drama. There is even greater likelihood of an early start by Thomas Lodge. There is reason to believe that he was the author of the lost *Play of Plays and Pastimes*, with which the actors defended their calling at the Theatre in 1582, and this may well be the *Delight* played by Leicester's Men at Court in 1580 after the pamphleteering attack on plays had got well under way.

The ages of the playwrights mentioned above would have made it quite possible for them to work for the players by the mid-seventies, in some instances perhaps furtively. Curiously, Gosson, Watson, Royden, Lyly, Peele, and Lodge were all Oxford men. We can imagine a sort of early Oxford movement toward the London playhouses, and even a possible relevance in the fact that Leicester, the chief London patron of players, was also Chancellor of the University. Admittedly these specific suggestions represent only a desperate peering into the dark backward and abysm of time, but the general probability remains—that truly poetic drama was pioneered on the popular stage before 1580, and some whom we usually think of as pioneers, Kyd, Marlowe, Greene, Nashe, belong to a second wave of practitioners. Shakespeare may well have begun writing as early as the earliest of these, with his actual "predecessors" belonging to the seventies and early eighties.

A concluding distinction must be made between what the facts reviewed above mean and what they do not mean. They mean that money was the triggering mechanism in launching the greatest era of modern drama. By taking in many pennies the actors could pay pounds to writers. The price paid for a playscript was £5 at first (more later), so that a writer who supplied four scripts a year could earn as much as most freemen of the livery companies. The average middle-class Londoner supported his family on £20 a year. For the first time it became feasible for a poet to live by his pen without patronage—providing, of course, that he was not incapacitated by temperament or by contempt for his actor-employers. The humanist manifestoes of the sixteenth century were more wise and human than some more recent ones because they took into account *both* immaterial yearnings and material needs. Starkey deplored penury and squalor because no one could live the good life unless he first could live. Stage history demonstrates that the rule applied to poets.

The facts do not mean that Elizabethan dramatic poetry was simply something bought. Before it could exist certain happy events had to occur in the fifties and sixties in London, Canterbury, Stratford, Norwich, and elsewhere. Babies had to be born with the appropriate kind of genes. And of course, the whole complex of new interests in classical and foreign literature, in the cultivation of aureate words and the flowers of rhetoric—

the "Endeavors of Art"—had to be there as shaping force. In speaking of the benign effects of rising prices and profits, Keynes once said that Shakespeare came when England was "in a financial situation to afford him." [19] It is one of those ideas which are true in a sense but silly if pressed too far. If great writers came with the ability of society to afford them, our present landscape would be cluttered with Shakespeares. There would have been no *Doctor Faustus* had not the means of paying for it been found, but its golden tribute to Helen of Troy, "fairer than the evening air/Wrapped in the splendor of a thousand stars," was something freely given, not bought. The five, or even six, pounds received by Marlowe scarcely compare with the reputed millions of dollars received by Mailer for his tribute to Marilyn Monroe. Perhaps between the 1570s and 1970s the alchemical process has been reversed, with gold turning into copper, or, as Nerissa would say, in one of her good sentences well pronounced, "they are as sick that surfeit with too much as they that starve with nothing."

G. K. HUNTER

Were There Act-Pauses on Shakespeare's Stage?

*T*HE PUBLICATION of T. W. Baldwin's
William Shakspere's Five-Act Structure in 1944 might seem to have
demonstrated with crushing finality that Shakespeare and his fellow
playwrights had available to them a system of play-structure which most
easily expressed itself in act-divisions, and that therefore the plays of these
men are not distorted by continuing the generally received custom of
printing and numbering them in five acts. But editors, both before and after
Baldwin, have been moving steadily in the opposite direction. It is true that
no one as yet has printed an edition of Shakespeare in scenes only; but
act-divisions have begun to retreat to the margins; and several recent
scholarly editions of minor Elizabethan plays have avoided the "temerity"
of imposing act-divisions on their undivided quarto originals, and simply
numbered scenes consecutively throughout the work. Looking back on the
whole range of the controversy about act-divisions in Elizabethan plays it
begins to appear that Baldwin's book was only an interlude—an interlude
which may prevent authors today from joining in John Dover Wilson's
insouciant claim that the unacademic Shakespeare would have scorned
such "newfangled" notions as five-act structure[1]—but one which has not
prevented recent critics from returning to pick up the threads of pre-
Baldwin antiact theory.

The recent books on this topic have all been hostile to the idea of
act-structure in Shakespeare. And one must be impressed by the fact that
their arguments are directed from different standpoints. Georg Heuser's
published dissertation, *Die aktlose Dramaturgie William Shakespeares*
(Marburg, 1956), undertook a very thorough examination of the gaps in
time and place implied by the progress of the action of Shakespeare's plays.
His work shows clearly that the time gaps in Shakespeare's structures are
not always aligned with the spaces between the acts. Occasionally there is a
gap in time inside an act-structure (the three days in *Twelfth Night* between

I.ii and I.iv is a case in point). Sometimes the act-division cuts across what seems to be genuinely continuous action (*Measure for Measure* IV.vi–V.i is an example; *Hamlet* III.vii–IV.i is another). Sometimes the stage is not properly cleared, as in the famous case of the act-division between III and IV in *A Midsummer Night's Dream* (F text), where the lovers *"sleepe all the Act."* From the point of view that acts are entities rigidly defined as requiring continuous time inside and a cleared stage and a time gap at either end, we must allow that Shakespeare either wrote with considerable carelessness or else deliberately ignored acts (as defined).

In another model thesis (written at Wisconsin under the direction of Madeleine Doran and Mark Eccles) and published with the title *Act Division in Elizabethan and Jacobean Plays 1583–1616* (Hamden, 1958), W. T. Jewkes tackles the problem from quite a different angle. He reports on the earliest printed form of some 236 plays from the period 1583–1616, and, listing the presence or absence of act-division in these quartos, allows the statistics to make the argument for him. A simple and significant pattern emerges (confirming what had been indicated earlier by E. K. Chambers [*Elizabethan Stage*, III,199]): the vast majority of the plays from the private playhouses are divided into acts on their first appearance in print; likewise, the vast majority of plays printed after 1616 show act-division, whatever their theatrical source; on the other hand, the vast majority of public theater plays, printed before 1616, are without act-division.

The work of Jewkes is in part repeated (unwittingly it would seem) in Henry Snuggs's *Shakespeare and Five Acts* (New York, 1960). Snuggs's work is worth reporting on, however. Less rigorously organized than Jewkes's, its specific arguments with Baldwin reveal the extent to which *William Shakspere's Five-Act Structure* has failed to convince not only because it tries to prove too much, but rather more because the argument runs counter to the emotional bias of the age. The commitment of both theatrical and textual scholars at the beginning of the modern movement in Shakespeare studies was to a conception of his theatrical art as immediate and accessible and totally unlike the theater of the nineteenth century; and this is still a powerful commitment. The line of theatrical renovation that runs through Poel, Craig, and Granville-Barker was designed to save Shakespeare from the fuss and clutter of Victorian staging. Thinking of an authentic Shakespeare performance as a completely continuous event, unbroken by scenery or the long intervals required to dismantle and assemble it, Granville-Barker was striking a blow against the recent past. One must certainly agree with him that the modern intermissions are inappropriate to Shakespeare. Nowadays the lights go up, our whole visual experience of the theater changes, the audience rises from its seats, parades in the foyer, consults the program. None of these things was possible in the Elizabethan theater. But the argument against such modernisms, as if they were the only possibilities to be derived from act-divisions, seems to measure commitment rather than logic. A less embattled position might view the evidence more variably. The real question is whether the play should be perceptible in the theater as a series of fifteen to thirty separate scenic units, marked off from one another by moments when the stage is clear, or whether a small number of larger units gives us a more effective hold on the material.

At much the same time as theatrical theorists were arguing for continuous performance, in another part of the island textual scholars were arguing for the authenticity of Shakespeare's (undivided) quarto texts, and their frequent superiority to the (usually divided) texts in the First Folio.[2] In addition, there was the exciting possibility that Shakespeare's hand could be found in the (undivided) MS play, *Sir Thomas More*, and that Shakespeare's manuscript could be detected behind some of the quarto texts, which led naturally to the argument that Shakespeare had thought of his plays as undivided by act-intervals. The hectic sureties of early modern Shakespeare bibliography, as represented, for example, by John Dover Wilson, have not, of course, survived intact. I shall argue below that the undivided state of the Shakespeare quartos is open to a number of alternative interpretations.

The purpose of the present study is to look again at all the evidence collected to support the prevailing modern arguments, to see if the arguments stem inevitably from the evidence, and then (since there seems to be space left for something more than mere repetition) with such hypotheses as the evidence makes appropriate, to reread the plays, looking for the expressive functions of pause or continuity. It must be confessed, to start with, that the argument between Jewkes and Baldwin could be well expressed by the image of the whale and the elephant that some medieval theorists thought appropriate to the Pope and the Emperor: each is monarch of his own realm; and neither is in contact with the other. Baldwin is concerned with a principle of construction derived from classical antiquity. Jewkes is concerned with the actual printed form of the plays. Their central questions do not coincide, so their answers do not really conflict. The answer to the question, "Were the plays built up on the basis of Donatus's description of Terence's plays?" in no way prejudges the answer to Jewkes's question, "Why were the public theater plays before 1616 printed without act-divisions?" These two scholars only come into direct conflict if they abandon their central knowledge and make inferences about theatrical practice. Clearly one should take a long skeptical look at this area of inference.

The tables of plays assembled by Jewkes and Snuggs show that before

1616 authors like Jonson, Lodge, Peele, Tourneur, men whose plays show the allure of classical learning, wrote (for the public as well as the private theater) plays whose earliest published forms contain act-divisions, while nonacademic authors, like Dekker and Heywood, wrote plays for the public theater which were published without act-divisions. Jewkes and Snuggs assume that this results from the fact that the "unlearned" playwrights were men of the theater, while the learned men were thinking of their works as literary artifacts and were careless or ignorant about actual theatrical practice. There seems no evidence to support this as a necessary explanation. Must we suppose that the author of *The Hog Hath Lost His Pearl* (1614) was a theater man because the quarto of his play is undivided? The probabilities are all against it. Robert Armin was one of the most celebrated of the actors in Shakespeare's company. And yet his *The Valiant Welshman* (1615) is divided into acts. Robert Wilson was another celebrated actor, of an earlier period, and again for the public theater. And yet his *Three Ladies of London* was published in 1584 with a confused act-notation, which I take to be evidence that division into acts was undertaken either by Wilson or his theater.

We know from *Henslowe's Diary* that "act" was a meaningful division of a play for him and for the purveyors of plays who serviced his public theater companies. Professor G. E. Bentley has written interestingly about the use of acts as units of composition in collaborative plays.[3] The clearest evidence of this in the public theater comes too late to be significant in itself,[4] but the dramatists involved included men like Dekker and Webster and Rowley, who had been writing long before 1616. It would be absurd to assume that such men changed their habits of composition in mid-career because the King's Men had moved into the Blackfriars, or because some other supposedly significant theatrical event had occurred. The rational deduction from the evidence that Bentley gives is that the habit of thinking about plays in acts prevailed throughout the whole period of public theater writing.

The evidence of the theatrical "plots" preserved at Dulwich with the rest of the Henslowe-Alleyn papers points in the same direction. What is usually admitted is that one "plot"—*The Dead Man's Fortune*—has lines of crosses at the ends of acts (with the direction *Musique* set against them). Other plots are, however, no less unambiguous. "The plot of the first part of Tamar Cam" has the rubric "Enter Chorus [Dick Jubie]: Exit" at each point where a new act begins. "The plot of the Battle of Alcazar" has lost that part of the sheet concerned with act V, but what we have is clear enough indication of act-structure. At the beginning of act I we find "Enter a Portingall" and then on a separate line "1 Domb shew." Act II likewise begins with "Enter the Presenter [= Portingall]: to him/2 domb shew"; and at the appropriate distance appear "3 domb shew" and "4 Domb shew." There can be little doubt that if the missing fragment were to appear it would include the words "5 domb shew." The complex structure indicated by the plot of the *Second Part of the Seven Deadly Sins* has been clearly divided into five acts by Dr. Greg, who remarks that the action consists of "three Sin plays, but two of these are clearly divided into two sections each, evidently with the object of providing a five-act plan." [5]

The evidence of these plots seems simple and unambiguous. Indeed John Dover Wilson, though seeking to prove that Shakespeare had no act-structure, admits that Henslowe's companies must have produced their plays in five acts. Allowing this, he is forced into the curious assumption that Shakespeare's company had different theatrical customs from the Henslowe public theater companies.

Alleyn's company inherited the dramatic tradition of Marlowe, Greene, and Peele, while dramatists like Heywood, Chapman, Day, and Jonson who worked for it in the 'nineties were all academic men, deeply imbued with the classical spirit. It was only to be expected that such a company would deal in acts.[6]

The argument being espoused here cuts across that pursued by Jewkes and Snuggs, based on the evidence of the early printings. Jewkes's statistics establish a distinction between the private theaters and the public ones, but none at all between the different public theater troupes. The former distinction has, of course, support from what we know about the theatrical life of the capital; the latter has none. We know that in the boys' theaters musical performances were given between the acts, and it is commonly surmised that no such interludes existed in the adult or public playhouses. The principal piece of evidence usually cited in this connection comes from Marston's *The Malcontent* where, in the Induction written for the adult performers, we hear of the new "additions" designed "to entertain a little more time, and to abridge the not received custom of music in our theatre." I have pointed out in my edition of *The Malcontent* (the Revels Plays, London, 1975) that this may refer not so much to the inter-act music as to the introductory concert of music which, when the Duke of Stettin-Pomerania visited the Blackfriars in 1602, lasted "for a whole hour preceding the play." The *Malcontent* reference, therefore, cannot be construed as *proving* the presence of inter-act music in the boys' theaters and its absence in the adult theaters. The public theaters must have had some musicians, to accompany songs and dances and to sound flourishes, tuckets, and so forth. I have mentioned above the direction *Musique* written between the acts in the "plot" of the public theater play, *The Dead Man's Fortune*. But even if the argument for distinction between the boys' companies and the men's is less clear-cut than commonly supposed, it is still much more plausible than that which Dover Wilson proposes between the Henslowe companies and the Chamberlain's Men. The plays that can be ascribed to Strange's Men, or The Admiral's or Worcester's Men (the Henslowe companies), appear in Jewkes's lists as predominantly undivided. If these undivided prints represent the stock of a company which divided its plays in the theater, then the undivided prints from Shakespeare's company may well be taken to imply the same mode of performance.

The difficulty of arguing from the playwright to the company is neatly illustrated by the case of Heywood. For Dover Wilson, Heywood is one of the "academic men, deeply imbued with the classical spirit," and so helps to explain the Henslowe practice. For Snuggs, however, Heywood is "like Shakespeare . . . closely identified with the theater as both actor and playwright, and far removed from the academic closet drama; thus his work reflects what actually went on on the boards" (p. 47), and so he is deduced to have written his plays for performance without act-divisions. Snuggs's observation that "every play of Heywood's published before 1610 is undivided, every one after that date divided" (p. 49) is a serious one; but the evidence is not clear enough to enable us to explain it in terms of "how Heywood wrote plays."

The fate of plays in the playhouse and the morals that may be drawn from this are illustrated by *The Battle of Alcazar*. As we have seen, the "plot" tells us that it was written and performed in five easily perceptible sections or acts. The first printed version of the play, however, yields only the statistic "imperfectly divided" in Jewkes's list; correctly enough, for only "Actus Secunda" and "Actus 4" are marked. One can see good reason why the printed version should be thus: the "plot" is clear enough for the prompter, even without numbering the sections. There is no reason to suppose that a playhouse manuscript needed further numerical indications any more than the "plot" did. The play is divided into five theatrical sections by structure, but the printer need not have had anything to guide him toward a formal and complete statement of act-numbers. Jewkes, however, draws quite a different moral from the situation. He says: "It seems quite clear that the play was originally divided, but lost the clear markings for the act divisions during its history in the playhouse" (p. 127). The danger in such an argument is of subsuming the thing in the word; the *words* "Act I," and so forth, may well have had this history, for they are of interest mainly to writers and readers; but the fact of division into five parts seems to have been preserved throughout the theatrical transformations of this play, and not to be open to serious question.

What is played down in such arguments is the role of the printing house. Ben Jonson's plays for the public theater are exceptions to the general rule that public theater plays are printed without act divisions. Why? We know that Jonson carefully prepared his plays for their publication, modeling the form on the Renaissance printings of Roman comedy. It is inconceivable that Jonson's plays should have appeared in an undivided form (unless surreptitiously), whatever the practice of the playhouse where they were performed. Jonson is exceptional in the degree of his care for the printed form of his plays. But the difference from other learned dramatists of the age is only one of degree; his reverence for the printed form of the classics was widely shared. These learned dramatists, Chapman, Marston, Daniel, Middleton, and so forth, printed almost exclusively the plays they wrote for the private theaters; the fact that these plays are nearly all divided may tell us less about the theatrical conditions of the private companies than about the self-image of the authors. The printed form of Marston's plays, for example, with their "classical" scene-structure, their Latin stage-directions and act- and scene-headings, bespeaks the involvement of the author in the printing process, as does other evidence.[7] Such printed versions cannot be relied on to give us direct information about the habits of the playhouse.

The appearance of regular act-divisions after 1610 or 1616 may likewise find its explanation in the printing shop rather than the playhouse. Jewkes and Snuggs follow Dover Wilson in supposing that the entry of the King's Men into the private Blackfriars theater was a crucial event in theatrical history and altered the whole nature of Elizabethan play-performance. This may or may not be so; it is not a matter on which I need let my skepticism appear. What is clear is that there was a general improvement in the social status of plays in the first quarter of the seventeenth century; and this was a development that affected printing styles as well as theater audiences. Clearly the expectations of the purchaser of playbooks was rising; larger margins and a more spacious layout became the rule. If the publisher or printer thought that the new audience would look for act-divisions, clearly stated, as a symptom of the classical status sought for modern plays, then he was perfectly capable of supplying them.

One of the two most significant monuments of the new status sought for plays—Shakespeare's First Folio of 1623—is particularly interesting, not only because it is by Shakespeare, but also because it reprints with act-divisions many plays which had been printed previously without them. The crux of the controversy lies here. Are we to suppose that the Folio's act-divisions derive from new theatrical habits acquired by the King's Men when they took over the Blackfriars? Or may we suppose that the undivided quartos are being brought up to the dignity implied by a volume in Folio on "farre better paper than most Octavo or Quarto *Bibles*"?[8] Jewkes's commentary, which is largely a paraphrase of W. W. Greg, *The Shakespeare First Folio* (Oxford, 1955), is prepared to allow in several places that the act-division in the Folio must have been introduced as part of the preparation of the text for printing. Commenting on *Love's Labor's Lost*, he says of the Folio act-division that "probably it was done at the time of printing" (p. 163); on *The Taming of the Shrew* he quotes Greg to the effect that the act-division was "probably introduced at the time of printing" (p. 161), and again on *Richard III* he quotes Greg's view that the act-division was probably introduced by the printer on his own initiative (p. 157). Once this has been allowed for some cases, there is no logical reason for denying it in any case. The form of the plays in the Folio can be cut completely adrift from any assumptions about the theatrical habits of the age. And if we attribute act-division to the printer, or (far more probably) the copy editor, we can leave the theatrical mode to be sought out in terms of the plays themselves. Some consequences of this freedom are studied in the second half of this essay.

But the argument (if it is to carry weight) must be tested against the quartos as well as the Folio, for the assumption that the Folio act-divisions do not need to reflect stage practice does not tell us anything about the quartos. Whatever the facts of the Folio, it is still easy to assume that the quartos are without act-notation because they faithfully mirror a public theater practice of performing without breaks or pauses or other indicators of act-structure. The Folio's acts may represent only a literary imposition on the theatrical truth revealed by the quartos.

The general assumption is that the quartos lack act-divisions but have scene-divisions. This is not strictly true. The Shakespeare quartos (both "good" and "bad") provide a record of entries and exits, and no more.[9] All clear-cut separation of scene from scene, and, of course, enumeration of scenes, is editorial in exactly the same way as is the act-division.[10] The documents behind the quartos seem to have given a clearly coordinated body of information about entries, speeches, and exits, and this limitation on what the printer saw before him seems to exist whether the documents derived from the author or the playhouse. Certainly, for texts that came from "pirates" or reporters we could not expect any more. Quartos derived from the author's "foul papers" or working drafts create less clear-cut expectations. But the absence of act-divisions in an author's draft does not necessarily imply either that the compositional method ignores acts or that the theatrical performance discounted them. We assume that the author's draft was handed over to the theater's book-keeper, who then made a promptbook out of the material, by greater or lesser adaptations.[11] The theatrical shape of the play was thus not finally crystallized when the author handed in his draft. One might indeed expect an author working closely with a theatrical company to avoid giving needlessly definite form to a text still to be worked over. What was liable to happen to painstakingly recorded divisions, even if no great adaptation is made in the text, can be seen in the surviving manuscript of Massinger's *Believe As You List*. Massinger has written out his text with clearly stated and centered numbers for each act and scene. The book-keeper then scored out all Massinger's indications, but reinserted the act-headings, in his distinctive prompter's script, in the margin, as if to say, "these things are my concern, not the author's."

The case of *Believe As You List* bears clearly on the third and most crucial class of manuscripts which can be deduced to lie behind the Elizabethan quartos—actual prompt copies. I call this class crucial, for the question it raises goes at once to the center of the issue being discussed: "If prompt-copy manuscripts of early public plays were printed without act-division, does this not mean that the plays were without act-division in the prompt-book and so without act-division in the public theater performance?" The evidence of *Believe As You List* and the surviving prompt-copy manuscripts does not make this a necessary argument. The book-keeper seems to have preferred to keep the nontextual matter of the plays in the margins. A printer not feeling that act-division was an essential part of his copy was obviously at liberty to ignore the marginal material, most of which was irrelevant to the reader. The surviving prompt-copy manuscripts, of a date early enough to be significant, certainly suggest that act-division is a pretty basic element in the existence of these plays. Only four surviving manuscripts seem to be involved: *Sir Thomas More, Edmond Ironside, Richard II/Thomas of Woodstock, John a Kent and John a Cumber*.[12] All of these except *Sir Thomas More* have marks of act-division. Jewkes, however, makes the point that "the manuscript prompt-books indicate clearly that the playhouses themselves were responsible for the addition of act divisions to plays which were originally undivided: both *Edmond Ironside* and *Thomas of Woodstock* have clearly had division added by a prompter, in the first decade of the seventeenth century" (p. 101). This overstates the evidence in a number of ways. Manuscripts "originally undivided" do not tell us anything about productions "originally undivided." The textual material of these manuscripts is simply a neutral base on top of which the prompter writes his production notes (including act-division). There is no evidence in them of a production which precedes the one with act-division mentioned. And one cannot ignore the comment of the Malone Society Reprint's introduction to *Richard II*: "C, who systematically inserted the act numbers, may be supposed . . . to have been concerned with the manuscript at an early stage" (p. xvi). The evidence that Jewkes takes to point to a revision of theatrical practice in the early seventeenth century seems in fact only to be telling us the same things as *Believe As You List*: act-division was part of playhouse preparation of the manuscript, and always was so.

The one early prompt-copy manuscript which is anomalous is *Sir Thomas More*. But *Sir Thomas More* is anomalous in so many ways that this is hardly significant. As Greg says, "I very much doubt whether the manuscript can be regarded as a 'live' Book [prompt copy] at all: in any event it is a quite exceptional example, and I am inclined to regard with suspicion certain far-reaching inferences that have from time to time been based on its peculiar features" (*Dramatic Documents*, p. 200). The Munday original of this play (such of it as has survived) does not seem to have been very seriously prepared for the stage. In such circumstances the absence of act-division is not really extraordinary. If we compare *More* with the other Munday autograph promptbook of the same period—*John a Kent*—and ask why the finished play has act-divisions and the work-in-progress (*More*) has none, we may well find that the logic of the situation requires us to depend on the nature of the documents rather than the conditions of production. The absence of act-division in the Shakespeare quartos seems likewise to define the nature of these documents rather than the customs of the Globe. And if the absence of act-division from the quartos, like its presence in the Folio, can be satisfactorily explained in these documentary terms, we are left, once again, with the plays themselves as the principal guides to the theatrical presentation we assume.

It has been the purpose of this essay up till now to examine the evidence put forward in favor of act-free composition and performance of Shakespeare's plays. It seems that the evidence so far adduced does not require the conclusions that have been drawn from it. It now remains to look at the actual texts of Shakespeare's plays, to see if they show any signs of act-breaks or pauses which would be detectable whatever the mode of presentation in print, to ask what purposes such pauses could have served in the economy of the play, and to find out if one can extrapolate, in terms of such purposes, from known or provable instances to unknown or problematic ones.

The obvious first case to pursue in such an enquiry is *Henry V*. We know that *Henry V* is in five acts because the choruses tell us so. If the choruses were absent from *Henry V*, would there be any other way of detecting the five-act structure that the choruses make clear? Act I is separated from act II in terms of place, and there seems also to be a gap in time. At the end of act I we hear Henry's declaration of war and his first resolution to invade France. The first chorus then informs us that the time-consuming mobilization for war has occurred. It also tells us that "The King is set from London, and the scene/Is now transported, gentles, to Southampton." It must be admitted that the separation in terms of place is less complete than the chorus suggests. We learn in II.iii that the subplot figures are on their way to Staines, and this clearly though retrospectively tells us that they were in London in II.i. We do not, of course, know this in II.i; it is not part of our consciousness as we follow the action. We believe what the chorus has told us because no one actually contradicts him; no counter-Southampton location is established; the characters in II.i have not appeared in the play before; they are given no local roots; and it is emphasized that they are on the move to France, taking part in the action that the chorus has described. But one must allow that the precise change of location belongs to the main plot alone; the subsidiary strands of the plot trail after the King. And this is something that occurs several times in Shakespeare.

Act I of *All's Well That Ends Well* locates the main action in Rossillion, and at the end of it Helena leaves for Paris. Act II locates the main action in Paris, to which both Helena and Bertram have moved. A chorus could quite well say "to Paris do we move our scene," even though II.ii takes us back to Rossillion again (yet another person is being sent to Paris). Such "lagging" scenes do not deny the truth of the imaginary chorus-line. The separation of place from place along the line of the act-division creates a sense of dramatic phrasing or punctuation, which is there for the sake of the effect, not (as some would prefer) for the sake of the rule. *As You Like It* repeats the point. Act I is set in the court. At the end of it Rosalind and Celia leave for the forest of Arden. Act II establishes the forest as the new seat of action. But II.ii takes us back to court, and II.iii shows Orlando and Adam belatedly following the ladies into the forest. The act-division again seems to be establishing, in terms of place, a new center of plot location, but not a prison for the action.

Act III of *Henry V* is separated from act II in a way that raises no problems. Between II and III the action has moved to France, and when we begin III we are already in the thick of war: "Once more unto the breach, dear friends, once more." Between III and IV on the other hand there is no break in terms of place, and in terms of time there seems to be a deliberate effort to convey continuity. Time seems to be of the essence in these scenes, and it is described with extraordinary precision. The last scene of act III shows us night in the French camp. "Would it were day" says the Constable in the opening remark; and even more exact are the last words: "It is now two o'clock; but let me see—by ten/We shall have each a hundred Englishmen." When the chorus enters he tells us:

> Now entertain conjecture of a time
> When creeping murmur and the poring dark
> Fills the wide vessel of the universe.
> From camp to camp, through the foul womb of night,
> The hum of either army stilly sounds.

That is, the time described is, so far as we can tell, the one we have already been living in at the end of act III.

When act IV begins we find only the "early stirrers" awake; it is still night. The function of the inter-act pause filled here by the chorus must be different here from what we have so far considered. I believe that it can, however, be understood. The Battle of Agincourt is the climax of the play; but Shakespeare intends to show it less as a Homeric action than as a demonstration of the social and psychological challenge it offers to the English and to their king. On the one side of the act-break we see the French, self-confident, vainglorious, backbiting; on the other side we meet the English, humble, pious, loyal. The chorus between them is not a narrative of actions but a meditation on the events we are about to witness. It is like taking a breath before making a maximum effort, or like the interim of which Brutus speaks, "Between the acting of a dreadful thing/And the first motion." The presence of the inter-act chorus, serving such a function, suggests that before we discount act-divisions between events because these are continuous in time or place, we should canvass more fully the exact textual situation. Between acts IV and V of *Henry V* there is again a very obvious break in time and place. Act V of this play may almost be regarded as an appendix, in which political virtue receives its comical reward. It is all the more clearly demarcated for that.

The second Shakespeare play one ought to look at, if one is seeking to study five-act structure in a protected environment, is *Pericles*. Here again the chorus tells us (unambiguously in the first three acts) that the play is designed to be seen as a series of movements, set off from one another by methods that can be duplicated in other plays without choruses. Act I of *Pericles* consists of three actions, each separated from the others in time and place. Apart from the number of lines involved, there is no way of telling whether scenes i, ii–iii, and iv are scenes or acts. The Gower chorus here seems to be an essential element to give us guidance. Act II, however, is not only clearly separated from I and III in place and time, but is continuous in itself and completes the action it deals with. Act III is also a continuous series of related actions, taking place within a circumscribed though not confined area of place and time, and ending (as often in Shakespeare) with a kind of nadir, the family dispersed, that which has been built up broken down, and the search for meaning apparently denied. Fourteen years must be supposed to elapse before act IV begins.

Act IV is composed of interwoven actions in two separate places, Tarsus and Mytilene. In addition it contains a choric interlude in which Gower tells us of Pericles' doings. Why should we not suppose that this Gower narration (and that other one usually called V.ii) is as much an act-separator as those between acts I, II, and III? One answer is that these two interludes differ in form and function from the inter-act choruses. In IV.iv Gower takes us forward in the plot of Cleon and Dionyza. But in terms of the other half of the narrative, Marina in the brothel, he leaves us exactly where he found us. This Gower scene is also stylistically assimilated into the play in a way that the inter-act narratives are not. In both versification and vocabulary he joins the action here, where otherwise he is separated from it.

Act V, scene ii, on the other hand, is in the distinctive archaic octosyllabics of the choric speeches. But here again he connects more clearly than he separates. He merely fills in the gap between V.i and V.iii so that the action of act V is not only single and unified but also continuous. In V.i Pericles is told by Diana to visit Ephesus. In V.iii he has arrived at the temple of Diana in Ephesus, not to create new action but to fulfill what has been forecast. In this, *Pericles* V.ii differs from the third chorus in *Henry V*. Both tell us about a journey by sea which carries a king from one land to another; but in *Henry V* the journey separates one stability from another, one mode of action from another. In *Pericles*, journeying *is* the action; once we have landfall at Ephesus the end is easy and inevitable.

These two clearly sectioned plays suggest that Shakespeare's five-act structure worked in the main by separating sections of continuous action by gaps in time and/or place. But they suggest that this rule was by no means mechanical, that both Continuity and Separation were concepts to be interpreted liberally, as are other forms of punctuation used in humane discourse. From time to time he seems to have been willing to insert a pause into the middle of material that is continuous in place and time. Shakespeare also seems to have been willing to dispense (when occasion required) with that other modern shibboleth, the cleared stage. Thus in act II, scene ii of *King Lear* Kent is placed in the stocks. At the end of the scene he settles down in his "shameful lodging," says goodnight, and falls asleep. Edgar now enters and tells us how he is being hunted. As far as the action is concerned we are (as the Folio tells us) in a new scene (II.iii). Edgar exits; Lear, Fool, and Gentleman enter. We are now in act II, scene iv. At line 4 Kent addresses the king and is noticed for the first time. To stage this by having Kent unstocked at the end of II.ii (F gives him no exit) and then restocked at the beginning of II.iv (he has no entry) would be patently absurd. Shakespeare clearly assumed here that a character asleep and not seen by others counts as absent. It is an eminently practical assumption.

When the same assumption impinges on act-division in *A Midsummer Night's Dream* it creates, however, a famous crux. As noted above, the Folio text of this play places at the end of act III a stage direction, *They sleepe all the Act*. Jewkes remarks on this: "Act division . . . was not there originally, since the heading *Actus Quartus* is placed in the middle of a continuous scene, where there is no clearing of the stage" (p. 168). The *Lear* example suggests that Shakespeare did not share Jewkes's reverence for the cleared stage. The act-break here brings to an end a particular phase of the action: this last sleep of the lovers finally sorts out their cross-purposes. But though one phrase-line ends here, the phrasing overlaps in another voice: the sleeping of the lovers ends their problems, but the physical fact of their sleeping is effectively added to the sleeping of Titania and Bottom (which begins act IV). The progressive and parallel awakenings of act IV requires the presence of the lovers on the stage; but their silence and apparent invisibility for the first sixty lines of the act is a mode of absence sufficient to justify an act-pause.

Other examples of a stage not cleared at the point of the act-break are more dubious. Jewkes has argued that *Titus Andronicus* I–II is such an example, and Heuser discusses *Hamlet* III–IV and *Measure for Measure* IV–V. At all these points it is possible that the stage is not cleared, but in all of them an exit followed by a reentry can be imagined. Let us look at one of these, however, and assume that the stage continues to be populated, deciding how important this fact alone is in establishing the presence or absence of an act-break. At the end of act IV of *Measure for Measure* Friar Peter tells Isabella and Mariana that "the Duke is entering"; he has found them a place where they can stand and deliver their petitions. It is possible that they do not exit at this point (even though the Folio prints *Exeunt*). They may simply retire to their vantage point, from which, at line 15, they come forward and make their pleas. If we allow this, have we ruled out the possibility of an act-pause? In terms of genuine theatrical effect I would judge not. The entry of the Duke (*in propria persona*) marks a new and climactic phase in the action. A pause before the actual entry seems eminently stage-worthy. But does it require that the stage be cleared? Surely not. Isabella, Mariana, and Friar Peter wait on the stage for a perceptible blank interval while the fanfares move nearer and the grand entry is prepared. The actual entry is not less a new paragraph because the petitioners are waiting for him. The issue here seems not to depend on presence or absence on the stage, but on the quality of the buildup for the new entry.

Romeo and Juliet is a play that offers one stage of openness in act-structure beyond what we have considered. It places one sonnet at the beginning of the play and adds a second before what the modern editors call act II (the Folio text of this play remains undivided). The act-division for the rest of this play is purely editorial. The gap between acts I and II, which is implied by the second chorus, is, however, the most problematical in the whole play. The action seems to run on continuously. Act I concludes with the Capulets' ball, when Juliet, stunned by discovering the identity of her new beloved, retires into the house. When act II opens, Romeo enters, also evidently coming straight from the ball: he has found himself unable to leave Capulet's house. We seem here to be in a situation similar to that found between acts III and IV in *Henry V*. And again a chorus assures us of the existence of a gap in the action. Heuser and Jewkes and Snuggs all argue that such continuity is incompatible with an act-pause. The evidence of the plays seems, however, to be stronger than the force of the theory. Perhaps we should amend the definitions to fit the assured and self-consistent technique of the author. It is our business to ask what function a gap has at this point in *Romeo and Juliet* rather than to assert that Shakespeare either did not know or did not mean what he was doing by separating the two acts.

It is worth noticing that the end of act I is marked by a crisis. The old Romeo is burned out by the experience of meeting Juliet, but the new direction of will seems totally self-frustrating. He tells us: "O dear account! my life is my foe's debt," and Juliet echoes him: "My only love sprung from my only hate." In both cases the stultifying discovery is followed by an exit. All the action that has been set up during act I seems to disintegrate. We are left, as at the end of *Pericles* act III (and even more obviously, *Winter's Tale* act III), at a totally negative point of bafflement and powerlessness. Romeo's entry at the beginning of act II marks, however, the defeat of bafflement and the recovery of willpower; he overcomes his despair and makes his decision: "Can I go forward when my heart is here?/Turn back, dull earth, and find thy centre out." In terms of clock time this may be virtually continuous with the end of act I, and place may be considered unchanged; but the pause between the acts has marked a crucial shift of direction, which is confirmed by the moment of entry. The Chorus is a meditation on this death and rebirth: "Now old desire doth on his deathbed lie,/And young affection gapes to be his heir;/ . . . But passion lends them power." Its presence makes clear Shakespeare's sense of the value of punctuation at such a point, to give what he thought the appropriate emphasis.[13]

The remainder of *Romeo and Juliet* provides copybook examples of the "phrasing" of the plot into a series of movements or acts. Act II ends at an obvious point of completion: Romeo and Juliet leave with Friar Laurence for the wedding ceremony: "you shall not stay alone/Till Holy Church incorporate two in one." The play seems to cry out for a moment of pause here, before act III begins again the violence of the feud. Act III ends also with a phase of the play clearly completed. Inside act III the climax of the play has occurred: Romeo has killed Tybalt and been banished. The last scene of the act fulfills every despairful thought that the action has given rise to: the lovers have to part; and Juliet is immediately assailed by the enforcement of another marriage. She is left alone with the one thought that is positive, "If all else fail, myself have power to die." Once again the end of an act is marked by a nadir. Act IV takes up the apparent fulfillment of that promise. It develops only one matter, the conflict between the father's plans and the daughter's resolve, and concludes with that conflict at an end, Juliet apparently dead and the marriage (naturally) abandoned, the household plunged into a comically distanced mourning. But act IV is separated from act V not only by the completion of its own concerns, but by the complete shift of place and of atmosphere when we arrive at act V. Romeo has been absent from the action throughout act IV—a recurrent feature in the period.[14] Now at the beginning of act V we meet him in Mantua, caught up in a charming version of that hybris which tragic heroes often show.[15] From this point the plunge to death is meant to be spectacularly rapid; and so it is here.

I have said that *Romeo and Juliet* provides a copybook example of act-structure. This is true in terms to the total movement of the play no less than in the detail of act-ends and act-beginnings. If we think of the subject of the play as being the conflict between personal love and family hatred, we can see that each of the middle act ends with an alternating implication of victory or defeat. The end of II (the marriage) seems to be a victory for love; the end of III (the separation) is clearly a defeat; the end of IV seems like a conditional victory (Juliet has defeated her family, and prepared the way for love's triumph). An act-pause, or other means of marking the crucial stage reached at the end of each act, seems desirable if we are to notice the structure. Such a view runs, of course, directly counter to that propounded by Harley Granville-Barker, who has devoted to "the question of act division" a whole section of his *Preface* to *Romeo and Juliet.* He remarks:

What we should look for, surely, in act-division is some definite advantage to the play's acting. Where, in this play, do we find that? But the gains are patent if we act it without check or pause. Whatever the Elizabethan practice may have been, and whatever concessions are to be made to pure convenience, everything seems to point to Shakespeare having *planned* the play as a thing indivisible. (P. 36)

Granville-Barker's principal argument for this last point derives from his sense that the play lacks moments at which all the action could be said to be at rest:

Nor is there any scene-division in the play, where an act-division might fall, over which some immediate bridge does not seem to be thrown. Either a strong contrast is devised between the end of one scene and the beginning of another that a pause would nullify, or the quick succession of event to event is an integral part of the dramatic effect Shakespeare is seeking. (P. 34)

One might well object that the sense of *pause* here is oversimple. It is argued that "formal pauses or intervals" allow the emotional tension to "not only relax, but lapse altogether" (p. 32). However, it often seems that a pause, of the appropriate length, can cause tension to increase rather than elapse. It is certainly so in music, as anyone caring to listen to the last bar of a Handel recitative can confirm. Also rather oversimplifying is the notion, found in both Granville-Barker and Snuggs, that "it is in the very nature of the play [*Romeo and Juliet*], of its precipitate passion, to forge ahead without pause" (Granville-Barker, p. 34; compare Snuggs, p. 109). The idea that a precipitate story can only be told effectively in a precipitate narration would seem to be a rather egregious example of the fallacy of imitative form. In any case, *Romeo and Juliet*, like other plays, combines one story that seems to rush through time to its conclusion with other elements that seem to demand a slow-moving and extended time-process—for example, the incarceration of Friar John in the infected house. No one formal structure can hope to mirror the movement of all the lives it imitates; some degree of arbitrary formal imposition is inevitable.

In the course of looking at some of the more guaranteed or explicit act-divisions in Shakespeare we have seen several different uses of such breaks to make dramatic or theatrical points. Several of these seem to recur throughout Shakespeare's work, and that of his contemporaries, as habits if not as rules. The movement of act V to a different location, where crucial decisions can be made meaningful, is obvious enough in *Hamlet, The*

Winter's Tale, A Midsummer Night's Dream, The Merchant of Venice, accompanied, in the more grave actions, by the reemergence of a principal character who has (in some sense) been absent from the immediately preceding action—the case of *Measure for Measure* may illustrate what is meant by that "in some sense." This fifth act convention is not, of course, a rigid requirement of the form, and uses of the same general effect without precise implications for act-structure can be seen in *Timon of Athens* and *The Comedy of Errors. All's Well* is an ambiguous case, for, though the beginning of act V is, I believe, deliberately contrived, the point is being made in terms of a continuous process rather than a sharp division. The habit is, however, recurrent enough to evoke something like expectation in the alert reader; and expectation, of course, makes its effect, when it is disappointed, as clearly as when it is fulfilled.

Measure for Measure is one of several plays in which a change of stylistic tone and (correspondingly) a change in the focus of illusion create a sudden shift of level corresponding to an act-division. At the end of act III the Duke steps forward and in thirty lines of octosyllabic couplets moralizes on the substance of the play so far and forecasts what is to come. For Georg Heuser this is a clear example of unbroken play structure, for the Duke tells us in the course of his couplets that "With Angelo *to-night* shall lie/His old betrothed" (italics mine). It is true that no gap in time is created. In III.ii we hear that "Claudio must die to-morrow" (220), and in IV.ii we are told " 'Tis now dead midnight, and by eight to-morrow/Thou must be made immortal" (67–68). We have already seen, however, that in both *Henry V* and *Romeo and Juliet* Shakespeare is willing to interrupt such a continuous action by a pause-creating chorus. What the *Measure for Measure* example seems to show is the use of the act-pause to transport us to a different stylistic level, whatever the time sequence may be doing. When we reach the beginning of act IV we are outside Vienna (for the first time in the play). We find ourselves in a moated grange; there we meet a new central character, Mariana, and a new atmosphere is engendered by the romantic song "Take, O take those lips away," inserted here, it would seem, only for its atmospheric power, for Shakespeare has to apologize, almost immediately, for permitting it. In some sense the act-pause allows us to take a new breath, to seem to start again. The obvious comparison with this is in the chorus of Time at the end of the third act of *The Winter's Tale,* where a wholly new world is discovered (sixteen years later) on the seacoast of Bohemia.

The end of act II in *King Lear* appears without benefit of chorus, and there is no startling gap of time to be found here. None the less the theatrical pacing of the play seems to cry out for a pause at this point. Acts

I and II of *King Lear* carry us forward in a continuous double span of attention from the initial surrender of power to the inevitable consequence of total powerlessness. I call this a double span because act II shows a repetition, carrying forward to an even more intense degree of desolation, the pattern established in act I. In I.iv Lear finds that Goneril is intent, not to protect him, but to deprive him. He storms out of her house at the end of act I, assuring himself (though not us) that there is a world elsewhere; Regan will treat him differently. In II.iv he discovers that what has been forecast (I.v) is true—Regan is as like Goneril as "a crab [is] to a crab"—and in the climactic section of the scene Goneril and Regan act together to deprive him systematically of everything except his rage. This time there is no one else to go to (Lear himself has seen to that). He rushes off the stage into a nowhere—"O fool, I shall go mad!"—to the sounds of a storm brewing. The wicked characters left behind on stage preen their plumage and justify themselves. Hearing the storm they withdraw into the comfort of the house: "Shut up your doors, my lord; 'tis a wild night./My Regan counsels well. Come out o' th' storm."

The big doors at the back of the Elizabethan stage bang shut; *Storm still*, as the stage direction says at the beginning of the next act. It seems essential to the theatrical phrasing of the play that there should be a pause here, while the audience stares blankly at the empty stage and is given the sense of nadir that (once again) the act-pause represents. The disaster that has been threatening the play since the beginning has occurred. It seems essential that we should be able to contemplate that fact before we advance into act III and discover that all is not lost in all dimensions of the world. We then move forward into the storm, the heath, and the desolations of act III and discover there a world as new as the seacoast of Bohemia. But it is essential that we register first the change of direction; mere continuity across this division destroys Shakespeare's artful organization.

The main line of my consideration of Shakespeare's plays has now proceeded from unambiguously external examples of division, in which choruses tell us where the act-breaks are placed (*Henry V, Pericles*), through partial external division (*Romeo and Juliet*), and choruslike but internalized division (*Measure for Measure*), to consideration of one case where the evidence is wholly internal (*King Lear*). Instances of the last kind could of course be multiplied; but perhaps enough has already been said to indicate the range of situations which can legitimately be considered. One modest conclusion at least seems inescapable: Shakespeare was aware of, and prepared to make evident, the act-pause (both with and without formal textual acknowledgement) to organize his material and direct our attention toward the shape of the organism. Some plays (*Romeo and Juliet* and *All's*

Well are examples) show an exact coincidence of structural breaks and act-divisions. Others (*Much Ado* would seem to be a case in point) reveal no interest in this effect. Over all, Shakespeare (and most of his contemporaries) show the power both to use act-division and to leave it alone, as a concealed part of the machinery. They are unsatisfactory witnesses if we wish their art always to answer Yes or No to the question posed in my title. Their art has, in fact, more interesting things to say about the possibilities of act-pause, and a candid examination of their plays will reveal this richly.

We have seen that there are aesthetic arguments for some act-pauses in the presentation of Shakespeare's plays, but this by no means should lead us to expect that there will always be an aesthetic justification for a pause at the end of an act. If we argue for a regular theatrical indication of a five-act structure we must allow that a fair proportion of the pauses thus generated will be placed arbitrarily. But is it not equally arbitrary to stage the plays without any breaks? At a merely subjective level I must confess to a sense of shapeless rush in performances in this mode which I have act-endings can only be passed over by arbitrary and doctrinaire decision. The plays themselves seem to demand a mode of staging halfway between five-act staging and the unbroken staging of Granville-Barker's dream. Emrys Jones has recently suggested that a middle-of-the-play pause is a recurrent feature of Shakespeare's dramaturgy;[16] and certainly some plays support the idea—for example, *Richard III, Measure for Measure, Macbeth, The Winter's Tale.*

But other plays resist this patterning, falling into threefold, fourfold, or even fivefold structures. The variety of shapes and forms in Elizabethan drama makes a strong argument for an *ad hoc* response in the theater, for an assumption that the Elizabethan public theater had no formal program of act-pauses, and responded to each individual play as a new situation. Such an *ad hoc* solution runs counter, however, to everything we know and suppose about the Elizabethan theater. The guilds of actors, like other elements in a highly regulated society, lived within traditional norms. One assumes that they were able to continue operating in a fiercely demanding repertory system because they kept the rules of the game identical in one performance after another. I must confess that it seems to me inconceivable that the Globe sometimes had one pause, sometimes two, three, or four, or that the spectator had no prior assumption about the structure of what he was going to hear. It would certainly be in keeping with Elizabethan habits of mind, revealed in other art forms, that an arbitrary and external formal structure should be imposed on the material.

The final stages of the argument depend for their force on the extent to which we find such analogies persuasive. Indeed, throughout this essay I have been assuming that the function of the act-pause may be compared with the function of pause in a musical performance. Even today the breaks in a sonata movement between first and second subject, between exposition, development, recapitulation, coda, are a matter of exposing the overall structure to an audience by tactful cooperation between the performer and the musical score. I should confess openly that I conceive of the act-pause in the Elizabethan theater as having a similar function: its existence allows the skillful performers to play the formal structure against the informally expressive material. The danger that I see in the modern tendency to deny formal pause in the name of "continuous performance" is that it runs counter to this pluralistic aspect of Shakespeare's art. Since he is continually playing the formal against the informal, we can only weaken the whole art if we deny the possibility of displaying the formal partitioning of act-structure.

BERNARD BECKERMAN

Shakespeare and the Life of the Scene

*L*IKE ALL fashions, fashions in criticism change. In Shakespearean studies, it is now the turn of dramaturgic criticism, thanks to a set of historic and esthetic circumstances. A glance at nineteenth-century conceptions of Shakespeare's dramatic art reveals how constrained writers were by prevailing assumptions about what good drama should be. Since then, the continuing breakdown of dramatic tradition and the extension of the limits of dramatic form, culminating in the recent theatrical experiments of the fifties and sixties, has obliged artists and critics alike to peer below the conventional arrangement of plays in order to regard the dramatic medium freshly. Concurrently, the art theaters, whether as summer festivals or as civic institutions, have captured Shakespearean production. This has increased the self-consciousness of presentation, and has led to recurrent debate over problems of style and interpretation.

These positive changes in dramaturgic outlook brushed but did not deeply affect Shakespearean criticism during the first half of the twentieth century. Notwithstanding the work of E. E. Stoll, L. L. Schücking, and M. C. Bradbrook on Elizabethan theatrical conventions, the trend of criticism was against contemplation of dramatic art. Given the available techniques for studying drama, it seemed, perhaps justifiably, to a person like G. Wilson Knight that the interpretation of language not the examination of dramatic form would yield deeper appreciation of Shakespeare's art. In effect, exploration of theater was discouraged. Instead, a generation of criticism plumbed the plays for their mythic themes, their overarching metaphors, and their moral philosophies. Unfortunately, in the course of revealing these mysteries, the critic often produced an interpretation that did not lead the readers back to the work but offered them an alternative, often striking in its imaginative suggestiveness but quite alien to the original vision of the poet. Creative interpretation, however, is no substitute for encounter with the original drama. Shakespearean writers and students have increasingly sensed this, and so have turned to the theater for insights into Shakespeare that might complement those insights stimulated by previous modes of criticism.

Ironically, increased attention to dramaturgy comes at a time when theatrical theory is in disarray. In fact, the attempt to understand Shakespeare's artistic mastery must go hand in hand with the attempt to construct a new dramaturgy. Because contemporary experiments as well as Shakespeare's plays do not readily fit Aristotelian formulation, it is necessary to find alternate ways of describing them. Happily, the search serves to illuminate not only the work of Shakespeare and his contemporaries but also the entire range of dramatic form.

Current efforts to deal with Shakespeare's dramatic art show three interlocking approaches. One approach—perhaps the most widespread at present—examines the importance of nonverbal elements in the drama. This is the approach often labeled *Shakespeare without Words*. The actor's gestures and even silences as well as the arrangement of the stage and the use of properties are studied in order to learn how Shakespeare employs them and what impact they are likely to have on the audience. A second approach traces the organization of the narrative and the juxtaposition of various scenes to one another. It is perhaps the oldest approach of all, apparent in Harley Granville-Barker's prefaces and still important in Madeleine Doran's and Wolfgang Clemen's writings.[1] Indeed, the analysis of narrative structure is frequently regarded as the entire subject of dramatic criticism. Lastly, and yet to be fully explored, is the approach that concentrates on the kind of scenes Shakespeare wrote. In a recent book, *Scenic Form in Shakespeare* (Oxford, 1971), Emrys Jones has rightly stressed that Shakespeare was foremost a writer of magnificent scenes. How to describe these magnificent scenes remains a challenge, however, for no matter how valuable the other two approaches are—and they are valuable —they have yet to elucidate the internal development of the Shakespearean scene.

We are all sensitive to the supreme and commanding utterance that Shakespeare places in the mouths of his characters. So attuned are we, in fact, to his dazzling play of images and rhythms that we often treat the verbal surface as though it had autonomous life. Words linked to words become themes and themes become the unearthed revelation of a work's meaning. Too often, in the process, the words as the exponents of acts are diminished.

But even as we weave our interpretations from the words alone, we sense that sustaining the fabric of language is a subterranean flow of energy. The most common name we have for that flow of energy is *action*. Unfortunately, the vocabulary and techniques for describing action are so limited that critics often despair of ever describing it precisely. The energy-system of a play, however, is so fundamental to its unfolding, so primary to the way incidents are shaped and how they are performed, that we have to treat action if we are to treat Shakespeare as a dramatist at all. To treat action means, in my view, to open ourselves to the impulses suggested by the words, to trace how these impulses are linked together into a structure, and to discover how the structure is realized in performance.

To gain an insight into structures, it is most useful, I believe, to contemplate the building block of drama, what Emrys Jones terms the *scenic unit*.[2] From an understanding of how a scene is shaped we can move to a fuller understanding of how scenes are connected and ultimately of how a play exerts its power. Scene-structure is a complex subject, however, and can hardly be examined exhaustively in so brief an essay. I propose therefore to deal only with one aspect of a scene's structure—the shape of its energy.

We experience a play through a sequence of temporal units. The scene, as it is usually defined, is one such unit. It is further divided into subsegments. Each of these subsegments embodies the dialectic of the thrust of one energy—usually expressed by one person—against some sort of resistance. In the opening line of *Othello* we can sense this dialectic immediately. "Tush, never tell me!" cries Roderigo, containing in his words the impress of that offstage remark by Iago which provoked the resistance. During the course of a scenic unit this dialectic assumes an intangible but palpable shape, a shape accented by moments of crux when accumulated energies break the tenuous balance between thrust and resistance. For instance, in the scene where Lady Macbeth persuades Macbeth to kill Duncan, the crux of the scenic unit occurs just before Macbeth proclaims, "Bring forth men-children only" (I.vii.72), for the line signals the end of his resistance and a shift to his acceptance of Lady Macbeth's scheme against the king's life.

We can speak of several degrees of abstraction in a scenic unit. Least abstract are the concrete words and gestures of the characters. These words and gestures gain coherence through the dramatic activity that binds them. Often the activity takes an elementary form such as persuasion or confession. Whether Shakespeare discovered the activity through the language or the language arose out of his conception of the activity, we shall never know. We only know the scenes as they come down to us, and the activity they contain. Coursing through that activity is an underlying thrust of energy, a thrust of energy that has a tendency to assume one of two primary shapes, an active shape or a reactive one.

Let me stress, I speak of a tendency, one full of subtle gradation. An impelling force courses through a scenic unit. On one hand, it may be so organized as to bring about a change in conditions. It moves *toward* the moment when the change will be effected. For example, one person persuades or fails to persuade another to do something. The shape of that effort I call *active*. On the other hand, the scenic unit may be arranged to show an adjustment to an impulse that has occurred previously. A classic instance is a scene of lamentation. The shape of that unit I call *reactive*. Both active and reactive tendencies may exist in the same scenic unit, but the overall shape of a scenic unit exhibits one dominant thrust or another.

This inclination toward one or the other shape is common to all dramaturgy, and is readily apparent in Shakespeare's work, as an example of each type of segment will show. In *Coriolanus* there is a particularly vivid illustration of the active scene (V.iii). It occurs when Volumnia pleads with her son not to destroy Rome. This scene has two parts.[3] The first is a scenic unit of greeting, played out in a strange ceremony of formal intimacy in which son kneels to mother and mother to son (V.iii.19–76). The second unit is an active persuasion segment (V.iii.77–189).

Persuasion is one of the simplest forms of dramatic activity, embodying an effort by one character to achieve a specific objective through bringing about a change in another character. The skill of the dramatist can be discerned in the arguments that the first character expresses, in the quality of the resistance exercised by the opposing character, in the gradations by which a moment of decision is approached, and in the theatrical force of the change achieved. In the segment we are considering, Volumnia impels the action, her objective is to effect a change in her son, and the resistance stems from Coriolanus's determination not "to infringe [his] vow" (V.iii.20). The event is thus future-oriented, from the very first pointing toward the crucial moment when Coriolanus will either yield to his mother or reject her importunities.

In the course of the segment Volumnia's persuasion shifts from lengthy formal argument to devastating scorn. Only at the beginning of her plea does Coriolanus defend his position. Otherwise, his mother has only his silence to attack. What I want to stress at this point, however, is not the activity of persuasion itself but how Shakespeare varies the primary shape of pressure and resistance by the particular way he dramatizes Coriolanus's resistance. When Coriolanus first sees his mother approach, he rejects filial instinct (V.iii.35). To his mother's face, he affirms:

> The thing I have forsworn to grant may never
> Be held by you denials.
> · · · · · · · · ·

> Tell me not
> Wherein I seem unnatural. Desire not
> T'allay my rages and revenges with
> Your colder reasons.

(V.iii.80–86)

Note that Shakespeare gives Coriolanus's unequivocal stand against Rome full vent immediately. He holds nothing back. In effect, he throws away Coriolanus's principal arguments. By doing so, he develops the scene as a portrait of the mute withering of Coriolanus's will. Only a few words by Coriolanus interrupt Volumnia's plea. They are addressed obliquely to no one in particular, self-justification for an abortive effort to flee his mother's tongue. But Volumnia perseveres, proceeding from rational persuasion to personal attack. She strikes at Coriolanus's pride. "Thou hast affected the fine strains of honour," she mocks (V.iii.149). There is no reply. She urges her son to speak; he says nothing. Yet his silence is more eloquent than any words can be. It is a speaking silence, through which the actor commands our attention by depicting the slow erosion of Coriolanus's resistance. The crux of the action starts with Volumnia's second kneeling (171), which echoes the earlier ceremony, and reaches full intensity with the stage direction indicating that Coriolanus *holds her by the hand, silent* (182). The family's abasement and imminent departure finally wrench a response from Coriolanus. "O mother, mother!/What have you done?" (182–83).

Throughout, Shakespeare need merely hint at Coriolanus's resistance. Because the primary thrust of persuasion excites expectation in the audience, Shakespeare can rely on the actor's skill and the audience's imagination to fill the contours that he has drawn. We thus have a scene of active energies embodied in persuasive activity, arranged to move from volubility to a crux of silence, and expressed through language which shifts from a certain formal stiffness to the most intimate appeal.

In contrast to this actively shaped segment is the reactive sequence of Hamlet's first soliloquy, "O that this too too solid flesh would melt" (I.ii.129). The impelling force of the speech emerges from the circumstances of Gertrude's "o'erhasty" marriage to Claudius. This marriage on the heels of the unexpected death of the elder Hamlet has induced a pervasive disenchantment in the young Hamlet. The speech gives voice to the disenchantment, but more than that, it is an effort to absorb the blow of the marriage and find some accommodation to it. Thus, the energy expended by Hamlet is not to bring about a change but to adjust to the change that has occurred. The first eight and a half lines serve as a prologue (I.ii.129–37). In longing for dissolution and in reaction to the world about him, Hamlet displays his state of mind. He announces his melancholy, as it were. Then the past asserts itself. As he dwells upon recent events, remembrance becomes increasingly painful. "Let me not think on't!" is the active thrust by which he tries to stem the involuntary flood of recollection. It is this flood that gives the primary reactive thrust to the speech. As the past reaches a point of anguish it merges into the present. "O, most wicked speed, to post/With such dexterity to incestuous sheets!" (156–57). And as he moves from the present—"It is not"—to the future—"nor it cannot come to good"—Hamlet accepts an impotent adjustment: "But break my heart, for I must hold my tongue!"

As we can see, in the reactive scene there is a discrepancy between the impelling force and the character's ability to cope with that force. The shape of the sequence traces the process of adjustment. Frequently, in a reactive sequence, the crux comes at a point when the character experiences an acute anxiety at his present state. He becomes keenly aware of the gap between fact and his ability to accept that fact. In the "too too solid flesh" soliloquy Shakespeare, after first displaying Hamlet's state of mind, then takes him by means of a recollective process through remembrance of the past, anguish at his present condition, and foreboding for the future. This pattern, employed here in a somewhat abbreviated form, is very common in reactive sequences and indeed can be found in all drama from the Greeks to the present, from the Orient to the Occident.[4] Again, it is his ability to erect on a common primal structure modulations of infinite suggestiveness that makes Shakespeare the supreme dramatic artist he is.

A sharper sense of the distinction between the two modes of shaping a scene might be gained if we were to consider the two scenes I have cited in another way. Suppose Shakespeare had chosen to write the Volumnia-Coriolanus scene as a reactive one, how might he have done so? Perhaps he would have started the action after Volumnia had already made her initial plea. The precipitating force would have been set off, and the action would be built on Coriolanus's attempt to resolve the dilemma he faces. The scene would then explore the complexity of feeling he has for his mother and for Rome, perhaps following the conventional pattern of reviewing his martial past, realizing the impossible present he finds himself in, and conjuring up the destruction that lies in his future.

It is harder to conceive of Hamlet's soliloquy in an active form. Nevertheless, if Hamlet struggled to speak out, if he schemed as to how he might attack the marriage, then we would have the elements of an active speech, obviously one that is far different from the original.

Naturally, what I have been describing is not drama in its entirety. The active-reactive duality is merely a shorthand way of schematizing the energies in a play. These energies compose the support system—the underlying life force—out of which the specific interaction among characters emerges. The control and projection of the energies are the foundation of an actor's work. That is why an actor who may have only a rudimentary idea of the meaning of Shakespeare's words can often convey the truth of a scene. The actor senses the patterns of energy, flows into them, and by projecting them finds the correct impulses for a thought or a word.

Moreover, the projection of these patterns provides the elementary magnetism that holds an audience's attention and shapes its response. Suspense in the theater, after all, relies upon active energy-shapes to create a gap between an audience's present awareness and its future expectation. Even when it knows how a play will end, an audience can be hypnotized by the underlying flow of energy if this is artfully structured, that is, if controlled shifts in increments of energy rather than the mere dispensing of information fill the gap between the known and the expected. When dramatic energy is given exquisite and subtle variability through word and gesture, as in Shakespeare's works, then the audience enjoys a range of sensations where elemental and subsidiary responses mingle.

No play, of course, is grounded solely on active or reactive sequences. These are arranged in varying combinations to give each dramatic work its own distinctive rhythm. Whether active or reactive scenes predominate, whether active scene follows active or reactive scene alternates with active, whether one type of scene or the other generates greater intensity—all such considerations affect a play's rhythm. By and large, English Renaissance drama relies heavily on reactive sequences, often short-circuiting the active by beginning a scene *in medias res*, and so focusing on a character's adjustment. In Shakespeare this tendency blends with his lyric power to produce those incomparable reactive scenes of Othello's jealousy, Lear's madness, and Hamlet's frenzy. But it is in *Antony and Cleopatra* that he most delicately spins a web of active and reactive patterns. The counterpoint of one energy to another is especially evident, not only because of the forty-two formally indicated scenes in the play but also because most of these scenes are subdivided into very brief scenic units. The shift from one thrust of energy to another thus occurs rapidly and repeatedly.

In criticism much is made of the contrast in the play between Roman and Egyptian life. And we do get the effect of that contrast. But we should also note that Roman life, as such, is never really portrayed. Instead, the active energies of Rome are set against the fluctuating energies of Egypt. Almost invariably Octavius Caesar is shown in an active state. He gives orders, makes announcements, or justifies himself. Even when he is on the verge of tears, apparently twice in the play, he says nothing (III.ii; V.i). Others observe him about to weep. In the two or three instances when he does have a reactive speech, his response is sustained to the end of the six or seven lines. Never in the play does he shift from an active to a reactive and then back to an active state.

By comparison, Antony exhibits a far more complex pattern of energies. In the first half of the play, while he does have brief reactive units, for instance, when he receives news of Fulvia's death (I.ii.121–31), he generally is active. In Rome he is almost completely active except when he mulls over the soothsayer's advice (II.iii.32–40). As a result, through the first half of the play Antony's temper becomes more and more like Caesar's. The symmetry of the parley scene (II.ii) deliberately accents the evenness of that temper and the directness of the force each man exerts. The parley itself is an active scene as are most of those involving the Romans.

The imminent break between Caesar and Antony is prefigured during the parting from Octavia (III.ii). As brother and sister bid each other farewell, the focus shifts first to Antony's reaction. He describes his bride's tears and tongue-tied manner, apparently moved by his observation. One is struck by the tenderness and yet the objectivity that suggests an alienation from the event. Immediately thereafter, Enobarbus and Agrippa comment upon Caesar's reaction. The contrasts are complex: Octavia's tears are set against Caesar's welling emotion that never quite overflows the eyes; Antony's sympathetic against Enobarbus's acerbic observations; and lastly, Antony's open reaction against Caesar's covert reaction. Throughout the rest of the play, this covertness of Caesar's reaction persists. We seldom see Caesar except in the most active state. When he receives word of Antony's death, he speaks elliptically. "The gods rebuke me but it is tidings/To wash the eyes of kings!" (V.i.27–28). He speaks of tears, but as in the earlier scene, another character is left to point out that "Caesar is touch'd" (V.i.33), thus making the reactive sequence a group affair rather than a personal adjustment.

After the first half of the play Antony reveals repeated shifts of energy. Naturally, with disaster come instances when Antony responds like a wounded beast to his own shame or his suspicion of Cleopatra. But even before the first battle with Caesar (III.vii) he displays a series of abrupt shifts. During the dispute over whether to fight by land or sea, he passes through a series of extremely brief segments: reactive, active, reactive. He reacts to messages (21–28), he gives orders (28–53), he reacts to further messages (54–57). Throughout much of the latter part of the third act and in the fourth act, this pattern of shifting energies occurs, and they reinforce our impression of Antony's unsteadiness. Yet in a curious way Shakespeare mutes Antony's irresolution. He does this by turning those scenes, which promise to be most fully developed in the reactive mode, into the opposite shape. After the first battle (III.xi), Antony enters on a reactive burst: "Hark! the land bids me tread no more upon't!/It is asham'd to bear me" (III.xi.1–2). But immediately he starts persuading his servants to leave him, thus making the scene active: "Friends, come hither./ . . . I have a ship/Laden with gold. Take that." And he continues: "Take it!" (11); "Friends, be gone" (15); and "Leave me, I pray, a little" (22). Only when he sits muttering aside as Cleopatra enters, is his reaction developed in a half-articulate manner:

> No, no, no, no, no!
>
> (29)
>
> O fie, fie, fie!
>
> (31)
>
> Yes, my lord, yes! He at Philippi kept
> His sword e'en like a dancer, while I struck
> The lean and wrinkled Cassius; and 'twas I
> That the mad Brutus ended. He alone
> Dealt on lieutenantry and no practice had
> In the brave squares of war. Yet now—No matter.
>
> (35–40)

What this arrangement suggests to me is that at the opening of the scene Shakespeare reverses and later diffuses an expected response in order to emphasize a blockage in Antony: his inability to find release in either active or reactive energy. Not until he and, later, Cleopatra approach death do they approach the suspension of effort which lies between the active and reactive. That Shakespeare moves the play toward such a state of quiescence is apparent in the way he mutes any tendency toward passionate exclamation and sustained reaction. By inducing in us a kinetic uncertainty, he prepares us to welcome Cleopatra's measured commitment to death.

These last remarks on *Antony and Cleopatra* verge on interpretation. Hitherto I have tried to be pre-interpretive, that is, to describe one of the dramaturgic features of the play. To my mind scene-analysis must precede interpretation. The active-reactive scheme is only one feature of drama. There are many other features that need definition and illumination. Drama is an extremely complex art, complex not only in its construction but in the responses it evokes in an audience. Yet ironically, our descriptive language for drama is pathetically simple, virtually childish. As a result, our observations on drama remain primitive. Because we have no commonly recognized form of discourse, we can not go beyond elementary discussion among ourselves. And if this inarticulateness affects drama as a whole, how much more does it affect Shakespeare's drama, which is simultaneously complex and simple, poetic and dramatic. Until we can speak a language of drama more fluently than we do, we shall only half understand Shakespeare's art.

G. P. V. AKRIGG

Shakespeare the King-Maker

$\mathcal{J}$T IS a point so obvious as generally to elude comment that in the Shakespeare canon kings possess a preeminence beyond that which they enjoy in the works of any of his contemporaries. Surveying the plays of Lyly, Greene, Peele, Marlowe, Jonson, Webster, and the rest, we find that none of them give kings the centricity and emphasis that they receive from Shakespeare. In making this statement, we take into account not only the ten "histories" entitled after English kings, but the tragedies which center in King Lear and King Macbeth, and those comedies in which rulers preside and intervene. The reason why the world of Shakespearean drama so often moves in orbit about a king is not hard to identify: the Ideal of Kingship was one of the richest and most potent in Shakespeare's imagination.

The importance of the monarch in Shakespeare's own society needs little comment. Foreigners in the seventeenth century, no less than in the twentieth, were impressed by the emotional attachment of the English to their monarchy. Writing in 1624, the Venetian ambassador to the court of James I could speak of "the royal authority, which the English reverence above everything else." [1] Head both of church and state, the sovereign was dominant in practically every area of national endeavor. The hierarchical society in which the monarch stood at the apex finds a formulation in Shakespeare's numerous king-beggar linkages and antitheses:

> The King's a beggar, now the play is done.
>
> > (*All's Well*, Epilogue, 1)

> the king lies by a beggar, if a beggar dwell near him.
>
> > (*Twelfth Night*, III.i.9–10)

> Sometimes am I king:
> Then treasons make me wish myself a beggar,

And so I am.

(Richard II, V.v.32–34)

The paradox of king and beggar, opposites and yet members within the same society, focused itself for Shakespeare in the story of "The magnanimous and most illustrate King Cophetua" and the beggar maid (*Love's Labour's Lost*, IV.i.66). In three of his plays Shakespeare refers to Cophetua by name, and there are other indirect references:

> Is there not a ballet, boy, of The King and the Beggar?
> (Love's Labour's Lost, I.ii.114–15)

> Our scene is alt'red from a serious thing,
> And now chang'd to "The Beggar and the King."
> (Richard II, V.iii.79–80)

> If your master
> Would have a queen his beggar, you must tell him
> That majesty, to keep decorum, must
> No less beg than a kingdom.
> (Antony and Cleopatra, V.ii.15–18)

The whole movement of history, cultural and political, in the Renaissance, the weakening of religious convictions, the emergence of the new centralized monarchies, inevitably brought a growing importance to kingship, steadily brightening its aura. Marlowe, in the spirit of the new age, sardonically switched a cliché about the importance of winning a heavenly crown, when he had his Tamburlaine speak of the final end of men's endeavors being "That perfect bliss and sole felicity,/The sweet fruition of an earthly crown." The Renaissance was in very truth an Age of Kings, and Shakespeare was very much of his age in his fascination by kings and kingship. M. M. Reese speaks truly of "the royalism that is the final value of Shakespeare's political drama." [2]

Other reasons, more peculiar to William Shakespeare, may account for his centering so often and so much upon his kings. A dramatic and, indeed, poetic element is intrinsic in the ritual and ceremony of kingship. Shakespeare obviously responded imaginatively to the "power, /Preëminence, and all the large effects/That troop with majesty" (*King Lear*, I.i.132–34). He dwells upon the details, dramatically emblematic of the coronation:

> She had all the royal makings of a queen;
> As holy oil, Edward Confessor's crown,

The rod, and bird of peace, and all such emblems
Laid nobly on her.

(*Henry VIII*, IV.i.87–90)

One of the great Shakespearean archetypal images, of course, is that of the world as a theater—"All the world's a stage." This image, however, was central not only for Shakespeare but for his age. Again and again we encounter the "Theatrum Orbis" motif in Renaissance art and literature. An associated image was that of kings as the principal actors upon the world's stage. James I has an apposite passage: "It is a true olde saying that a King is as one set on a stage, whose smallest actions and gestures, all the people gazinglie doe beholde." [3] Shakespeare, dreaming of the epic drama he hoped to achieve in *Henry V*, called for "A kingdom for a stage, princes to act" (Prologue, 3).

Philosophically as well as poetically, Shakespeare was bound to make kings and kingship central. It is one of the truisms of Shakespearean criticism that Shakespeare was a great law-and-order man, a great believer in "degree," to use the Elizabethan term. And for Shakespeare, born into Tudor England, law and order were inseparable from the office of the king. The Lord Chief Justice in *2 Henry IV* speaks succinctly of "The majesty and power of law and justice,/The image of the King whom I presented" (V.ii.78–79).

Perusing the plays, we gradually get Shakespeare's vision of the Ideal of Kingship. We see the ideal king as just, generous, magnanimous. With equity and insight he directs the government of society. An almost religious aura surrounds him, a tremendous distance in rank separates him from the subjects he commands, though, paradoxically, he is himself a part of the society they constitute. Poetry and drama surround him. Ceremony and circumstance mark him as the KING. The centrality of this Ideal of Kingship is emblazoned on the pages of Shakespeare. It is there in the imagery. The king is like the sun blazing in the heavens. Images of sunshine illuminate Richard II before he, a king of snow, melts before "the sun of Bolingbroke." Prince Hal, as heir to the Crown, is described by Vernon as "gorgeous as the sun at midsummer" (*1 Henry IV*, IV.i.102). Become king, he displays "A largess universal, like the sun" (*Henry V*, IV, Prologue, 43). Conversely (the sun reigning as a king in the heavens) "The sun ariseth in his majesty" (*Venus and Adonis*, 856). Another image emphasizing the dominance of the monarch is that of the king as the lofty tree towering above the garden that is the state. This has been noted by Caroline Spurgeon as one of the "running images" in the plays. Thus Edward IV is seen as "the royal tree" that has left royal fruit, Henry VI is "the cedar" that falls to the axe, and imperial Mark Antony is "this pine . . . That overtopp'd them all." [4]

Interesting too is Shakespeare's vocabulary. The plays are studded with references to the "sacred king," "anointed king," "crowned king," and most of all to the "royal king." Similarly we have mention of "anointed majesty," "most imperial majesties," "high imperial majesty," and, very frequently, "royal majesty." "Royal king" and "royal majesty" are phrases which normally we might dismiss as obvious tautologies, but not here. Shakespeare knew well enough that many kings are less than "royal" in any absolute sense. "Royal king" and "royal majesty" spring from his distinction between the Real and the Ideal King. Thus the bestowal of the epithet "royal" is the ultimate encomium. He does not reserve it for his English kings. Julius Caesar, who never did accept a crown, becomes "royal Caesar" (*Julius Caesar*, III.ii.249), and Mark Antony declares "Caesar was mighty, bold, royal" (III.i.127). Cleopatra dies amid a shower of "royals"; Iras calls upon her as "Royal Queen," and Charmian declares that golden Phoebus will never "be beheld of eyes again so royal!" Octavius confirms the epithet: "She level'd at our purposes, and being royal,/Took her own way" (*Antony and Cleopatra*, V.ii.339–40). Dimension is added to Othello by making him fetch his life and being "from men of royal siege."

The word "royal" escapes in fact from literal contexts. In *Measure for Measure* the epithet properly belonging to Duke Vincentio is "ducal" (a word which oddly enough Shakespeare never uses in his plays). Instead we find Isabella crying "Justice, O royal Duke!" (V.i.20), and subsequently Friar Peter declares "I have heard/Your royal ear abused" (138–39). Possibly there is something to the old theory that Shakespeare modeled Duke Vincentio on James I, and used "royal" because of a blurring of character and original; but a more likely explanation is that Shakespeare, concerned in these final scenes to build up the grace and worth of the Duke, brought into the play one of his own ultimate value words. "Royal" in fact becomes for Shakespeare a word for the utmost in goodness, magnanimity, and generosity. Thus Timon of Athens, in the days of his bliss, is hailed as "noble, worthy, royal Timon" (II.ii.177). In *The Merchant of Venice* the bourgeois Antonio is twice referred to as a "royal merchant" (III.ii.239; IV.i.29). When Shakespeare wishes to pay his greatest tribute to England he employs concentrated language of kingship: "The *royal throne* of *kings,* this *scept'red* isle,/This earth of *majesty*" (*Richard II*, II.i.40–41; emphasis added). Only if we appreciate what the Ideal of Kingship meant to Shakespeare can we get the full impact of Lear's famous line: "Ay, every inch a king."

Despite his rich, romantic, poetic, and somewhat anachronistic ideal of kingship (what Harold Hobson with a touch of hyperbole has recently termed "Shakespeare's adoration of royalty" [5]), Shakespeare was not blind to the actual condition of kings, the human frailties of the individuals who may wear the crown, their vulnerability in sharing in the general human condition. Almost with a sense of paradox he notes that physical nature is oblivious of kingship. The storm on the heath spares Lear nothing because of his royal boood. At the beginning of *The Tempest*, amid the waves that break upon King Alonso's ship, the boatswain asks, "What cares these roarers for the name of king?" With a strange fascination Shakespeare dwells upon the cares which come with the crown, so that sleep which comes to the "wet sea boy" is denied to the king in his luxurious bed. Observations such as "the King is but a man, as I am" (*Henry V*, IV.i.105–6) and "kings and mightiest potentates must die" (*1 Henry IV*, III.ii.136) stud the plays. The recurrence of such commonplaces is part of a technique of chiaroscuro in Shakespeare's portrayal of his kings.

Once we come to deal with individual monarchs, we find that Shakespeare the psychologist and the historian determines the treatment, and accordingly his kings are made real and not ideal. Of Henry VI one can say little. That hapless monarch appears intermittently and ineffectually amid the swirl of the plots and counterplots, coups and counter-coups of his barons and his queen. Practically a saint in his guileless simplicity, he bears testimony to one fact at least—Shakespeare understood from the outset that, where sovereignty is concerned, goodness is not enough. With Richard III we come to the polar opposite, the Machiavellian villain who with a bloody axe can cut his way to the crown. But the individual personal wickedness of Richard is not for one moment allowed to contaminate the Crown itself. There is no reason why the Crown should diminish in brightness. The homilies of the Church of England had sufficiently instructed the English that kingship is not the less to be honored because an evil king may be sent by God as a punishment for the people's sins. W. M. Merchant has pointed out how, for the Elizabethans, a parallel existed between monarchy and priesthood. In both there was to be observed "the practical distinction between the status sacramentally conferred and the moral person upon whom it is conferred." [6] At the end of *Richard III* the crown, unstained, moves from the temples of the vicious Richard to the forehead of that champion of goodness, Richmond.

Richard II is a particularly interesting play because, in fashioning his Richard, Shakespeare has contrived to set in contrast the ideal king and the real king. At the outset, Richard appears to us as the Ideal King. The radiant handsomeness of His Majesty, emphasized by the imagery of roses and sun, seems the outward sign of a truly royal spirit within. When he speaks, it is with the accents of majesty:

> Now by my sceptre's awe I make a vow,
> Such neighbour nearness to our sacred blood
> Should nothing privilege him nor partialize
> The unstooping firmness of my upright soul.
>
> (I.i.118–21)

But this is only a role, one of the many which the histrionic Richard is to provide for himself in the play. And part of the fascination of *Richard II*, if properly produced, is that sense of near incredulity induced in the audience when it first senses that Richard, despite his royal presence, is weak. Here is the demonstration of how, in real life, it may happen that "kings grow base." The end of the play is instructive. Richard secures at the last a sort of rehabilitation in the eyes of the audience, but not in terms of kingship. Richard, being but a man, must like all men find within himself and not in any office the key to his redemption. It is as a man that each individual king must in the end be evaluated. Richard finally finds within himself the courage which allows him to die bravely.

Hardest to date, and least successful, of all Shakespeare's history plays is his *King John*. Here he fails to distinguish sufficiently between the wickedness of John, the wearer of the crown, and the integrity of kingship as such. The two concepts become very badly confused, and the audience, after turning against John the criminal, finds itself confused at being expected to applaud John the king.

We come to Shakespeare's ultimate achievement with the theme of kingship, the Henriad. Henry IV is, in much less lurid fashion, a species of Richard III, a usurper who has desecrated legitimate kingship. On his deathbed he must confess "By what bypaths and indirect crook'd ways/I met this crown" (*2 Henry IV*, IV.v.185–86). But Shakespeare's interest in these plays is never really in Henry IV, that somewhat prosaic Machiavellian. His concern is with Prince Hal, who becomes Henry V. For a number of reasons, including the unsuitability of the drama as a medium for the epic,[7] *Henry V* is only a partial success for most audiences. But all that concerns us now is that Henry V is Shakespeare's embodiment of the Ideal King. He speaks with the accents of majesty, and his spirit is majestical. There is no false note when he speaks of rousing him in his throne of France. Wise and farseeing in statecraft, he provides for England's defense against the weasel Scot before he leaves her shores. With a special insight into the hearts of his subjects, he knows the hidden thought of old Sir

Thomas Erpingham. With the intuitive touch of a true leader he can give to each of his soldiers "a little touch of Harry in the night."

This Henry is intensely religious. Piety, let it be noted, is one of Shakespeare's central requirements of a truly royal king. Note how in *Macbeth* Edward the Confessor, saint and king, is made the center from which Good emanates in its triumphant counter-invasion upon Evil, which (possessing Macbeth) has invaded Scotland. Note also the praises of "gracious" Duncan and his religious queen. Certainly we are left in no doubt of Henry V's deeply religious nature. He will not take in hand the invasion of France until he secures from his spiritual director, the Archbishop of Canterbury, an absolutely unequivocal declaration that he may "with right and conscience" claim the French throne. Alone on the eve of Agincourt he prays to the God of battles, and after a miraculous victory is won he declares, "O God, thy arm was here!/And not to us, but to thy arm alone,/Ascribe we all!" (IV.viii.111–13). He orders that all holy rites be performed with the singing of the "Non Nobis" and the "Te Deum."

Henry's role as warrior is central to Shakespeare's picture of him as the ideal king. An anachronistic part of his idealization of kingship makes him think in terms of medieval kings personally leading their armies into battle. A curious consequence of this strain in his thinking is that "royal" becomes a word associated with battle. The Induction to *2 Henry IV* speaks of "that royal field of Shrewsbury." Richard II contemplates the trial by combat between Mowbray and Bolingbroke as "this royal fight." In a play as remote from the English histories as *Antony and Cleopatra*, Antony, using the same idiom, will "drink carouses to the next day's fate,/Which promises royal peril" (IV.viii.34–35). Earlier he has exclaimed to Cleopatra, "O love,/That thou couldst see my wars to-day, and knew'st/The royal occupation" (IV.iv.15–17). The fact that historically Henry V was a great soldier helps to make his stage representation an incarnation of Shakespeare's idealized concept of kingship. But it is part of Shakespeare's rounding out of Henry that, while he makes him a military hero, he gives him at the same time a feeling apprehension of the horrors of war, set forth graphically in his warning to the citizens of Harfleur.

After writing *Henry V* and presenting the ultimate in kingship, Shakespeare seems to have lost his momentum in writing about sovereignty. By now he had touched upon all its aspects, paradoxes, and implications. Not surprisingly Shakespeare ceases to write plays dealing with English kings. Only at the last does he make a final return with *Henry VIII*, though here he seems to be interested chiefly in Wolsey and the wronged Queen Katherine.

His history plays behind him, Shakespeare turned to the writing of his great tragedies. The spiritual issues here are so profound that even kingship must take a subordinate though not always a minor role. In the tragedies and Shakespeare's later comedies and romances, kings, princes, and dukes will still walk the stage; but, though the royal chord will be heard upon occasion, it will be less frequent.

The time has come for us to take our leave of Shakespeare's individual kings and to concentrate upon the philosophical and psychological issues which are involved in the whole subject of Shakespeare as King-Maker. There were, of course, two views of kingship held in Shakespeare's day. The first was that of Machiavelli's *realpolitik* which saw power, sovereignty, as something to be won by the strong and ruthless and to be held independent of any theological or idealistic sanctions. Shakespeare has kings of this school. Richard III, King Claudius, and King Macbeth force their way to their thrones by stratagem, fraud, and crime. They are part of the power mechanism so prominent in Shakespeare's political awareness. But there was a more traditional view of sovereignty, that carefully nurtured by the ministers of Elizabeth I and, in greater degree, by those of James I, the view that the sovereign is God's Elect, chosen and appointed to this throne by God himself, and responsible only to Him. Shakespeare presents the Divine Right view in his plays less frequently than is commonly realized. Claudius may declare "There's such divinity doth hedge a king/That treason can but peep to what it would,/Acts little of his will" (*Hamlet*, IV.v.123–25). But an irony nullifies these lines when we recall that they are spoken by a man who has come to the throne through high treason, murdering King Hamlet. In *Macbeth*, Macduff announcing Duncan's murder cries,

> Confusion now hath made his masterpiece!
> Most sacrilegious murther hath broke ope
> The Lord's anointed temple and stole thence
> The life o' th' building.
>
> (II.iii.71–74)

But Macduff is not saying that Duncan had been elected by God to be King. Rather he speaks of the sacrament at his coronation, when the anointing gave a religious sanction to his rule.

The only person in the Shakespeare canon who makes specific Divine Right declarations is Richard II. It is Richard who declares

> Not all the water in the rough rude sea
> Can wash the balm off from an anointed king.
> The breath of worldly men cannot depose
> The deputy elected by the Lord.
>
> (III.ii.54–57)

But Richard is a desperately weak character, and all his talk of God electing and defending him is a psychological prop. There is an interesting parallel between him and James I who, haunted all his life by fears of assassination, iterated and reiterated his conviction: "Kings are in the Word of GOD it selfe called Gods, as being his Lieutenants and Vicegerents on earth, and so adorned and furnished with some sparkles of the Divinitie." [8] But nowhere in his plays does Shakespeare vindicate the theory of Divine Right. He may let poor, pathetic, weakly vicious Richard II vaunt,

> For every man that Bolingbroke hath press'd
> To lift shrewd steel against our golden crown,
> God for his Richard hath in heavenly pay
> A glorious angel. Then, if angels fight,
> Weak men must fall; for Heaven still guards the right.
>
> (III.ii.58–62)

The only comment needed is that in fact the rebel Bolingbroke does win and becomes king, while unkinged Richard goes to his lonely death at Pomfret.

As noted earlier, it was an important part of the Divine Right theory, sedulously taught by the Church of England, that the people must accept as a divine punishment a cruel and wicked king who had come to his throne by lawful succession:

Shall the subjects both by their wickedness provoke God for their deserved punishment to give them an undiscreet or evil prince, and also rebel against him, and withall against God, who for the punishment of their sins did give them such a prince? Will you hear the Scriptures concerning this point? *God,* say the holy Scriptures, *maketh a wicked man to reign for the sins of the people.* [9]

Nowhere does this doctrine find statement within Shakespeare's works. We need not be surprised at his silence on this point. As Godfrey Goodman, Bishop of Gloucester in the final days of James I, noted, the doctrine of Divine Right never won general consent from the English people. [10] John Chamberlain spoke for the majority when he observed in 1610, "I heare yt bred much discomfort; to see our monarchicall powre and regall prerogative strained so high and made so transcendent every way." [11] Shakespeare may have been fascinated by the mystique and ceremony of kingship (though his Henry V has some penetrating comments to make upon that "idol ceremony"). No doubt his intense conservatism made him cherish kingship as the source of social law and degree, and accordingly recoil at the very thought of usurpation. No doubt he did see the anointing of a king in his coronation at Westminster as a profoundly significant religious sacrament. But it is impossible to make Shakespeare a champion either of Divine Right or of its attendant doctrine of the necessity of submitting to evil but legitimate monarchs. His position in these matters was almost certainly that of most of his fellow countrymen.

Sycophantic courtiers and chaplains might be voluble on how God defends his deputy, but Shakespeare sees the deposition of a king who has signally failed as a fact of political life, however jarring or disastrous the ultimate consequences might prove. He knows that an unkingly king in a sense ceases to be King. In *2 Henry VI*, York contemptuously declares to Henry VI "King did I call thee? No! thou art not King/Not fit to govern and rule multitudes" (V.i.93–94). In the succeeding play, Warwick announces to Edward IV: "When you disgrac'd me in my embassade,/Then I degraded you from being King" (*3 Henry VI*, IV.iii.32–33). In *Richard II* John of Gaunt in metaphor unkings Richard before the actual deed is performed by Bolingbroke: "Landlord of England art thou now, not King" (II.i.113). The very intensity of Shakespeare's devotion to the Ideal of Kingship probably made not unattractive to him such ringing declarations addressed to unworthy monarchs.

Merchant, in an article already cited, sees a dilemma for Shakespeare in this matter of the unroyal king:

But the king is sovereign, having logically no judicial superior. His moral failure to fulfill the functions conferred sacramentally upon him, the apparent necessity of his deposition, involve therefore the tragedy of an insoluble difficulty.[12]

Shakespeare, however, found one way out of this dilemma. Let a ruler swerve too far from the duties of kingship and he ceases to be a king. Instead he is generally recognized as a monstrous aberration, stigmatized with the name of "tyrant."

"Tyrant" is just as powerfully emotive a word as "King" for Shakespeare, being its total negation. The antithesis is clearly set up for us. "We are no tyrant, but a Christian king" (*Henry V*, I.ii.241). Tragedy occurs when kingship gives way to tyranny: "Yield up, O love, thy crown and hearted throne/To tyrannous hate!" (*Othello*, III.iii.448–49). Tyranny cancels out all the rights of kingship. Macbeth may have been formally crowned at Scone, but he is "an untitled tyrant bloody-scept'red" (IV.iii.104). King Leontes, we gather, came to his throne by lawful succession, but his kingship is lost in the infamy of his tyranny. Paulina warns him,

> this most cruel usage of your queen
> (Not able to produce more accusation

Than your own weak-hing'd fancy) something savours
Of tyranny, and will ignoble make you,
Yea, scandalous to the world.

> > (*The Winter's Tale*, II.ii.116–20)

"Tyranny"—that single word is a flaming indictment, and the no longer kingly Leontes furiously retorts, "On your allegiance,/Out of the chamber with her! Were I a tyrant,/Where were her life?" (120–22). Restored by shock and penitence, Leontes ceases to be a tyrant and regains his kingly identity. But for those, in other plays, who are irreclaimable in their tyranny there awaits death at the hands of those who fight under God:

> Then if you fight against God's enemy,
> God will in justice ward you as his soldiers.
> If you do sweat to put a tyrant down,
> You sleep in peace, the tyrant being slain.

> > (*Richard III*, V.iii.254–57)

After the tyrant is slain, Shakespeare ushers a true king to the vacant throne. Richard III is succeeded by Richmond, founder of the Tudor dynasty. When Macbeth's tyranny is ended, Malcolm comes to the throne, pouring forth honor and justice:

> My Thanes and kinsmen,
> Henceforth be Earls, the first that ever Scotland
> In such honour nam'd. What's more to do
> Which would be planted newly with the time—
> As calling home our exil'd friends abroad
> That fled the snares of watchful tyranny,
> Producing forth the cruel ministers
> Of this dead butcher and his fiendlike queen,
> Who (as 'tis thought) by self and violent hands
> Took off her life—this, and what needful else
> That calls upon us, by the grace of Grace
> We will perform in measure, time, and place.
> So thanks to all at once and to each one,
> Whom we invite to see us crown'd at Scone.

> > (V.viii.62–75)

The nightmare of Macbeth's tyranny ended, Scotland passes into the quiet haven of rule under a true king, brave, magnanimous, and generous. To the sound of trumpets is inaugurated the reign of a royal king.

Something more needs to be said before we take leave of Shakespeare and his dream of majesty. Perhaps, in some corner of that incredible mind, he knew that an unreality attended upon all his rich poetic vision of ideal kingship. Perhaps he sensed that he was only indulging his imagination in a resplendent dream. How often that word "dream" becomes associated with kingship in his plays!

> This dream of mine—
> Being now awake I'll queen it no inch farther.
> (*The Winter's Tale*, IV.iv.458–59)

> Learn, good soul,
> To think our former state [of sovereignty] a happy dream.
> (*Richard II*, V.i.17–18)

> thou proud dream,
> That play'st so subtilly with a king's repose.
> (*Henry V*, IV.i.274–75)

> I do but dream on sovereignty.
> (*3 Henry VI*, III.ii.134)

> I'll make my heaven to dream upon the crown.
> (*3 Henry VI*, III.ii.168)

> I could be bounded in a nutshell and count myself a king of infinite space, were it not I have bad dreams.
> (*Hamlet*, II.ii.260–62)

> the very substance of the ambitious is merely the shadow of a dream.
> (*Hamlet*, II.ii.264–65)

> We are a queen (or long have dream'd so).
> (*Henry VIII*, II.iv.71)

> I dreamt there was an Emperor Antony.
> (*Antony and Cleopatra*, V.ii.76)

> Stay we no longer, dreaming of renown.
> (*3 Henry VI*, II.i.199)

To Sigmund Freud the creation of literary fictions was akin to dreaming. What of Shakespeare personally? Did he himself, in reverie or slumber, dream of kingship? The protean psychology of an actor sends him into many roles, but it is surely worth noting that during Shakespeare's own lifetime John Davies of Hereford singled out for mention the "Kingly parts" which Shakespeare played.[13] For what it is worth, we have John Manningham's recounting the jest of how Shakespeare, likening himself to William the Conqueror, claimed precedence before Burbage, as Richard III, when he arrived before the latter at a woman's bedchamber.[14] May these things reveal some dream pattern within Shakespeare? Did he, besides creating kings within his plays, tend in sanguine mood to dream of himself in kingly terms? Caroline Spurgeon suspected that such was the case:

One might almost deduce that he often dreamed himself a king of men, surrounded by homage and sweet flattering words, and had awakened to find this but empty and vain imagining, and that he was, after all, only Will, the poor player.[15]

If we incline to the fascinating thought that Shakespeare at the end of *The Tempest* may have presented himself in the persona of Duke Prospero, we may find some significance in Prospero's comment that our world with its gorgeous palaces and solemn temples is but such stuff as dreams are made on. We may let our minds linger on passages from the sonnets:

> doth my mind, being crown'd with you,
> Drink up the monarch's plague, this flattery?
>
> (Sonnet 114:1–2)

Thus have I had thee as a dream doth flatter—
In sleep a king, but waking no such matter.

(Sonnet 87:13–14)

CLIFFORD LEECH

The Moral Tragedy of
Romeo and Juliet

*H*OW ADVENTUROUS Shakespeare was in writing *Romeo and Juliet* in 1594 or 1595 we do not always realize. First, there had been few tragedies written for the public theaters before then, and none in the first rank except Marlowe's. Shakespeare himself had doubtless already written *Titus Andronicus*, an exercise after Seneca and with many memories of Ovid. Kyd too had popularized Seneca in *The Spanish Tragedy*. Marlowe had had his imitators: Greene's *Alphonsus King of Aragon* had echoed the enthusiasm for the aspiring mind, but with none of the ambivalence that was deep in Marlowe. *Selimus*, which may also be Greene's, presented the other side of the picture—an Asian king who tyrannized and manifestly deserved to be destroyed. Marlowe's plays continued as a prominent part of the repertory, but only Shakespeare gives evidence of responding to their complexity.[1] Moreover, few tragedies before *Romeo and Juliet* had taken love as a central theme. It is true that *Dido Queen of Carthage*, attributed to Marlowe and Nashe on its title page of 1594 (where it was also declared to have been acted by the Children of the Queen's Chapel), was a play about love. But it is dubious whether we can accept this as a love-tragedy: "ironic comedy" would seem to fit it better.[2] It did indeed end with three deaths, and we must recognize that the idea of love leading to disaster was an occasional concern of the private stage in these years. *Gismond of Salerne* was acted at the Inner Temple in 1566 or 1568: it is a Senecan play, and the lovers never appear on the stage together. The lost *Quintus Fabius* of 1574, acted by the Windsor Boys at court, apparently had for its subject Xerxes' violent passion for the daughter of his sister-in-law.[3] Richard Edwardes's lost play *Palamon and Arcite* was acted at Christ Church, Oxford, before Elizabeth in 1566: coming from Chaucer's *The Knight's Tale*, its ending must have included destruction for one of the lovers. All these, however, clearly belong to the private stages. Arthur Brooke in the address to the reader prefixed to his poem *Romeus and Juliet*

(1562) refers to having "lately" seen the story on the stage—there is no indication whether the stage referred to was public or private. Until Shakespeare wrote *Romeo and Juliet*, love on the public stage appears to have been solely an element either in comedy or in those romantic plays which Sidney mocked in his *Apology for Poetry* and which are vestigially preserved for us in *Sir Clyamon and Clamydes* (ca. 1570) and *Common Conditions* (ca. 1576).

Shakespeare, however, in the early years of his career showed a readiness to try every mode of playwriting. He had contributed to, and perhaps even invented,[4] the history play based on the English chronicles; he had written various types of comedy: a derivative from Plautus in *The Comedy of Errors*, a romantic wandering play in *The Two Gentlemen of Verona*, an Italianate intrigue affair in *The Taming of the Shrew*; now he wanted to try tragedy again—though he was to neglect that kind for some years afterward—and chose to make a play out of Arthur Brooke's thirty-year-old poem. It was a fascinating tale that had come from Italy, dramatized also in Spain by Lope de Vega in *Castelvines y Monteses* (though we have no reason to believe that either dramatist knew the other's work), and Shakespeare took over from his own comedies much that seemed to fit his new purpose.

But if he was to write a tragedy about love, what attitude should he take up to it? His inheritance was complex. From Galen in the second century A.D. there came the idea that love was a form of "melancholy," an idea that continued to be held fast in the late sixteenth- and seventeenth-century mind. The frontispiece to the original edition of Burton's *Anatomy of Melancholy* shows "Inamorato" as a chief "melancholy" type. Nevertheless, Aristotle had declared that melancholy was a privileged state which enabled men to see more clearly into things than a normal man could.[5] Moreover, there was Plato, with his notion of a ladder leading from the simplest sensual love to love of the highest. The Neoplatonists, exemplified splendidly in Castiglione's *The Courtier*, seemed to demand a kicking away of the lower rungs of the ladder as one ascended higher (which surely Plato never demanded), but nevertheless they saw love as an ultimate, a mode of experiencing the ideas of Goodness and Beauty. There was, too, the legacy from Courtly Love, which Spenser responded to, but which was perhaps now growing rather thin. And there was the attitude of churchmen, varying from a total contempt for women to a more discreet insistence on the need for man not to put any woman in the place that God alone should occupy. A Courtly Love poet customarily ended with a palinode, rejecting the devotion that he had before exhibited, and in *The Romance of the Rose* Jean de Meun's satiric presentation of the love-condition followed on Guillaume de Lorris's much briefer account of the lover's devotion. An Elizabethan sonneteer could see his love as his way to an apprehension of the godlike, or he might, as Shakespeare does, find submission to his mistress "Th' expense of spirit in a waste of shame." In addition we must not forget the surely ever-recurrent view of the lover, or of the husband, as an essentially comic figure. In *The Second Shepherds' Play* in the Wakefield cycle, one of the shepherds makes the common medieval joke about his wife's shrewishness and warns the young men in the audience not to let falling in love lead them into marriage. In the early sixteenth century the lover's comical extravagances are at the center of Udall's *Ralph Roister Doister*. To write a play about love and to disregard this common view of it would be to exclude a major part of human experience in relation to the play's subject. Thus a playwright choosing to make love central in a tragedy had little warrant for presenting the condition as simply ennobling: other views of it were exerting a good deal of pressure in Elizabethan times.[6]

Romeo and Juliet has proved a problem for Shakespeare critics. Franklin M. Dickey has seen it as exhibiting a simple moral lesson: to be taken up wholly by one's passion for another human being would, he argues, be seen by an Elizabethan as a moral imperfection, as likely to induce a general disregard of the moral law: so Shakespeare's play, despite its sympathy with the lovers, must be seen in relation to the contemporary idea of moral responsibility.[7] But to argue in this way is to take *Romeo and Juliet* as Roy Battenhouse has taken Marlowe's *Tamburlaine*:[8] Battenhouse tries to disregard the grandeur that goes along with the evil in Marlowe's hero; Dickey misses the sense of an enhanced degree of life which Shakespeare's lovers experience along with the danger they freely encounter. Nicholas Brooke is aware of the problem that faced Shakespeare: he suggests that the love of Romeo and Juliet is tested against the presentation of the normal current of life, which is indeed strong in the play, and that this love just—and only just—makes itself acceptable as an achieved good.[9] Indeed, when we remember the likely date of Shakespeare's play, we shall not be surprised at this. In *Love's Labour's Lost* he had made fun of the devotion that the King of Navarre and his three lords had manifested to the Princess of France and her three ladies: the men are made to endure a year-long penance, and Berowne's required sojourn in a hospital is, Berowne himself recognizes, almost an impossible demand. Can love outlast the waiting-time? Can it be related to the agony of the sick and the dying? In any event it must, the ending of the play suggests, be put into a total context, not being capable of replacing that context. In *The Two Gentlemen of Verona* love is juxtaposed with the idea of friendship, which, being as it was alleged purely altruistic, had a high standing indeed in the Renaissance, and love was there mocked through the figures of Launce and Speed, who took a more commonplace view of relations between the sexes. At the end it is the sympathetically opportunistic Julia who gets things straightened out. If the heroic lover and friend Valentine had been solely in charge of the play's termination, only disaster would have been possible. In writing a play in which the love of a young man and a young woman was to be considered a proper motive for tragedy, Shakespeare was bound to draw on his earlier treatments of love in comedy, but he would need to make a major departure too.

Certainly there is plenty of comedy here. Were it not for the declaration of the Prologue, with its references to "star-cross'd lovers" and to the ending of the feud through their deaths, we might well take the first two acts as moving toward a fortunate issue for the young people. The atmosphere is here generally one of pleasurable excitement, although Shakespeare has given Juliet a moment of premonition in the first balcony scene:

> Although I joy in thee,
> I have no joy in this contract to-night.
> It is too rash, too unadvis'd, too sudden;
> Too like the lightning, which doth cease to be
> Ere one can say 'It lightens.'
>
> (II.ii.116–20)

More of such premonitions will be noted later. But, until the moment when Mercutio is killed, the threat is not anywhere heavy. When Romeo and Juliet declare their love, there are moments of pure comedy. Thus Romeo compares himself to a schoolboy, reluctant to go to his books as Romeo is reluctant to leave Juliet: "Love goes toward love as schoolboys from their books;/But love from love, toward school with heavy looks" (II.ii.157–58). And there is a touch of absurdity, which we shall applaud when we remember what we all have done in distantly comparable circumstances, when Juliet says she has forgotten why she called him back, and he says he is ready to stay till she remembers:

> I have forgot why I did call thee back.
> *Rom.* Let me stand here till thou remember it.
> *Jul.* I shall forget, to have thee still stand there,
> Rememb'ring how I love thy company.
> *Rom.* And I'll still stay, to have thee still forget,
> Forgetting any other home but this.
>
> (II.ii.172–77)

We may remember too that Romeo has wished to be the glove on Juliet's hand, a mildly ludicrous idea, and that both lovers would like Romeo to be Juliet's pet bird:

> *Jul.* 'Tis almost morning. I would have thee gone—
> And yet no farther than a wanton's bird,
> That lets it hop a little from her hand,
> Like a poor prisoner in his twisted gyves,
> And with a silk thread plucks it back again,
> So loving-jealous of his liberty.
>   *Rom.*   I would I were thy bird.
>   *Jul.*   Sweet, so would I.
> Yet I should kill thee with much cherishing.
>
>   (II.ii.178–85)

They will speak differently in the second balcony scene, but even there they will only dimly apprehend the world that threatens them.

Before this, of course, Romeo had been almost totally a figure of fun when he was giving voice to his love for Rosaline, and after meeting Juliet he is in a situation of some embarrassment when he goes to tell the Friar of his new love and of his wish for a secret marriage. When he admits that he has not been in his bed during the night that has just passed, he has to hear the Friar exclaim "God pardon sin! Wast thou with Rosaline?" (II.iii.144), and there is a particularly ludicrous touch when the Friar claims to see on Romeo's cheek a tear shed for Rosaline's love and not yet washed off. Even so, Shakespeare makes it plain that the new love is a thing of true moment. This is made evident not only in the authority of language that the lovers are sometimes allowed, during their interchange of words at their first meeting in the Capulet house and in the first balcony scene, but also in Romeo's premonition of disaster when he is on his way to the first meeting:

>   my mind misgives
> Some consequence, yet hanging in the stars,
> Shall bitterly begin his fearful date
> With this night's revels and expire the term
> Of a despised life, clos'd in my breast,
> By some vile forfeit of untimely death.
> But he that hath the steerage of my course
> Direct my sail! On, lusty gentlemen!
>
>   (I.iv.106–13)

Because we have hints enough that disaster lies ahead, we cannot see the love merely in terms of comedy.

Moreover, Romeo's behavior when he meets Mercutio and Benvolio again after he has talked with the Friar shows him as a young man ready to cope with danger for his love's sake and also ready, as now an adult lover, to give over affectation and to feel able to parry Mercutio's jests. Then, after the marriage, he has dignity both in his first refusal to fight with Tybalt, his new kinsman, and in his entering into the fray because he has by ill luck been responsible for Mercutio's death. At least, it may at first seem like ill luck, but we are made to see that Romeo's refusal to fight, Mercutio's indignation, and Romeo's revenge for his friend's death all arise, by necessity or at least probability, out of the nature of the characters and their situation in Verona. "O, I am fortune's fool!"—Romeo's cry after Tybalt's death—is comment enough on his inability to cope with the situation engendered by the feud, which previously he had been overconfident about. How precarious is his hold on his new adult status is underlined in the scene in the Friar's cell, where his love is expressed again in ludicrous terms:

> More validity,
> More honourable state, more courtship lives
> In carrion flies than Romeo. They may seize
> On the white wonder of dear Juliet's hand
> And steal immortal blessing from her lips,
> Who, even in pure and vestal modesty,
> Still blush, as thinking their own kisses sin;
> But Romeo may not—he is banished.
> This may flies do, when I from this must fly;
> They are free men, but I am banished.
>
> (III.iii.33–42)

The poor girl, with those flies on her hand and lips; those lips, so beautifully red because they are kissing each other; that shocking pun of "flies" and "fly": Romeo had uttered no more immature lines when the thought of Rosaline was on him. His extravagance here is similar to that of Valentine in *The Two Gentlemen of Verona*, who was similarly banished from the town where Silvia lived. And the mocker or rebuker is present with both: Launce the clown makes fun of Valentine; Romeo is described by the Friar as "with his own tears made drunk." He will recover dignity before the play's end, but he has lost hold of it here.

Juliet, on the other hand, has not Romeo's initial disadvantage of a previous, and ludicrous, love-attachment. We see her first as the dutiful daughter, ready to prepare herself to fall in love with Paris, as her parents would like her to. But Romeo is her first true commitment, and if she expresses herself comically at times in the first balcony scene, that is only a reminder of her extreme youth. And she is much more practical than he is: it is she who suggests how the wedding shall be arranged. Shakespeare has, moreover, given two almost parallel scenes in which she is the central figure: II.v, when she awaits the Nurse's return from her mission to Romeo, and III.ii, when she is looking forward to the coming wedding night. In both instances we have first a soliloquy from Juliet, expressing impatience that time goes for her so slowly, then the Nurse entering and delaying the news she has to give, and finally the Nurse's assurance that things after all will be well. But the differences between the scenes are remarkable. The news that the Nurse withholds is good in the first instance: everything is in order for the secret wedding. In the second instance it is bad news: Tybalt is dead and Romeo banished. The Nurse's delay, moreover, is a matter of teasing in the first scene, the result of incoherent grief in the second. And, although at the end of the second scene the Nurse promises to find Romeo and bring him to comfort Juliet, there is now true darkness here. Act II, scene v ended with Juliet's cry "Hie to high fortune! Honest nurse, farewell." The pun is evidence of pure excitement, and we can imagine Juliet giving the Nurse a quick and affectionate embrace as she goes off to her wedding. The second scene ends also with words from the girl: "O, find him! give this ring to my true knight/And bid him come to take his last farewell" (III.ii.142–43). The echo of Courtly Love in "true knight" has something forced and pathetic in it, and "last farewell" will prove to be a fact. Now, too, it is the Nurse who goes. Juliet must wait.

Yet in both scenes Juliet's youth is most poignantly brought out. Her impatience in II.v is of course amusing: for the moment we forget the omens, and know that the Nurse will truly impart her good news. And III.ii opens with one of the most famous speeches in the play, Juliet's soliloquy beginning "Gallop apace, you fiery-footed steeds/Towards Phoebus' lodging!" Here we find Juliet trying out image after image to give appropriate expression to her love, her desire to be wholly at one with Romeo. There is an overelaborateness in her invocation of Phoebus and Phaeton, of the "sober-suited matron," "civil night" ("civil" because she gives privacy to her citizens), who will teach Juliet "how to lose a winning match,/Play'd for a pair of stainless maidenhoods"; there is a playing with the idea of contrast when she sees Romeo as lying "upon the wings of night/Whiter than new snow upon a raven's back"; and she reaches a grotesque extravagance in the famous lines:

> Give me my Romeo; and, when he shall die,
> Take him and cut him out in little stars,
> And he will make the face of heaven so fine
> That all the world will be in love with night

And pay no worship to the garish sun.

(III.ii.21–25)

The extravagance is, of course, understandable: we do not have to forgive it. Juliet has seen Romeo only at night: she will never see him by daylight, except for the brief moment of their wedding and that half-light of dawn in the second balcony scene. So she can reject the "garish sun" that has never shone on them out of doors. Something more mature immediately follows: "O, I have bought the mansion of a love,/But not possess'd it; and though I am sold,/Not yet enjoy'd" (III.ii.26–28). R. W. Bond noted how the words of Valentine in *The Two Gentlemen of Verona* provided an earlier use of the same image: "O thou that dost inhabit in my breast,/Leave not the mansion so long tenantless,/Lest growing ruinous, the building fall/And leave no memory of what it was! [10] The change of sex is interesting here: Juliet knows that the man is possessed by the woman while he merely penetrates her. Yet we still feel that this inexperienced girl is straining after an appropriate image, trying to be more "grown-up" than she really is. Suddenly the speech ends with an image wholly fitting this character who so recently was herself a child:

> So tedious is this day
> As is the night before some festival
> To an impatient child that hath new robes
> And may not wear them.

(III.ii.28–31)

She is no longer a child, but her childhood memory is here linked with the new experience. Because the memory is now only a memory (yet a vivid one), because Romeo's body will be so startlingly her new clothes (Donne said: "What needst thou have more covering than a man," Elegy XIX), she in using this image from childhood grows suddenly mature as we hear her speak. It will take a good deal longer for Romeo to produce any comparable utterance. Doubtless Shakespeare realized that he had gone further with the girl than with the boy: it was convenient therefore to give the whole of act IV to her concerns, Romeo leaving for Mantua before act III is over and not entering the play again till act V begins.[11]

In giving us these two related scenes in *Romeo and Juliet*, II.v and III.ii, Shakespeare was repeating a device he had twice used in *Richard III*. There he had two wooing scenes and two "lamentation scenes" (to use A. P. Rossiter's term),[12] both pairs being marked by resemblance and difference. Richard wooed Anne successfully against all the odds, and then he wooed his brother's widow Elizabeth for the hand of her daughter: there is an obvious difference between wooing a potential bride and wooing a potential mother-in-law. Moreover, the second of these scenes is left open-ended, and only later are we told that Elizabeth has agreed that her daughter shall marry Richmond, the future Henry VII. Both scenes leave Richard confident. He thinks he has won, and in his second apparent triumph expresses contempt for Elizabeth as he had earlier done for Anne. But the later use of the earlier kind of approach suggests in certain lines both obstinacy and fatigue. The two "lamentation scenes" are also differentiated in that at first Margaret is the adversary, the denunciator of the house of York, and then in the second scene she joins with the women of York in expressing their grief and their horror at the evil that Richard for them represents. Indeed, parallel with variation was one of Shakespeare's special devices in these early plays, as in those scenes of *The Two Gentlemen of Verona* where Launce echoes or indirectly comments on the love-preoccupations of Proteus and Valentine.

In act V of *Romeo and Juliet* Romeo at once shows signs of a new status. His response to the false news of Juliet's death has a directness very different from his behavior in the Friar's cell when he was lamenting his banishment: "Is it e'en so? Then I defy you stars!" And he at once gives directions to Balthasar on the journey he plans to Verona and Juliet's tomb. Of course, he could have explored the matter more fully. It occurs to him to ask if no letters from the Friar have come with Balthasar, but when he receives a negative answer his "No matter. Get thee gone/And hire those horses" shows the rashness we have seen in him throughout. Left alone, with the desire for poison in his mind, he turns his attention to the apothecary's shop and to the situation of poor men. This is psychologically true, for in a moment of anguish we naturally tend to take refuge in a thought of something other than a demand that is immediately on us. After that, Romeo's recognition that the gold he gives is a worse poison than the one he buys is largely a Renaissance commonplace, but the eloquence with which he expresses it gives him an authority he has previously lacked:

> There is thy gold—worse poison to men's souls,
> Doing more murther in this loathsome world,
> Than these poor compounds that thou mayst not sell.
> I sell thee poison; thou hast sold me none.
> Farewell. Buy food and get thyself in flesh.
>
> (V.i.80–84)

Earlier Romeo had to face the distinction between "loving" and "doting" that the Friar insisted on: the young man "doted" on Rosaline, which the Friar could not approve, and he must love Juliet "moderately." Yet of course he did not follow the Friar's advice, though he thought that his love for Juliet was something the Friar could understand. Shakespeare suggests another distinction between love and love: the kind you simply like to maunder over, the kind that ultimately commits you. We do not, as Romeo does, usually kill ourselves for love, but we remember to the end a girl that truly mattered. The utterances from the sympathetic Friar, who thinks the Capulet-Montague feud may come to peace through the marriage, are an echo of the church's view of love in the Middle Ages. The total commitment to another person is, we have seen, in that view a dangerous thing if not kept properly subordinate to one's love of God. Romeo cannot follow the Friar in this: he is so totally committed to Juliet that he will kill himself in her tomb. There is indeed a threefold presentation of love here, not a dichotomy: there is the affected, superficial concern with Rosaline, there is the fatal commitment to Juliet, and there is the "moderation" counseled by the Friar and illustrated in the play's older married couples. Shakespeare gives utterance to the church's counsel, neither endorsing nor rejecting it. If the play's lovers could have lived, some different things would have conditioned their relations to each other: perhaps they were lucky to avoid it. We may be reminded of the ultimate return to Lisa in James Branch Cabell's *Jurgen.*

When Romeo and Juliet commit suicide rather than live without each other, their last words have a special eloquence. Suicide, we must remember, was a mortal sin, yet many men of the Renaissance took a dissident view of it. In particular, Montaigne saw it as man's last available card to play.[13] The classical precedents, moreover, were numerous and powerful.[14] Nowhere in this play is it suggested that damnation lies in wait for the lovers. The audience were likely to feel that Romeo and Juliet had dared greatly: they could not be, in the absence of any comment from the chorus or from the characters who survived them, likely to have in their minds the idea of damnation.

There is, after all, a kind of "happy ending." The feud will be ended, the lovers will be remembered. We may be reminded of the commonplace utterance that we have two deaths: the moment of actual ceasing to be, and the moment when the last person who remembers us dies. These lovers have their being enshrined in a famous play. So they are remembered in perpetuity, and their lives, according to the play itself, will be recorded in their statues.[15] Certainly this is a sad affair, like that of Paolo and Francesca in *The Divine Comedy.* But we may ask, is it tragic?

Tragedy seems to demand a figure or figures that represent us in our ultimate recognition of evil. We need to feel that such figures are our kin, privileged to be chosen for the representative role and coming to the destruction that we necessarily anticipate for ourselves. The boy and girl figures in *Romeo and Juliet* are perhaps acceptable as appropriate representatives for humankind: after all, they do grow up. What worries us more, I think, in trying to see this play as fully achieved "tragedy," is the speech of the Duke at the end, which suggests that some atonement will be made through the reconciliation of the Montague and Capulet families. We are bound to ask "Is this enough?" It appears to be offered as such, but we remember that the finest among Verona's people are dead.

Shakespearean tragedy commonly ends with a suggestion of a return to normality, to peace. Fortinbras will rule in Denmark, Malcolm in Scotland, Iago will be put out of the way. But these later tragedies leave us with a doubt whether the peace is other than a second-best, whether indeed it is in man's power ever to put things right. In *Romeo and Juliet* the ending of the feud is laboriously spelled out.

But there is also the matter of Fate and Chance. Romeo kills Paris: at first glance that was a quite fortuitous happening. Paris was a good man, devoted to Juliet, who unfortunately got in the way of Romeo's approach to Juliet's tomb. At this point Romeo's doom is sealed: he might kill Tybalt and get away with it; he could not get away with killing an innocent Paris, who was moreover the Prince's kinsman. Now it is inevitable that he will die, whatever the moment of Juliet's awakening. There is indeed a "star-cross'd" pattern for the lovers, there is no way out for Romeo once he has come back to Verona. But perhaps Paris's important function in the last scene is not sufficiently brought out: the spectator may feel that there is simple chance operating in Romeo's arrival before Juliet wakes, in his killing himself a moment too early, in the Friar's belated arrival. Later I must return to the matter of the play's references to the "stars": for the moment I merely want to refer to the fact that tragedy can hardly be dependent on "bad luck."

Even so, though simple chance will not do, we may say that tragedy properly exists only when its events defy reason. The Friar thought the marriage of the young lovers might bring the feud to an end, and that was a reasonable assumption. Ironically, it did end the feud but at the expense of Romeo's and Juliet's lives, at the expense too of Mercutio's, Tybalt's, and Lady Montague's lives. The element of *non sequitur* in the train of events common to tragedy—despite the fact that, with one part of our minds, we see the operation of "probability or necessity," as Aristotle has it—is well described by Laurens van der Post in his novel *The Hunter and the Whale*:

I was too young at the time to realise that tragedy is not tragedy if one finds reason or meaning in it. It becomes then, I was yet to learn, a darker form of this infinitely mysterious matter of luck. It is sheer tragedy only if it is without discernible sense or motivation.[16]

We may balk at "luck," as I have already suggested, but "mysterious" is right indeed (as Bradley splendidly urged on us in the First Lecture of *Shakespearean Tragedy*), for what "sense" or "motivation" does there seem to be in tragedy's gods? The sense of mystery is not, however, firmly posited in *Romeo and Juliet*. Rather, it is laboriously suggested that the Montagues and the Capulets have been taught a lesson in a particularly hard way.

Thus we have several reasons to query the play's achievement in the tragic kind. Do the lovers take on themselves the status of major figures in a celebration of a general human woe? Is the ending, with its promise of reconciliation, appropriate to tragic writing? We have seen that the lovers grow up, and they give us the impression of justifying human life, in their best moments, more than most people do. But the suggestion that their deaths will atone, will bring peace back, seems nugatory: no man's death brings peace, not even Christ's—or the Unknown Soldier's. The play could still end tragically if we were left with the impression that the survivors were merely doing what they could to go on living in an impoverished world: we have that in *Hamlet* and the later tragedies too. Here the laboriousness with which Shakespeare recapitulates all the events known to us, in the Friar's long speech, is surely an indication of an ultimate withdrawal from the tragic: the speech is too much like a preacher's résumé of the events on which a moral lesson will be based. We can accept Edgar's long account of Gloucester's death in *King Lear*, because we need a moment of recession before the tragedy's last phase, where we shall see Lear and Cordelia dead, and because no moral lesson is drawn from Gloucester's death; but at the end of this earlier play, when Romeo and Juliet have already eloquently died, we are with difficulty responsive to the long reiteration of all we have long known through the play's action.

Shakespeare has not here achieved the sense of an ultimate confrontation with evil, or the sense that the tragic figure ultimately and fully recognizes what his situation is. Romeo and Juliet die, more or less content with death as a second best to living together. Montague and Capulet shake hands, and do what is possible to atone. The lovers have the illusion of continuing to be together—an illusion to some extent imposed on the audience. The old men feel a personal guilt, not a realization of a general sickness in man's estate. But perhaps only Lear and Macbeth and Timon came to that realization.

We can understand why Shakespeare abandoned tragedy for some years after this play. It had proved possible for him to touch on the tragic idea in his English histories, making them approach, but only approach, the idea of humanity's representative being given over to destruction, as with the faulty Richard II, the saintly Henry VI, the deeply guilty yet none the less sharply human Richard III. He had given his theater a flawed yet impressive Titus Andronicus and in the same play an Aaron given almost wholly to evil but obstinately alive. But in these plays the main drive is not tragic. The histories rely on the sixteenth-century chronicles, *Titus* on that tradition of grotesque legend that came from both Seneca and Ovid. The past was to be relived and celebrated in the histories; *Titus* was more of a literary exercise in antique horror than a play embodying a direct reference to the general human condition. In *Romeo and Juliet* Shakespeare for the first time essayed tragedy proper—that is, by wanting to bring the play's events into relation to things as they truly are—and he used a tale often told but belonging to recent times and concerned with people whom the spectators were to feel as very much their own kin. He may well have been particularly attracted to the story he found in Brooke's poem for the very reason that its figures and events did not have the authority of history and belonged to the comparatively small world of Verona. No major change in the political order can result from what happens in this play's action. No individual figure presented here is truly given over to evil. Without any precedents to guide him, he aimed at writing about eloquent but otherwise ordinary young people in love and about their equally ordinary friends and families. Only Mercutio has something daemonic in him, in the sense that his quality of life transcends the normal level of being.

We have seen that, if Shakespeare had no useful dramatic precedents in this task, he had a manifold heritage of ideas about the nature of love; and many parts of that heritage show themselves in the play. The immoderateness and rashness that the Friar rebukes seem, on the one hand, to lead—in the fashion of a moral play—to the lovers' destruction. On the other hand, not only is our sympathy aroused but we are made to feel that what Romeo and Juliet achieve may be a finer thing than is otherwise to be found in Verona. Both views are strongly conveyed, and either of them might effectively dominate the play. Of course, they could coexist and interpenetrate—as they were to do much later in *Antony and Cleopatra*—but here they seem to alternate, and to be finally both pushed into the background in the long insistence that the feud will end because of the lovers' deaths. The "moral" is thus finally inverted: the lovers' sequence of errors has culminated in the error of suicide, but now we are made to turn to their parents' error and to the consolation that Romeo and Juliet will be remembered through their golden statues. And it is difficult for us to get interested in these statues, or to take much joy in the feud's ending.

Yet the deepest cause of uneasiness in our response to the play is, I believe, to be found in the relation of the story to the idea of the universe that is posited. We are told in the Prologue of "star-cross'd lovers," and there are after that many references to the "stars." So there is a sense of "doom" here, but we are never fully told what is implied. Many coincidences operate: Romeo meets Tybalt just at the wrong moment; the Friar's message to Romeo about Juliet's alleged death goes astray; Romeo arrives at the tomb just before Juliet awakens; the Friar comes too late. I have already drawn attention to Shakespeare's device by which Romeo has to kill Paris, so that, even if he had arrived at the right time, there would have been no way out for him. We may feel that a similar sequence of chances operates in *Hamlet*: if Hamlet had not killed Polonius in a scared moment, if he had not had his father's seal with him on the voyage to England, if he had not managed to escape on the hospitable pirates' ship, if the foils had not been exchanged in the fencing bout with Laertes, if Gertrude had not drunk from the poisoned cup, things might indeed not have been disposed so as to lead him to Claudius's killing at the moment when it actually occurred. Even so, we can feel that, after all, the end would have been much as it is. Hamlet was a man in love with death, far more in love with death than with killing: we may say that only in the moment of death's imminence was he fully alive, freed from inhibition, able to kill Claudius: somehow or other, whatever the chances, this play demanded a final confrontation between the uncle-father and nephew-son. In *Romeo and Juliet*, on the other hand, we could imagine things working out better: the lovers are doomed only by the words of the Prologue, not by anything inherent in their situation. It is not, as it is in Hardy's novels, that we have a sense of a fully adverse "President of the immortals": there is rather an insufficient consideration of what is implied by the "stars." Of course, in *King Lear*, in all later Shakespearean tragedy, there is a sense of an ultimate mystery in the universe: "Is there any cause in nature that makes these hard hearts?" Lear asks in his condition of most extreme distress. Bradley recognized that this mystery was inherent in the idea of tragedy,[17] as is implied too in the passage from Laurens van der Post I have already quoted. But in *Romeo and Juliet* there is no sense of the mystery being confronted: rather it is merely posited in a facile way, so that we have to accept the lovers' deaths as the mere result of the will of the "stars" (the astrological implication is just too easy), and then we are exhorted to see this as leading to a reconciliation between the families.

The final "moral" of the play, as we have seen, is applied only to Old Montague and Old Capulet: they have done evil in allowing the feud to go on, and have paid for it in the deaths of their children and of Lady Montague. But, largely because Romeo and Juliet are never blamed, the children themselves stand outside the framework of moral drama. They have, albeit imperfectly, grown up into the world of tragedy, where the moral law is not a thing of great moment. They have been sacrificed on the altar of man's guilt, have become the victims of our own outrageousness, have given us some relief because they have died and we still for a time continue living. I have argued elsewhere[18] that we can hardly forgive ourselves for accepting such a sacrifice, can hardly accept a frame of things which seems to demand such a sacrifice. To that extent, *Romeo and Juliet* is "tragic" in a way we can fully recognize. But its long-drawn-out ending, after the lovers are dead, with the pressing home of the moral that their deaths will bring peace, runs contrary to the notion of tragedy. There is a sanguineness about the end of it, a suggestion that after all "All shall be well, and/All manner of thing shall be well," as Eliot quotes from Julian of Norwich in *Little Gidding*, and we can hardly tolerate the complacency of the statement.

So in *Romeo and Juliet*, understandably in view of its early date, we cannot find that tragedy has fully emerged from the moral drama and the romantic comedy that dominated in the public theaters of Shakespeare's earliest time. Here he attempted an amalgam of romantic comedy and the tragic idea, along with the assertion of a moral lesson which is given the final emphasis—although the force of that lesson is switched from the lovers to their parents. But tragedy is necessarily at odds with the moral: it is concerned with a permanent anguishing situation, not with one that can either be put right or be instrumental in teaching the survivors to do better. When Shakespeare wrote "love-tragedy" again, in *Othello* and in *Antony and Cleopatra*, he showed that love may be a positive good but that it was simultaneously destructive and that its dramatic presentation gave no manumission from error to those who contemplated the destruction and continued to live. Nowhere, I think, does he suggest that love is other than a condition for wonder, however much he makes fun of it. But in his mature years he sees it as not only a destructive force but as in no way affording a means of reform. That *Romeo and Juliet* is a "moral tragedy"—which, I have strenuously urged, is a contradiction in terms—is evident enough. It is above all the casualness of the play's cosmology that prevents us from seeing it as tragedy fully achieved: we have seen the need for a fuller appreciation of the mystery. As with *Titus Andronicus*, the nearest play to *Romeo and Juliet* overtly assuming a tragic guise in the chronology of Shakespeare's works, the march toward disaster is too manifestly a literary device. At this stage in his career Shakespeare had not worked as free from the sixteenth-century moral play as Marlowe had done in *Tamburlaine*, *Faustus*, and *Edward II*.

Even so, there is a small achieved tragedy embodied within this play. I have described Mercutio as "daemonic," and that is an adjective we can appropriately apply to every tragic hero: he has fire within him—whether he is Oedipus, Orestes, Hamlet, Macbeth, Racine's Phèdre, Ibsen's Brand, or any of the men and women who occupy the center of Lorca's stage—and the fire ultimately consumes. We can call this "hubris," but the rashness implied in that word is not a matter for moral comment. Mercutio has no Friar to counsel "moderation" to him: even if he had, we cannot imagine him as paying more attention than Giovanni did in Ford's *'Tis Pity She's a Whore.* Certainly Benvolio urges him not to stay in the sun when the Capulets are abroad, but this friend speaks as one man to another, hoping to save his friend from physical danger, not as concerned with his moral health. Mercutio, careless of what may come (as Hamlet was to be), draws his sword and goes to his death. His last words are ironic and resentful. The wound was so small, yet fatal. The quarrel between the "houses" was no concern of his. Yet the wound is "enough," the feud has finished him. No lesson is drawn from this destruction; there is no suggestion that good may come out of it. It has simply happened, to the world's impoverishment.

We cannot certainly know whether Shakespeare had already planned Mercutio's death when he gave him the "Queen Mab" speech. What we do know is that the character is virtually Shakespeare's own invention, hardly a trace of it being in Brooke's poem. But we can guess that the speech prefigures the death and that Shakespeare knew, as early as the first act of the play, that its speaker was soon to die. That does not excuse the crassness of some recent directors who have made the actor of Mercutio's part show a trepidation of his own when, near the end of the speech, he refers to a soldier's dream: our anguish at his death is all the more poignant if he does not show fear or anticipation. All sorts of reasons have been given for the insertion of the speech in the play: it makes Mercutio prominent in our minds, as he needs to be because he will play a crucial role in the plot; it hints at a fantastic dreamworld which will make us aware of a mystery not sufficiently explicit, as we have seen, within the play as a whole; it provides a choric commentary on the loves, for Rosaline and then for Juliet, that Romeo experiences; it mocks indeed not only at sex-relationships but at all men's dreams—and Romeo, just before Mercutio enters on his fantasy, has referred to an ominous dream that he has just had. Does Romeo ever have anything more than a dream, though a splendid and entrancing one? But what is perhaps most important is that the speech puts Mercutio outside the general Christian framework of the play. He is surely a pure pagan: his last call is for a surgeon, not a priest. There is an angriness in him that is a link with Hamlet, Othello, Lear, Macbeth: these characters are by no means all unbelievers, but their final acts are those of men standing alone, without help from the general current of thought in their world, with a full realization too of their loneliness. They take the Protestantism of Shakespeare's time to a desperate limit. Here, not in the oblivious *Liebestod* of the lovers, for all its pre-Wagnerian eloquence, we find the true germ of Shakespeare's later development. One may suspect that Mercutio haunted this playwright, that the character and his death provided a foundation on which the later tragedies could be securely built.

JOAN WEBBER

Hamlet and the Freeing of the Mind

*W*E ARE apparently invited to regard *Hamlet* as a revenge play, whose rules we know, just as we know those of the history plays that preceded it. In both kinds of drama, the characters' consciousness is limited by the genre: the protagonist's first obligation is to be a revenger or a king, and he thinks of himself as a person primarily in relation to this role. But the problems in regarding Hamlet as such a protagonist are apparent from the beginning and come to a crux in act IV. Here, having seen Fortinbras's army pass by on its way to overrun a patch of Polish ground, Hamlet again laments his own inactivity, saying, "O, from this time forth,/My thoughts be bloody, or be nothing worth!" (IV.iv.65–66). Then, obedient to the orders of Claudius, he takes ship for England, obviously unable to be sure even of his return; when he comes back, his thoughts are the opposite of bloody.

Great gaps in time, motive, and credibility occur elsewhere in Shakespeare, but nowhere, perhaps, as unsettlingly as here. Elsewhere such gaps are either explained, concealed, or rendered unimportant, but Hamlet's about-faces seem so blatant that one is almost forced to take account of them, and, I think, to argue either that Shakespeare's art is flawed or that some of our assumptions about the play are wrong.

The problem of the so-called delay—the putting-off of the revenge—is very similar. Generations of readers have found in it their key to Hamlet's character: for them he is a contemplative incapable of action, or a man who cannot make up his mind. But although he chides his own tardiness, Hamlet never seems idle: he engages in all kinds of swift actions, and, except for his willingness to go to England, any failure to act (as in killing the king at prayers) has obvious contextual justification. Rather, the play delays: scenes and motions are repeated; seemingly extraneous scenes (even the whole of act II) are included; much of the imagery in no way forwards what appears to be the plot.[1] We ought to ask, then, whether we have misread the main line of the plot: does it appear to delay because, like Hamlet, we have expected it from the beginning to move toward revenge, and are we possibly mistaken in that expectation? Once having arrived at these questions, we are free to observe what in fact the play is doing when it seems to stand still.

The major business of the play is partly a matter of new business for Shakespeare as a playwright, together with a resolution of old problems never before so fully understood. In the history plays he had been concerned with relationships between self and role, a concern here removed from history and drawn into a new dimension in Hamlet's effort to find his own way. At the same time, the sense of world-disgust which shadows several of Shakespeare's plays of this period not only emanates from Hamlet but also surrounds him in major thematic imagery. Because the *de contemptu* theme occupies a larger space in the play's atmosphere than could have been created by Hamlet's consciousness alone, it might be possible to argue that Hamlet's self-conscious isolation is triggered by world-disgust. But one could just as well work the other way around: his personal losses make him vulnerable to this more general kind of alienation. The two go together and intensify one another. Hamlet, encountering them together, gradually learns a kind of detachment that allows him essentially to remake himself, to act, to care without caring about the world.

Characteristically for Shakespeare, a conscious antagonist, Claudius, sparks the crisis, bringing about, successively, his own change of status, Hamlet's awareness and self-re-creation, and, finally, Claudius's downfall and Hamlet's death. *Hamlet* is unique among Shakespeare's plays, not in this usual tragic pattern, but in the intensity of its focus on problems of awareness. Knowledge of both the world and the self demands encounter with ambiguities and paradoxes which must be resolved rather than solved: that is, reason and good sense are not always enough. And knowledge, which includes knowledge of death, is not a key to anything, except, perhaps, itself. Consciousness of one's human condition can be heroic. *Hamlet*, the first of Shakespeare's major tragedies, poses for both protagonist and reader the question of whether or not, if one should have any choice in the matter, such awareness is worthwhile.

The many history plays that Shakespeare wrote before *Hamlet* exhibit a great deal of conflict between characters living according to a code that is losing its power, and others who are shaking off the code. *Richard III* is a good example of such a play: Richard can victimize others easily because they expect the rules and relationships of a medieval Christian society to operate for them even though they are incapable of contributing energy and commitment to these old designs. Richard, unillusioned and committed to his own welfare, has no trouble seeing the limitations of his contemporaries and playing upon them: because they want security and direction, and lack both energy and imagination, he can make them obey him even against the evidence of their own senses, until the future Henry VII, who has both energy and plausibility, arrives on the scene.

Claudius is in the same situation. Surrounded by people who accept the way things are, and who depend upon authority for security and direction, he can quite easily substitute himself for the former ruler. The Polonius family and their like have no way to organize their lives except in relation to the king, whoever he may be. In *Richard III*, even when perception and energy are available, the alternative is civil war. But in *Hamlet*, Shakespeare has ceased to give primacy to the limiting framework of history. Simply to do a revenge or to make a war cannot bring everything right for the human soul in which the ordering sanity of familiar relationships and rules has been destroyed by external events. Other characters, like Richard II, have come close to this condition, admitting their vulnerable, isolated state. Hamlet begins about where Richard ends, and the "delay" is one indication of a subordination of history to character. Less intellectually and historically limited than Richard, Hamlet is given ability and time to comprehend and respond to a world in which standard responses are wrong.

Claudius has attacked the medieval scheme of things, the unchanging patterns of relationship that exist among members of a family or a kingdom. The exhaustion of the pattern is indicated by the ease with which it can be manipulated without anyone's being the wiser. Although Hamlet continues to believe, during most of the play, that he has to get revenge on Claudius, the task he implicitly sets himself is to turn his suffering awareness into an individual conscious force, and then to decide whether he will contribute that force to the renewal of the traditional schemes. He has to find out why and how he should live.

Hamlet's disgust for life, which is at first painfully immature, is initially felt in reaction to broken or falsified relationships. Because of the specific nature of his perceptions, he becomes a threat to other characters in the play. These others, analogous in many ways to characters in *Richard III* as well as other history plays, are about at the end of that line, and look worse than some, though certainly not all, of their predecessors because Shakespeare emphatically dramatizes their unwillingness or inability to use their minds honestly. Committed to the scheme of things in Denmark, not on account of its intrinsic truth or strength, but because of their own weakness, greed, or inflexibility, they are dangerous to themselves and to the very society in which they believe. Choosing to manipulate or be manipulated, participating willingly in the ambiguities of life at court, they are overtaken by their own mistakes, and get what they deserve. It seems moralistic, perhaps, or melodramatic to say that such people as Rosencrantz and Polonius are evil; one may find them merely ignorant. But their ignorance is culpable by Shakespearean standards, and their destruction is guaranteed by their own actions.

Beyond the uneasy assertion, and the deterioration, of role-identities and assumed relationships, the atmosphere of the play is the world-disgust so familiar to medieval and Renaissance life.[2] Scholars have shown that contempt for the world increases during the late Middle Ages in proportion to an increase in worldliness and love of life, as if contempt were a kind of safeguard, a protective alienation from what might absorb a person too completely.[3] In *Hamlet* Shakespeare can almost be said to have made of the whole play a shifting emblem of the simultaneous glory and vanity of man's estate. This common paradox appears in *Hamlet* in peculiarly Shakespearean garb, and in different, overlapping degrees of profundity that account for much of the tenseness, confusion, and fascination of the drama.

The play opens brilliantly with what amounts to a verbal portrayal of the seventeenth-century perspective-picture that from a distance is a skull, close up a feast. Hamlet Senior is dead and Hamlet believes that "things rank and gross in nature/Possess it [the world] merely" (I.ii.136–37). Yet, seen close up, the funeral has brought forth a wedding feast; seen very close, without perspective, Elsinore is a place of peace and even of celebration. Claudius wants his entourage to forget about the skull and react simply as courtiers to their king. Hamlet provides a somewhat different viewpoint, which may nevertheless be read in traditional terms: as a university student and as a prince, he could scarcely have avoided the pervasive influence of the idea of contempt of the world.[4] Looking at the skull-feast picture, without even knowing that anything is wrong, some people might be able to see death, and others, life.

A great deal of skull-feast imagery will follow in the course of the drama. Shakespeare's own canon, seen in retrospect, provides us with another ambiguous perspective on the wedding banquet. It is of course a commonplace that most of his comedies end with weddings because they symbolize the renewal and security of society, an end to misery, confusion and doubt, the assurance of a happy future. In these plays, no one is forced farther into self-awareness than is necessary to enable some character reformations, and the enabling process tends to be pleasurable rather than painful. Death scarcely exists except as a threatening impetus toward renewal—as, for example, the threat of death sends the couples in *A Midsummer Night's Dream* and *As You Like It* into the forest. Marriage finally binds these lovers together in affirmation of the goodness of life.

But marriages have another function in Shakespeare's plays, less often observed. They tend to occur at the openings of tragedies, or very near the openings: such is the case in *Othello, King Lear, Antony and Cleopatra,* and *Hamlet*; in *Macbeth*, murder is facilitated by a fateful marital combination. In these plays, marriage is no security at all; in fact, the very pattern that has elsewhere been equated with life often brings forth or results in death. The union of Gertrude and Claudius is particularly striking in this respect because Claudius excuses it by listing all the social benefits usually ascribed to weddings. And so this most unlikely union—hasty and incestuous at best—is accepted by almost everyone as a right ordering of things.

The wedding-funeral, then, can legitimately be seen, by those unaware of the murder, either as a happy and healing event or as a characteristic example of human folly. Any medieval person might see it as both, given the availability of both responses to his time. Thinking of Shakespeare's comic use of marriage as well as of the tendency of young men toward melancholy posing, we might find it reasonable to be irritated by Hamlet's apparent preference for contempt of the world. At the outset he knows nothing of the murder, nor do we. A break in society has been skillfully repaired, and the second scene of the play portrays the results reassuringly. The king first explains the altruistic reasons for his marriage (including the information that he was open, in taking this step, to the advice of others, who "have freely gone/With this affair along" (I.ii.15–16). He proceeds with delicacy to try to make peace with Norway, to enable Laertes to return to France, and, in the face of extreme provocation, to try to build a relationship between himself and Hamlet. Alone in the court, Hamlet wears mourning and is deaf to the arguments of the king and queen that fathers must die and life must go on. It is easy enough to see him initially as a tragic character misplaced in comedy, or even as faintly comic himself in his intellectual's insistence on contempt of the world, his insistent use of the pat phrases and images of that tradition.

If, as Claudius would have us believe, nothing more serious than accidental death were involved, then Hamlet might belong in a category with the melancholy Jaques of *As You Like It*. The ambiguities of the king's opening speech are intended to set our minds at ease by acknowledging the world's doubleness, and pleading, nevertheless, for affirmation on the grounds that the reasons for the marriage are too important to allow extended time for mourning:

> Therefore our sometime sister, now our queen,
> Th' imperial jointress to this warlike state,
> Have we, as 'twere with a defeated joy,
> With an auspicious, and a dropping eye,

With mirth in funeral, and with dirge in marriage,
In equal scale weighing delight and dole,
Taken to wife.

(I.ii.8–14)

And he immediately turns to both business and rejoicing. He assumes that his audience is superficially inclined to peace and merriment, to contempt of the world, or to a bit of each—in any case, that his rhetoric can settle his listeners to his advantage. He cannot yet understand that Hamlet's melancholy "passes show." As for us, Horatio has compared Denmark to a Rome filled with the unnatural and fearful portents surrounding Caesar's assassination, but his speech easily slips by as a mere metaphor in the general confusion of the first scene.[5] Because Norway is an enemy, we are still likely to share Claudius's scorn of Fortinbras's assumption that Denmark might be in disorder because of Hamlet Senior's death.

Claudius has employed to his advantage an ambiguity traditional to the medieval world view; he has said, in effect, "These two views of things are both possible, but under the circumstances we have to proceed positively." Under cover of that easy tradition, he has really perpetrated something more like a *trompe-l'œil*—a deception of his people's minds and senses. For what looks like a healthy ordering of the kingdom is his own outright enjoyment of the rewards of crime. To take up Horatio's implicit comparison of Hamlet Senior's death with that of Caesar is to see that the success of the funeral-wedding mirage rests upon the effectiveness of a previous *trompe-l'œil* by Claudius, even more brazen than this. It is remarkable that none of the characters, with the possible exception of Horatio, has ever questioned the manner of Hamlet Senior's death and Claudius's ascent to the throne. Coming to *Hamlet* from Shakespeare's history plays, most Renaissance audiences, like his modern readers, must have wondered why the son has not succeeded the father. At the end of the play there is some talk of an election, so one might suppose that Claudius had been popularly chosen, but Hamlet complains that he has been cheated of the throne: Claudius "Popp'd in between th' election and my hopes" (V.ii.65). If Claudius has legitimately taken power, one would expect Shakespeare to have him provide this information, together with his other reassurances in his opening speech, but he does not, and the matter remains as surprisingly unquestioned as the sudden death of a king in the prime of life. " 'Tis given out that, sleeping in my orchard,/A serpent stung me" (I.v.35–36). The murder may have been more subtle than Macbeth's assassination of Duncan, but not that much more subtle. Claudius succeeds in his deceptions at least partly because he has a willing audience.

To some extent, the ease with which he perpetrates his tricks may be explained as analogous to Richard III's ability to deceive people with their own commonplaces. The Janus' face that allows comedy to coexist with tragedy, that is amused by the conflicting absolutes that govern the medieval world, could, given men's natural tendency to superficialize, look indifferently upon a wedding-funeral. The aesthetic patterning by which the dance of life and the dance of death, or the feast and the funeral, can merge or metamorphose into one another, depends for its energy upon an understanding of the moral relationship between the two as parts of a natural process. Claudius has first engineered, and then dismissed as natural, the death of Hamlet Senior. The pattern has become sinister, death-dealing. Yet just because the pattern still appears to exist, acknowledged by Claudius's speech, no one notices its debasement.

Why is Hamlet so different from the rest of the palace community? In numerous ways we are given to understand that his present state of distrust and alienation is of recent origin. He was in love with Ophelia; startling as it may seem, Rosencrantz and Guildenstern really were his friends. He liked plays and fencing, and was, no doubt, the glass of fashion and the mould of form. No tragic hero, he was everything that Ophelia admired. He himself thought his imperfect father to be perfection itself and in fact continues to think so in the face of contrary evidence. There is no reason to suppose that his life before his father's death was any different from the lives of those around him.

But with the funeral-wedding, his character becomes obscure. Despite his many soliloquies, no one has been able to interpret his mind in a way that is finally convincing. He has been said to be a weakling, a scholar, in love with his mother or death, afraid of death or exposure, deterred from vengeance by uncertainty about the ghost's origin and honesty, or by conscience or religious scruples; all these explanations are true, yet just because they *are* all in some sense true, no one of them really suits. Hamlet's pain is as great before he knows that his father was murdered as it is afterward: the apparent necessity of action neither increases nor diminishes his grief. All that one can say, initially, is that his father's death and his mother's hasty remarriage have triggered in him a recognition of the imperfectness (or fallenness) of human nature. The contempt of the world that he learned as scholar and courtier has become something that he can taste. A limited cause led to a comprehensive insight, the more devastating because of his previous innocence.

But he is not simply disillusioned. His knowledge of the goodness of the world is still real, perhaps more real than before; his medieval double vision is as intense as the power of his language suggests when he tells Rosencrantz and Guildenstern that man is both the beauty of the world and the quintessence of dust. True, it has all been said before. True, we may still find in Hamlet some kinship with the posing melancholy man of his age. Still, the personal immediacy of his responses and their lack of self-interest give them a validity that is to become more and more convincing as the play goes on. It is important now simply to acknowledge, as a counter to Claudius's reading of the ambiguities of his *coup d'état,* Hamlet's own recognition of the real duality of life. The intensity of that vision holds him paralyzed, unable to plunge blindly into revenge.

At the beginning, world-disgust is too new in him, too immediately connected with an immediate situation, to give him the detachment for which it was ordinarily valued. Eventually he will reach even beyond this remedial condition to a state—almost beyond that intended by the contempt writers—in which contempt turns into a protective alienation that will allow him to love without desire or pain. It is a kind of stoicism. This achievement comes slowly, as he absorbs the lesson that the play is here to teach. The necessity for detachment is borne in upon him from the beginning, however, in the extensiveness of the losses that he sustains.

Just as his very personal, immediate absorption of these antithetical commonplaces of worldly love and hate limits his capacity to act, so does the destruction of his formal identity. Beginning with the death of his father and continuing through act IV, Hamlet is almost systematically deprived, by Claudius, of everything that bound him to his society. His parents, his love,[6] his friendships,[7] his education, perhaps the kingship, and finally his native country, are taken from him; when he writes to Claudius that he has been set naked on the land of Denmark,[8] he means what he says. He has been cut off from the very relationships which make society work, which keep people's lives consistent and predictable, and make them unwilling to jeopardize the way things are.

One might say that Hamlet asked for this treatment by refusing Claudius's effort to retain Hamlet in his former position, with nothing changed except the person of the king. Hamlet is accepted as son and heir but, unlike the rest of the palace people, finds it impossible to believe in his part. Once having chosen to believe in personal relationships rather than assigned roles, however, he is utterly distinguished from everyone around him. Inevitably his isolation destroys in him all societal deterrents to consciousness or action. More and more he is capable of seeing everything (and, potentially, of doing anything) because he has lost all the responsibilities, commitments, and ordinary human rewards that usually influence and limit one's perceptions. He has nothing to lose except his life, and at first he thinks he doesn't even want that. Nothing prevents him from free and painful vision.

It is important to observe that for Hamlet this whole process is set in motion independently of his knowledge of the murder. His powerful, antithetical love-hate for the world and his separation from a normal context of relationships are both fully in evidence before he has seen the ghost. Thus, while his father's death is obviously the specific cause for his state of mind, the changes in his character do not hinge on this discovery of the murder. *Hamlet* is not a revenge play primarily, but rather a more comprehensive study of human awareness.

Everyone else at court can, and therefore does, use the version of reality concocted by Claudius to maintain the life with which he is familiar. The palace community has its foundation in Renaissance commonplaces about kingship which are in normal circumstances entirely accurate and justified. The king's well-being is that of the nation. So Rosencrantz and Guildenstern defend their employment:

> *Guil.* . . .
> Most holy and religious fear it is
> To keep those many many bodies safe
> That live and feed upon your Majesty.
>   *Ros.*   The single and peculiar life is bound
> With all the strength and armour of the mind
> To keep itself from noyance; but much more
> That spirit upon whose weal depends and rests
> The lives of many.
>
>   (III.iii.8–15)

The game of the *trompe-l'œil* is eagerly entered upon by everyone at court except Hamlet because without it their world would fall apart. Applied to the false king, the commonplaces make everything seem all right. And Claudius can shift his axioms according to the situation. When he needs Hamlet to be disposed of, he calls for the reasoning just cited (the king's life must not be endangered), but when he is threatened by Laertes, whose mind he can easily bend, his position on kingship is this:

> There's such divinity doth hedge a king
> That treason can but peep to what it would,
> Acts little of his will.
>
>   (IV.v.123–25)

Even Richard II had discovered that argument to be of little practical use (*Richard II*, III.ii.56–62 and ff.). Claudius knows that Laertes is easily impressed by routine sentiments, yet for him to speak in front of Gertrude of the king's claim on divinity is so callous as to suggest that he has momentarily convinced himself of his own role.

So far it would seem that Hamlet is simply a contrast of painful awareness with simple ignorance, but Shakespeare does not allow us to believe that ignorance is all that easy to maintain. Claudius, after all, did at least commit incest, and the murder itself should not have been that difficult to suspect for those who were on the scene. For the palace people, the effort to continue the lives they know seems to depend upon a reduction or unwitting denial of awareness. But, denied, it manifests itself insistently in 1) a nervousness about appearance that often takes the form of a pointless spying in the wrong places, or inquiring either into the wrong issues or in the wrong way into the right issues; 2) a chosen ignorance that has its own polluting atmosphere; and 3) efforts to manipulate reality in such a way as to make one's own view of things correct. These not entirely separable phenomena have a single meaning and effort: when awareness is blocked off, suspicion, illness, and corruption ensue; these effects largely create the atmosphere of the play. Ignorance of the murder is a symptom of character.

The nervous tone of the play is set by the sentinels on the platform, who in a supposedly friendly environment require formal identification of each other; the relief goes so far as to challenge the guard on duty. Whether or not there will be war between Denmark and Norway, what Danish drinking customs are like, what's wrong with Hamlet, where the ghost comes from, what Laertes is doing in France, whether or not Hamlet loves Ophelia, what success the child actors are having—all these and others are, for the most part, unreal or irrelevant problems, or real problems wrongly focused. Yet the characters (including Hamlet, who is not yet free of such preoccupations) spend their attention upon them, almost willfully failing to find any satisfaction.

Most of the characters are capable of extremely detailed, accurate observation, often manifested in comments on styles of dress and speech, but more frequently used for anxious, compulsive spying. Ophelia reports on Hamlet and Polonius on Ophelia. Polonius sets his servant Reynaldo to spy on Laertes; and Rosencrantz and Guildenstern, Hamlet's former friends, gladly take on the commission to spy on him. In fact, most of the characters are involved in Hamlet-watching, while Claudius moves about unimpeded. Again, the contrast with *Macbeth* is striking.

The language of the play emphasizes the characters' chosen uncertainties in such repeated words as "show," "discretion," "believe," "faith," "swear," "question," "doubt," "honest," "treason," "watch," "seem," and "appear"; there is imagery of locks, keys, and traps.[9] Sentence structure is unusually interrogative, frequently cast in such a way as to demonstrate the characters' unwillingness to come to their own conclusions, that is, to deal directly with reality: "Looks it not like the king?" "Is not this somewhat more than fantasy?" "What does this mean, my lord?" "What should we say, my lord?" And to this last question, from Rosencrantz and Guilden-stern, Hamlet replies, "Why, any thing, but to the purpose."

Playacting as a device for the manipulation of reality is common enough in Shakespeare's theater. In the comedies it is often a furtherer of truth. But the role-playing set up in I.ii by Claudius and Gertrude is a denial of truth that almost forces Hamlet to adverse response. In the court so beautifully ordered by Claudius, Claudius is the king, Gertrude the queen, and Hamlet the son of both parents and the king's heir. Hamlet Senior is not merely dead but cancelled. This is the most blatant effort made in the play to alter reality, and it forces Hamlet to opposition, since he is not and cannot be Claudius's son. Here perhaps more than anywhere else in that strange second scene, the ambiguity of appearances is stressed. To take one's brother's son as one's own is a loving act under some circumstances; to insist upon this nomenclature with a full-grown man still suffering from his father's death would seem to show less sensitivity than the rest of the scene has led us to expect from Claudius. But the fact that he has effected equally outrageous deceptions, without hindrance, justifies his assurance.

Superficial meddling and spying, willed and malicious ignorance, and gross manipulations of reality thus form one important characteristic of the play; these are born of and feed upon ambition and a desire to maintain the *status quo* even contrary to fact. Obviously behavior that denies or mutilates consciousness must affect the mind and the senses, and another dominant strain of language and imagery directly concerns the means of perception: there are innumerable references to mind, brain, eye, ear, and tongue (for talk, not taste). Sensory images are contemptuous. The play focuses us on the centrality of thought and thought-processes to the human character, and on the abuses of thought and of perception. Eye and ear are traditionally the purest of the human senses, even though easily deceived. Words like "look," "watch," and "see" run like a motif through the play: people use their eyes to observe or spy; they rivet them upon one another's faces. Pictures, images, plays-within-plays are constantly used or discussed; if eyes have grown unseeing, they must be retrained in observation. Appearances are totally untrustworthy, of course, but it is not altogether necessary to trust superficial appearance. Chosen ignorance has willed this course. Hamlet sees his father with his mind's eye before he sees the ghost; similarly, he turns his mother's eyes, as she says, into her soul.

This desirable mental sight is too often impeded. The eye weeps. Although it is an instrument of vision, it may be incapacitated by what it sees: at the fall of Troy, Hecuba is blinded with tears ("bisson rheum"); the sight "would have made milch the burning eyes of heaven" (II.ii.540), while Pyrrhus, causer of this woe, is pictured as having eyes like carbuncles. Laertes, at sight of his mad sister, asks his tears to "burn out the sense and virtue" (IV.v.155) of his eyes in order, apparently, that he may be readied for revenge.

Ears, like eyes, are frequently mentioned. As the first suspicion of wrong comes from the vision of the ghost before he speaks, confirmation (temporarily believed, at least) comes from the ghost's story. Hearing and sight are invoked almost line-by-line in the opening scene, whose darkness and suspicious atmosphere seem to cause a straining of those senses emphasized by constant reference to them. Hearing remains important throughout the play, and it is clear that the ear, like the eye, is easily misled. Cruel language may cause madness: Ophelia's "hard words" to Hamlet are thought to have driven the prince out of his senses, and his to her certainly contribute to her undoing. The pain that causes weeping also results in a "broken voice," words difficult to understand. Voice and mind are closely connected: Hamlet's hysteria at his father's message leads him to speak his pain in "wild and whirling words" that bewilder his followers.

Ears may be more purposefully assaulted. Hamlet Senior was killed by having poison poured into his ears. The ears of the people of Denmark and the court are constantly filled with rumors, with lies and gossip; flattery is a familiar technique. Thus the ear can be incapacitated by false seeming just as the eye can; and the ear can also choose to accept false rumor as the truth. Hamlet Senior says that "the whole ear of Denmark/Is by a forged process of my death/Rankly abus'd" (I.v.36–38). Hamlet complains that Rosencrantz and Guildenstern are trying to play him like a pipe, make him sing for the benefit of others' ears. Claudius, complaining of the troubles come upon him, says that Laertes, newly arrived from France,

> Feeds on his wonder, keeps himself in clouds,
> And wants not buzzers to infect his ear
> With pestilent speeches of his father's death,
> Wherein necessity, of matter beggar'd,
> Will nothing stick our person to arraign
> In ear and ear.

> (IV.v.89–94)

Of all the characters in the play, Gertrude has most significantly preferred unthinking self-indulgence to the disciplined use of her senses. In attacking her adultery with her husband's unlovely murderer, Hamlet gets at the same blindness in her that summarizes the condition of most of the characters in the play. In the scene in her closet, he asks,

> What devil was't
> That thus hath cozen'd you at hoodman-blind?
> Eyes without feeling, feeling without sight,
> Ears without hands or eyes, smelling sans all,
> Or but a sickly part of one true sense
> Could not so mope.

(III.iv.76–81)

This wild and frightening image describes the self-imprisonment of those who have chosen not to know.

Mind-brain-head-skull: these words flash out continually from the context of the play. Minds are deceived, abused. In order to get along, Hamlet allows everyone to think he is mad, and his seeming madness threatens their faith in appearances. That Polonius will say a cloud resembles anything at all in order to placate Hamlet only repeats in little the function he has performed for Claudius in helping to preserve the image of a well-ordered state. Just as the treatises on contempt of the world would have it, the human mind is sinful, corrupt; all that gives it life is subject to decay, and in life it allows its covering of skin to be painted with cosmetics, its senses to be plastered with lies.

And yet what alternative is there? So long as one stays within the guidelines of textbook rules for behavior, he can be terribly misled, as are Polonius with his platitudes, Ophelia with her efforts to be a faithful daughter and sister, Laertes in his eagerness to obey the revenge code. Hamlet too wants to revenge, doesn't know why he can't. His vision of a corrupt mankind appears to bring him confusion rather than wisdom. He is nearly paralyzed by double vision, as in his famous speech on the nature of man, another feast-skull picture of man as angel and quintessence of dust, the earth as majestical and a foul congregation of vapors. Reality taints, the world is a prison, and Hamlet feels himself captived in one of its lowest dungeons.

Between culpable ignorance and an awareness that nearly drives one mad, a clever person of limited morality can function fairly well. We may in fact admire such characters as Claudius for their ability to get what they want, keeping their eyes open only enough to enable them to appreciate and extend the blindness of others, using it for their own ends. In a world like this, where deception consistently obscures distinctions between good and evil, truth and falsehood, it is indeed difficult to see how consciousness can be used for good. From the very beginning, despair and isolation drive Hamlet to want to die. Yet he fears that death may be only another deception, seeming to promise oblivion, but instead extending awareness into an unknown dimension. Consciousness—and fear of more conscious-ness—make Hamlet's cowardice, preventing acceptance of either life or death.

Almost instinctively, he adopts the guise of madness. He himself becomes a *trompe-l'œil* that by its very nature threatens the survival of all the deceptions at court. For he is not only a puzzle; the nature of his deception makes him a mirror to others, forcing upon them things they do not want to see. Gertrude, Ophelia, and Polonius would rather talk double-talk than accept the truths that Gertrude sees as death-dealing. While he is truly sometimes at the end of his wits (approaching the divine sense that is madness in Shakespeare), Hamlet uses his perilous balance to increase his consciousness and to force consciousness on those around him. His madness is specialized and finely controlled: "When the wind is southerly I know a hawk from a handsaw" (II.ii.396–98). With his antic disposition and his teasing out of others' brains, he throws himself knowingly into their game and passes through it to the other side, thereby finding his way to some kind of reality or providence or nature behind the unending shiftiness of surfaces.

Before he can say that readiness is all, Hamlet must recover his own identity and become reconciled to his comic-tragic world. The resolving of those problems should coincide with the larger resolution of the ills of society. The way in which Hamlet progresses toward self-knowledge and self-definition is by means of a constellation of self-conscious devices involving mirror imagery, or reflexivity, in which possible actions or ways of being are seen as in a mirror and then either absorbed or broken through. Mirrors reflect; people reflect one another; and for Shakespeare every act returns in some way upon its maker. Images of reflection are characteristic of the sixteenth and seventeenth centuries. If it is in any way possible to separate medieval from Renaissance matter in this play, one might say that Shakespeare holds up a Renaissance mirror to a medieval world.

The most frequently repeated fact is the explicit subject of the play. The murder of Hamlet Senior is endlessly reflected, as in the story of Julius Caesar, the story of Claudius's own confession, Hamlet's holding up the mirror to his mother. The murder is very much the texture of the play, the unexpurgatable fact of life at Elsinore.

Just as intrinsic and as endlessly reflected is the course that Hamlet is supposed to take. Revenge is advertised by the ghost, again by the story of Caesar, and, most prominently, in Hamlet's counterparts and foils, Fortinbras and Laertes. Hamlet weeps at his inability to do what these men do, and yet it is just at the moment when the list has grown intolerable, when he sees Fortinbras's men passing and declares that his thoughts from now on will be bloody or worthless, that he takes ship for England. The obvious reflection and its lesson—see the murder, do the revenge—is a reflection of the past, of a time when it could still be believed that social action could preserve a social pattern.

But Hamlet's search must be for self-knowledge, and his first efforts, confused as some of them may be, are to force self-knowledge upon those people who have been so easily converted from his friends and relatives to spies and enemies. He spends a good deal of time looking at other people and trying to make them look at themselves. In the scene in Ophelia's bedroom, Hamlet goes backward out of her presence, keeping his eyes fixed on her. She is unable to return his gaze, understand his trouble, or see anything about herself in any of his speeches to her. She dies by drowning, falling into her own image as it were, because she has refused to know herself or him. By the wise clowns of the graveyard scene, this death is construed as self-murder, the reflexive action which for himself Hamlet finally rejects.

When Hamlet insists that the queen look at herself in a mirror, she responds by calling for help. Perhaps she is afraid for her life, but, taken most literally, the language of the play expresses her fear of self-knowledge, and later on she again associates self-knowledge with death: "These words like daggers enter in mine ears" (III.iv.95); "O Hamlet, thou hast cleft my heart in twain" (III.iv.156). To her cry for help, Polonius, behind the arras, responds by calling for help. That is, Hamlet says she should look in the mirror; she cries for help, and Polonius reflects her cry unthinkingly. For this mutual opacity, Polonius dies at once, while the queen, after her initial fright, apparently continues her self-destructive course to the end. At hearing the news of the murder, the perceptive king sees the image of his own death at Hamlet's hand and determines to murder Hamlet. This determination seals the king's death warrant.

Hamlet is as explicit with Rosencrantz and Guildenstern as with the Queen, but with them the whole underlying social problem of the play is raised. They have given up any effort at individual energy in order to be pipes for fortune's fingers. To say this is to acknowledge that Claudius is a principle not of order but of chaos. The medieval subordination of the individual to the common good resulted in purposeful and coherent design in which each individual is as fully realized as those who form the self-generating patterns of eagle and cross in Dante's *Paradise*. That Rosencrantz and Guildenstern have lost all individualizing energy is symbolized by the comic interchangeability of their names, and shown in all their puppetlike responses to Claudius's manipulation of them.

Obviously, reflection of ignorance can be mere repetition, or, worse, a confirmation and expansion of corruption such as occurs in the efforts of all these people to maintain a state beneficial to them. In making themselves pipes for fortune's fingers, Gertrude, Polonius, Ophelia, and Laertes deny whatever personal histories they might have achieved in order to become the king's echoes or their own. Hamlet Senior, repetitiously calling for revenge, is also asking Hamlet to deny himself: the phrase, "taint not thy mind" can suggest little more than "don't think," since the images of corruption with which Hamlet Senior himself describes his murder could not possibly leave his son's mind untainted.[10]

Polonius and the others are really spiritually dead before they die physically; that is one reason why we do not think of Hamlet as a murderer. They do not know how to save themselves; to try to repeat the actions they have done before, or, by spying to discover what they want to be true, is an effort to preserve a familiar past that died symbolically with Hamlet Senior. Their commitment to it is a denial, not an affirmation of present realities. At best they are in the way, and their deaths happen in the course of a much more important action, which is the opposition of Claudius and Hamlet.

Claudius took Hamlet's friends and relatives away, and either destroyed them or allowed them to destroy themselves. His ability to do this indicates that his intelligence is of the nature of Richard III's or Macbeth's; he has seen the existing pattern of life objectively, and knows that others depend upon it as a given to which their own individuality and perceptions are submitted to the point of being atrophied. But Hamlet is free of this dependence and has better vision. When he looks at his uncle, he sees a corrupted version of Hamlet Senior; but he also sees such a version of himself. In some sense, Hamlet and Claudius are mirror images of each other, reflecting one another as good and evil so often do in the Renaissance. When Claudius says to Hamlet, "Be as ourself in Denmark" (I.ii.122), he invites both the prince and the audience to make that dangerous identification. Hamlet cannot regard himself as king so long as Claudius is there; yet in some sense he must so regard himself. On the one hand, in looking at Claudius, he sees his own rightful glory; and on the other, his own corruption. Claudius, in turn, saying "Be as ourself" to

Hamlet, comes to see how dangerous to the throne is this potential king. While Claudius has assigned to the prince the part of son and heir, their real roles are now one.

In their supreme self-consciousness, both men are well equipped to look out for their own interests, although they do it differently. Their obligation to themselves is ironically summarized in a remark of Rosencrantz cited earlier:

> The single and peculiar life is bound
> With all the strength and armour of the mind
> To keep itself from noyance; but much more
> That spirit upon whose weal depends and rests
> The lives of many.
>
> (III.iii.11–15)

Both commoners and king are bound to keep themselves from harm and obviously, to begin with, to stay alive. When Hamlet first takes action, it is to save himself, whether one thinks of the first time as his murder of the spy in his mother's room or the spies on board ship. In both cases he is pleased with himself because he thinks they ask for it; he is particularly happy to see Rosencrantz and Guildenstern hoist with their own petard. He has been deprived of everything except his life and his increasingly free consciousness. When these are threatened, he fights for them with a joyous energy that is remarkable in contrast to some of his other behavior:

> For 'tis the sport to have the enginer
> Hoist with his own petar; and 't shall go hard
> But I will delve one yard below their mines
> And blow them at the moon. O, 'tis most sweet
> When in one line two crafts directly meet.
>
> (III.iv.206–10)

The deaths that Hamlet brings about are all wrought in this reflexive way: when his own life is endangered, his reaction turns that threat back upon the threatener.

Reflexivity, clearly, is another aspect of the mirroring imagery that in *Hamlet* so often indicates the degree or quality of a person's self-consciousness. An act returned upon its doer is reflected back upon him. The threatener is visited by the threat. Hamlet's efforts to save himself primarily reflect the behavior of the king, his chief mirror and mirrorer. Hamlet's self-defensive actions respond to Claudius's aggressive efforts to save himself, efforts which he admits, in his attempts at prayer, are wasted so long as he cannot give up the rewards of crime. While losing everything, Hamlet has become absolutely free; in contrast, Claudius has sold his freedom, and all his efforts to save himself return upon his own head.

Oddly enough, Danish drinking customs, deplored by Hamlet at the beginning of the play but heartily subscribed to by the king, help to bring about the king's downfall. The cannon shot accompanying the toasts implies reflexivity:

> No jocund health that Denmark drinks to-day
> But the great cannon to the clouds shall tell,
> And the King's rouse the heaven shall bruit again,
> Respeaking earthly thunder. Come away.
>
> (I.ii.125–28)

And in the final scene of the play, the king's language is even more telling:

> Give me the cups;
> And let the kettle to the trumpet speak,
> The trumpet to the cannoneer without,
> The cannons to the heavens, the heaven to earth,
> "Now the King drinks to Hamlet."
>
> (V.ii.285–89)

In his custom of shooting off a cannonade to mark a toast, the king literally defies the heavens that Hamlet invokes in his belief that "there's a divinity that shapes our ends." And even as the king's speech decrees, his own weapon returns upon him. If he is struck dead by heaven's thunder, it is thunder of his own making. Claudius himself feared such reflexive vengeance, as he told Laertes, explaining why he would not bring Hamlet to trial for the murder of Polonius:

> The other motive
> Why to a public count I might not go
> Is the great love the general gender bear him,
> Who, dipping all his faults in their affection,
> Would, like the spring that turneth wood to stone,
> Convert his gyves to graces; so that my arrows,
> Too slightly timber'd for so loud a wind,
> Would have reverted to my bow again,
> And not where I had aim'd them.
>
> (IV.vii.16–24)

Such conscious descriptions of reflexivity, and the whole complex of imagery of reflection of which they are part, are so common in Renaissance literature as to seem almost inseparable from the sorts of self-ignorance or self-awareness that they portray. They are undoubtedly indicative of an age whose self-consciousness is particularly intense, an age therefore especially concerned with the problems inherent in rejecting or fostering a sense of individual existence.

As Shakespeare uses it, the language of self-realization is moral. Reflexivity provides a clear means for describing both the likeness and inherent differences between good and evil actions. The reflexivity of evil is a moral of the play. The queen sees that "So full of artless jealousy is guilt/It spills itself in fearing to be spilt" (IV.v.19–20). Laertes, dying, says "The foul practice/Hath turn'd itself on me" (V.ii.328–29); and Horatio's explanation speaks of "purposes mistook/Fall'n on th' inventors' heads" (V.ii.395–96).

It is apparent, I think, that the fates of Claudius and Hamlet are bound up together, and that Hamlet cannot risk facing Claudius until he has come to terms with himself and life. Otherwise, he may be made simply another pipe for Claudius's fingers. One kind of repetition in the play, the structural delaying, occurs partly in order to give Hamlet a chance to become a knowing person, who in suffering all need suffer nothing. The contempt theme, meanwhile, is worked out in the atmosphere and imagery, not so much as a developing motif as one whose controlling presence must finally be understood.

At the beginning of this essay, I associated the combined love-hate for the world, with its distancing ambiguity, with the forms of comedy and tragedy, as the two kinds of opposed ideas are brought together in the funeral-feast imagery. From the beginning Hamlet is part of this thematic association, and by the end he has assimilated its meaning. Throughout the play comic and tragic elements are juxtaposed, as are worldly love and hate, but they do not come together to form a satisfactory philosophy in Hamlet's mind until the fifth act. Hamlet undergoes a sea-change that is symbolized, though not contained, by the voyage to England, and in the course of that change the comic-tragic alternation draws near to tragicomedy. Even in the earliest of Shakespeare's great tragedies, we are reminded of the late romances.

Act V, where we see Hamlet's return from his voyage, begins in a graveyard. Two peasants, called clowns, dig Ophelia's grave while alternately singing and discoursing obscurely and comically on the central meanings of the play. The reader is forcibly reminded of the many ways in which comedy and tragedy have come together throughout the story. The funeral and wedding feasts were one. As in the picture of the feast that forms a skull, so Hamlet, brooding, transforms the happy second scene into an image of corrupt mortality. Hamlet himself is both mad and sane, and from the time of his first interview with the ghost, comedy and tragedy constantly threaten to displace one another in his actions. When he bids his mother goodnight while dragging Polonius offstage, murder, while undeniably murder, somehow seems a jest. Hamlet blackly tells Ophelia that he is her jig-maker, and in fact he is frequently a maker of riddles, songs, and jokes. We are puzzled as to how he could have made love to Ophelia since his father died, or kept himself continually in fit shape to fence with Laertes (and even had pleasant words with Claudius on the subject); it would seem that a mere blink of the eyes can make Hamlet even in the midst of his pain appear before us as the glass of fashion.

The funeral-wedding feast is part of a stream of paired death-feast images running through the play. There are feasts of worms; the king drinks to Hamlet at the fencing match; at Ophelia's funeral, the queen wishes she were decking the bride-bed with flowers rather than the grave; and Fortinbras exclaims at the end of the play,

> O proud Death,
> What feast is toward in thine eternal cell
> That thou so many princes at a shot
> So bloodily hast struck?

> (V.ii.375–78)

Hamlet's designation of Polonius as fishmonger recalls many kinds of deaths and celebrations. Examining Yorick's skull, the prince recalls his "flashes of merriment that were wont to set the table on a roar" (V.i.210–11).

Hamlet inquires of Horatio how it is possible that the clowns can sing at their work of gravedigging, and Horatio suggests that custom makes it so. In life as in this play, custom bears it out, as Plato tells us Socrates argued, that the muse of comedy is one with the muse of tragedy. In Yorick's skull the two modes become a single vision. The conversation of the two clowns epitomizes and explains the drama's display of contempt for a loved world. They remind us of the reflexiveness of a history in which Fortinbras will recover what his father lost, the casuistical conditions under which chosen death is or is not to be labeled suicide, the identity of tragedy with comedy, and the indifference with which man must regard his life. At this point Hamlet becomes a member of the audience, watching as we do this rendition of his story. He has been a philosopher, with anguish meditating upon his skull. Now he sees two clowns tossing skulls in the air, as if they were gods indifferently making a game of human life. It is a scene almost exactly comparable to that in *The Tempest*, where Prospero, a spectator at his own masque, remembers the plot that Caliban's crew are laying against him. Suddenly seeing himself as a character in the plots and dreams of others, and dreams and life forever merging into one another, he knows that he must give himself up to destiny. It is the one place in the play where Prospero loses control of himself, just because he has seen so deeply into the meaning of things. Hamlet's jumping into Ophelia's grave is an analogous response; life now means everything and nothing, and he is simultaneously a tragic and comic figure with his seemingly absurd announcement, "This is I, Hamlet the Dane." "Hear you, sir," he says,

> What is the reason that you use me thus?
> I lov'd you ever: but it is no matter.
> Let Hercules himself do what he may,
> The cat will mew, and dog will have his day.
>
> (V.i.311–15)

The sign of the Globe theater is said to have been a figure of Hercules bearing the world on his shoulders. Even one strong enough to carry the world cannot change it; in some way nothing matters. Yet this realization does not bring Hamlet to despair; rather, like Prospero, after a moment of intense agitation, he is able to accept and believe in whatever may come. Recognizing inevitability, recognizing the limitedness of human power and the indistinguishability of tragedy and comedy, he is reinforced in his instinctively right reaction to the death of Polonius: he shocks Horatio by the amusement with which he relates the deaths of Rosencrantz and Guildenstern. The nearness of tragedy to comedy does not make life meaningless; rather, as in Shakespeare's last plays, it makes it possible and even funny.[11]

One frequently-observed difference between comedy and tragedy is that comedy always allows its characters a way out—a forest, another city, or a sea voyage, to free them from oppression and enlarge their understandings. Tragedy has its own grimmer analogy; the characters may suffer madness, from which at best they emerge with a surer self-knowledge to endure whatever fate is theirs. But Hamlet goes from a madness half-real, half-feigned, to a sea voyage never completed. Thrust jarringly against the protagonist's assertion that from now on his thoughts will be bloody, and composed of unlikely coincidences and luck, the voyage would seem like a comic intrusion, almost an authorial machine, if we had not been prepared for it both in the theme of self-knowledge and awareness and in the tragicomic theme of contempt of the world. Even so, the device is oddly symbolic, used to intensify our attention to these meanings. The play has all along been teaching Hamlet how to achieve a detachment from his sufferings that will enable him to reclaim a place in life. The voyage provides us with a specific point at which we can say this detachment is a reality.

At the same time the voyage collapses the world of the audience into that of the play, comically insisting that the themes of the play are those of real life. Thus, of course, the story literally was played out in England, although it is fictionally laid in Denmark. The "local color," in act II, of the conversation about child actors, breaks through the fiction and turns "Denmark" into England. So, when Hamlet is exiled to England, he is in some sense sent to where he is already, yet he never arrives. Instead he returns to where he started from, which is also England. Exile to England is said by many to have cleared Hamlet's mind, untainting it, yet the gravediggers are of the opinion that if Hamlet doesn't recover his wits in England, it won't matter, since there "the men are as mad as he." More sinisterly, Denmark has ordered England to have Hamlet's head struck from his shoulders, an undeniably permanent solution to the problem of a burdensome consciousness.

That Hamlet refuses. In the speech averring that from now on his thoughts will be bloody, he has insisted on the importance of human thought, of reason, as that which distinguishes men from beasts. Yet he has had somehow to get beyond the tainted reasoning forced on him by the ghost of his father, and, at least temporarily, beyond the context of medieval conventions and a priori assumptions. He now turns from revenge in order to find himself. He has thought he wants to die, but when his life is threatened he chooses to fight for it. The sequence beginning with the sea voyage shows that first. In some sense that trip is unreal, never happens, as all its comic paradoxy suggests. But it absolutely (though still paradoxically) exists as Hamlet's opportunity to decide to be himself. In some sense, it is his to decide whether to live, whether simply to live as a revenger, and whether or not, if he lives, to come back to England at all. Having asserted his life, he puts aside the mourning that would commit him either to inaction or to narrow revenge; surely a freedom from these aspects of his past confusion is also implied in his announcement to Claudius that he is set naked on the kingdom. Now, having in effect declared himself for a life with human meaning, he deliberately claims those things which once made up his identity. He announces himself Hamlet the Dane (reclaiming his country); he has used his father's signet ring, model of the Danish seal (sign of his right to the kingship), and Horatio calls him a king for his imperious language; he says that he loved Ophelia and Laertes; he calls Laertes his brother; with his vote, he leaves the kingdom to Fortinbras. And he says that the world makes sense: "there's a divinity that shapes our ends" (V.ii.10).

By the end of the play, then, Hamlet is a quite different person from the melancholy man of the second scene. His alienation is mature. He has resolved the pains and paradoxes of human consciousness, not by attempting to repress, sort out, or impose patterns, but by first making himself altogether free and then choosing his identity and his fate. The "readiness" that is all will be called ripeness in *King Lear*. And as in *King Lear*, that readiness could not have come about without a crisis; without Claudius, Hamlet could not have been so terrifyingly aware. The pattern of mirroring and repetition runs its course in the final meeting of the two, when Claudius tries to repeat the kind of action that he used on Hamlet Senior, poisoning a sleeping or unconscious man. Hamlet cannot now be a victim, or an instrument, because he has so fully created himself and thereby willed his own destiny.

If it is true that "there is nothing either good or bad but thinking makes it so," then Hamlet's own self-knowledge has made the meaning of the play. That is a satisfactory enough conclusion, yet I think that Shakespeare's philosophy is less sheerly existential. There is a difference between good and evil, and in Shakespeare's plays evil always recoils upon itself. The extremity to which Hamlet has wrought his consciousness has brought him in tune with the natural processes that guarantee this action. These processes are neither comic nor tragic; they simply happen. But felt by men as a funeral feast of life, or as a dance of life with death, they require and help to bring about a detachment that is somewhat different from simple contempt of the world. In its context, and at its strongest, the contempt tradition seems intended to balance excessive delight in worldly things. The funeral-feast deception is philosophically no deceit at all, but an effort to neutralize in the mind these opposing inclinations and enable people neither to love nor hate their lives. This detachment allows Hamlet in his final scenes to suffer all while suffering nothing.

Ophelia, Polonius, Laertes, knowing somehow that everything was wrong with their world, responded with rote behavior that made them easy victims. Hamlet now responds as readily as they, but instinctively rather than by rote, from a place almost beyond human awareness that allows him to contribute himself to the natural tendency of life eventually (and obviously at overwhelming expense) to come right. The fact that the world comes right by means of Hamlet's reassertion of the societal and familial relationships that had been debased and deadened indicates Shakespeare's conservatism, or perhaps a skepticism that any other structure would be less vulnerable to human folly. It is Hamlet's free acceptance of his given character and responsibilities, an acceptance that has to occur only because Claudius forces the issue, that brings about the king's downfall.

Hamlet is much concerned that his story can be told, and Horatio's way of announcing that story to Fortinbras is so like a prologue that we have the sense at the end that the play is just about to begin (another mirroring). Of all the self-ignorant people in the play, he is the only one who has been saved, and he seems no more horrified by the general carnage than he is pleased to have arrived at so timely a moment for the furtherance of his career. This last set of mirrorings in the play obviously allows for the fact that Fortinbras here rightly takes back what his father lost. It is both chilling and just to juxtapose the "defeated joy" with which wily Claudius claims to have married Gertrude, with Fortinbras's "For me, with sorrow I embrace my fortune" (V.ii.399). Obviously Shakespeare is offering Fortinbras the opportunity to be enlightened by the rehearsal. Also present are the English ambassadors who want to be thanked for England's unquestioning execution of Rosencrantz and Guildenstern: in their macabre ignorance, they make a fitting substitute for Rosencrantz and Guildenstern themselves. Shakespeare's own audience, mad Englishmen, are here too. These are the people (together with ourselves) who are to be told the story of Hamlet, with its infinitude of mirrors within mirrors. But the playwright doesn't know whether this mirror, art, will enlarge anyone's awareness or not. If the way to understand the play is to let it shock us into consciousness, as Hamlet was shocked by the death of his father, and at the same time to imitate its artistic detachment from the story it portrays, then the playwright is merely inviting his audience to be fully human, while making clear the price of accepting and the price of rejecting the invitation.

VIRGIL K. WHITAKER

Still Another Source for *Troilus and Cressida*

*J*N 1953 I wrote in a note to *Shakespeare's Use of Learning*, "I hope shortly to investigate the possibility that Shakespeare may have derived from Robert Greene's *Euphues His Censure to Philautus* (1587) the notion of subjecting the Troilus and Cressida story to ethical analysis, and even considerable guidance in doing so" (p. 194). "Shortly" has now become twenty-three years, and the possibility, despite all efforts, remains only that, although I should have written "the Trojan war" rather than "the Troilus and Cressida story." But, even as it recalls the rich achievements of a life devoted to scholarship, a festschrift also reminds us that Time's winged chariot is at all our backs. It is high time, therefore, that the promise be kept, and the possibility explored, uncertain and ultimately undemonstrable as it may be.[1]

Like most of the progeny of *Euphues*, Greene's work involves neither Euphues nor Philautus, although it certainly achieves the prolixity of the original and occasionally the mannered and ingenious style. It concerns, as the title page goes on to tell us, "a philosophicall combat betweene *Hector* and *Achylles*, discouering in foure discourses, interlaced with diuerse delightfull Tragedies, The vertues necessary to be incident in euery gentleman: had in question at the siege of Troy betwixt sondry Grecian and Troian Lords: especially debated to discouer the perfection of a souldier." [2]

More specifically, the siege of Troy, by which Priam "was with his sonnes and daughters brought to ruine: (the ende of voluptuous appetites) which they mayntained with the sworde" (p. 156), had continued for two years when a thirty-days truce was concluded. First, Andromache, Cassandra, Polixena, Hector, Troilus, Aeneas, and Helenus went to the Greek camp, where they were received by Achilles and later entertained by Agamemnon. After some sharp exchanges over the moral basis of the war (to be discussed later), Ulysses to change the subject related a "tragedy" of a queen who fled from Ithaca to Samos with her lover, poisoned him for a new infatuation, but was moved by a letter from her husband to repent and kill herself. The topical reference was obvious; so, after supper, Agamemnon, to keep the conversation on safer subjects, proposed that they discuss the ideal soldier. His chief qualities were agreed to be fortitude, wisdom, and liberality.

Helenus was chosen to treat of wisdom, first with a discourse and then with a "tragedy" telling how a neighboring king, having failed repeatedly in assaults upon Lydia, gained by trickery both Lydia and the princess whom he was after. But she and her ladies poisoned their cups of wine at a banquet and shared them with their captors, finding revenge along with their own deaths. The ultimate value of such wisdom was not questioned by the gathering. Meanwhile, Cressida, a member of the Greek camp, feasted her eyes on Troilus and then thought of him all night.

On the next day the Greeks visited Troy in return and were entertained by Priam. After dinner Hector discoursed on bravery—"What can a captain . . . attempt by pollicie, but he must performe by Fortitude?" (p. 245)—and then told his "tragedy" of two younger brothers, devotees of philosophy and liberality respectively, who tried to cheat their oldest brother of his throne when their father died while he was away pursuing his love of fighting. After fighting each other, they allied against their oldest brother upon his return but were both killed by him. Hector's insistence in this story and subsequently that fortitude is all that matters is perhaps significant.

Finally, after supper Achilles spoke of liberality and then told his story of an Athenian general who always let his soldiers share the booty of sacked cities and who was able, upon return from exile, to get the Athenian forces to destroy the Thebans after they had refused even to fight under more parsimonious generals. Greene's notion of warfare is about as barbarous as Greek practice actually was.

The work is a strange and unexciting mixture of genres. It would surely not justify such extended summary were it not for the possibility that it may explain several aspects of Shakespeare's play that are not derived from the sources usually considered. It may even have contributed something to the puzzling tone of the play.

A striking feature of *Troilus and Cressida* is the parallel council scenes which contain so much of the philosophical commentary that Shakespeare wrote into the play. That in the Greek camp (I.iii) is apparently based upon the council of Book I of the *Iliad*, although Shakespeare makes no mention of the quarrel over Chryseis. Details of the speeches are also based upon Book II, and Ulysses' dominant role in Shakespeare's council may also stem from his achievement in stemming the departure of the Greek army in Book II.[3] His great speech on degree seems derived from Richard Hooker's

Of the Laws of Ecclesiastical Polity, I, iii, 2, although the concept of chaos comes from elsewhere, perhaps from Ovid.

For the parallel Trojan council scene, no source has been found. But the discussion involves ideas that occur in the conversation about the rights and wrongs of the war early in Greene's work. Ulysses begins the discussion with a compliment to thè Trojan ladies who are visiting the Greeks: why did Paris cross the seas when the Trojan ladies, if those present are representative, were far more precious jewels—beautiful, wise, "sober & silent, as portending a temperate & vnfained chastity"? (p. 165).

I maruell *Paris* woulde make his choice of such a peece, and hasard the welfare of his father, countrey, and friendes, for a woman only indewed with the bare tytle of beawty, such a fading good as scarse can be possessed before it be vanished? (Pp. 165–66)

Cressida then breaks in with a more vehement attack:

And as great maruell my Lordes haue we the Ladies of Gretia, that *Hector* and his brethren, so famous through all the world for their martiall exploits, should beare armes in her defence, whose dishonesty ruinates both theyr fame & theyr countrey. Iustice gyuing euery man his due, allots lyttle pryuiledge to defrawde a man of his wyfe, which is the surest fee simple. The fayth of a knight is not limited by valour, but by vertue: fortitude consisteth not in hasarding without feare, but in being resolute vpon Just cause. (P. 166)

Thereupon,

Hector as Chollericke as she was scrupulous, roundly without longer debating with him selfe, made hir this answere.

As Madame, Iustice is a vertue that giues euery man his owne by equall proportion, so reuenge the sweetest content to parsons thwarted with iniuries, lookes not to end hir actions with an euen ballance, but useth *Legem Talionis*, repaying like for like: styrring vp the fire with a Swoorde, and for brasse weighing downe the scales with Leade. As my brother hath brought a trull from Greece, so myne Aunt, perforce (a fault farre surpassing this fact) was stolne from Troy, and from the daughter of a King made a seruile Concubyne. Nature, that despight of tyme will frowne at abuse and honour: that hurte thirsteth to salue hir selfe with reuenge, hath taught vs (although wee offer *Helena* thoughtes fit for hir offence) to mayntayne my Brothers deede with the Swoorde, not to allow such a fact honorable, but as holding it princely, with death to requite an iniury. (Pp. 166–67)

Achilles then asserts that the Greeks, too, "choose rather to dy satisfied than liue dishonoured." To him Troilus replies: "Greece complayneth of iniury, Troy is impatient of dishonour: both greeued ayme at reuenge. The Truce expired, let the doubt by the fauour of the gods and fortune be decided" (p. 168).

As the talk turns to threats, Ulysses tries to excuse his raising the subject of Helen but only leads Iphigenia to lecture the Trojans on their indifference to Philosophy:

> I thought to discouer the force of fancy, which partiall in her Cenzures prooueth beawty more predominant in affection, then virtue. *Helena* was fayre and a Queene, witty and therefore the sooner woonne, but yet dishonest, a cooling Carde to desire, a stayne manifest to the mynde, and yet so quickly ouerslipt by the eye, as it showes how little Juditiall the thoughtes bee of vnbridled affection.
>
> Had the Troians (quoth *Iphigenia Academis*) like to the Gretians, or were their cytties peopled as well with Philosophers as Souldiours, *Paris* had learned by their wise precepts to haue preferred Vertue before Beawty, & not to haue bought repentance so deare. . . . They pen downe volumes of martiall discipline, but knowe not *Apian* of morrall Philosophy, which is the cause they measure all their passions by will, and call Venus a goddesse onely for hir outwarde glory. (Pp. 168–69)

This speech effectively diverts the discussion to the Greeks' philosophy and to matters not parallel to Shakespeare's scene.

Except for Hector's speech on the laws of nature, which will be discussed later, there are no close verbal parallels. It has been necessary to quote the relevant passages from Greene in their entirety, furthermore, because Shakespeare picks and chooses and rearranges points to suit his purposes. This is, of course, exactly what we should expect in view of his practice in plays where he was following his sources closely. For example, in *Julius Caesar* II.i, the scene in which Brutus joins the conspirators, Shakespeare tries to show his poor judgment and his determination to govern by having him overrule Cassius and the rest on three crucial points. The three details come from different contexts in Plutarch's lives of Caesar and Brutus, and in only the last, Brutus's refusal to have Antony killed along with Caesar, does Shakespeare follow his source exactly. In the first, Brutus's rejection of the proposal that they swear an oath, Plutarch cites their complete fidelity without an oath as proof of their devotion to the cause and does not mention Brutus. In the second, Brutus's vetoing the proposal to include Cicero because "he will never follow anything/That other men begin" (151–52), Plutarch relates that the conspirators decided not to include Cicero because he was timorous and would hesitate to take vigorous action.[4] Shakespeare, in short, adapted details that he found interesting to the particular dramatic purpose that he had in mind. This seems to be essentially what happened as he wrote the Trojan council scene.

Except for Cassandra's prophecy, the themes upon which Shakespeare's Trojan council scene (II.ii) is based all occur in the passages quoted. Shakespeare's Hector argues, like Greene's Ulysses and Cressida, that Helen has cost many thousand lives and is not the Trojans', nor worth the keeping (18–25). Just as in Greene, Troilus rests his case on honor (25–28, etc.) and spurns reason (in Greene, philosophy) as merely an excuse for cowardice (46–50), and Hector later tells him and Paris that they "Have gloz'd, but superficially; not much/Unlike young men, whom Aristotle thought/Unfit to hear moral philosophy" (165–67). In Aristotle, incidentally, it is political philosophy, but moral philosophy in Greene. Hector's somewhat enigmatic lines, "And the will dotes that is attributive/To what infectiously itself affects" (58–59), as well as a later and clearer passage (168–73), parallels Iphigenia's charge that the Trojans "measure all their passions by will" (p. 169). Troilus and Paris take over arguments given to Hector in Greene, namely that the Greeks keep their aunt captive (77–80) and that the soil of Helen's rape should be "Wip'd off in honourable keeping her" (148–49).

If one is interested in *Troilus and Cressida*, as I have been, for its somewhat misplaced and dramatically unproductive parade of Shakespeare's knowledge of contemporary philosophy and psychology, the most important passage in the scene is Hector's application of the laws of nature to prove that Helen should be returned to the Greeks. It begins:

> Nature craves
> All dues be rend'red to their owners. Now
> What nearer debt in all humanity
> Than wife is to the husband?
>
> (173–76)

This clearly parallels Cressida's argument: "Iustice gyuing euery man his due, allots lyttle pryuiledge to defrawde a man of his wife, which is the surest fee simple" (p. 166). Hector accepts her premise (though he draws a different conclusion): "As Madame, Iustice is a vertue that giues euery man his owne by equall proportion . . ." (p. 166). Hector's speech in Shakespeare is developed, of course, in terms of commonplaces of moral philosophy. But it probably derives from the same context in Richard Hooker as Ulysses' speech on degree.[5] If so, Shakespeare's reading in Hooker would provide an obvious explanation for his substituting Nature, Hooker's subject, for Justice and also, incidentally, for his writing "reason," another theme of Hooker's, in place of Greene's "philosophy" as the antithesis of honor.

Hector's speech is interesting because it is also an example of the way in which I believe that the entire scene was constructed. Greene furnished themes and details that stimulated Shakespeare's imagination. These he fleshed out with material from contemporary philosophy, a misquotation of Aristotle and a parody of Marlowe, and most of all, of course, his knowledge of the way human beings argue to justify what they have done.

But Greene may well account for more of Hector than the passage just discussed. His portrayal of Hector is that of a fire-eating and not very bright devotee of fortitude. The remark quoted above reads in its entirety:

As Madame, Iustice is a vertue that giues euery man his owne by equal proportion, so reuenge the sweetest content to parsons thwarted with iniuries, lookes not to end hir actions with an euen ballance, but useth *Legem Talionis*, repaying like for like. (Pp. 166–67)

In Shakespeare, Hector, after arguing most philosophically, does a sudden and quite unmotivated reversal:

> Hector's opinion
> Is this in way of truth. Yet ne'ertheless,
> My sprightly brethren, I propend to you
> In resolution to keep Helen still;
> For 'tis a cause that hath no mean dependence
> Upon our joint and several dignities.
>
> (188–93)

This is similar to his resolution in Greene "to mayntayne my Brothers deede with the Swoorde, not to allow such a fact honorable, but as holding it princely, with death to requite an iniury" (p. 167). One can only conjecture that, as elsewhere in his plays, Shakespeare sacrificed consistency to dramatic expediency. Up to the lines just quoted, Hector serves as a foil for Troilus, who must be portrayed as young and impetuous and driven by his emotions. But the war had to go on, and Hector had to be adjusted to that fact. At any rate, from that point on he has important similarities to Greene's Hector. In his discourse on fortitude, the latter is taking issue with Helenus, who has spoken in praise of wisdom. His position is fairly well indicated by the Greeks' interpretation "that where courage manaceth reuenge with the Sworde, there it is folly to bring in wysedome in his Purple Roabes" (p. 259), and even better by Hector's own reaction:

Hector, a little chollericke that so brauely they went about to prooue his haruest in the grasse, stammered out these or such like woordes. I tell you brother *Helenus*, both you and the rest are deceiued, & that I will prooue against the wisest soldier in the world with my sword, that Senators who sit to giue counsaile for Ciuill pollicie, had neede to be wise, sith their opinions are holden for Oracles, & Captaines valiant, whose deedes are accounted peremptorie conquests: put case wisedome & fortitude be in a Generall, yet is hee called wise as hee giues iudgement, and couragious as with a hardy minde hee attempts the victories. Let men haue science in their heades, and no weapons in their hands, and whom can they preiudice: I say therefore, which none rightly can gainesay, that fortitude is most necessarie for a souldier, sith our common phrase confirmes my reason with euidence, in saying, hee is a wise Senator and a hardy souldier. (Pp. 260–61)

Shakespeare's portrait is much subtler. Hector foolishly thinks that war is a game. He is reproved by Troilus for "a vice of mercy" that is "fool's play" (V.iii.37–43), and he meets his death because he disarms on the field of battle (V.viii.1–10). The wisdom that Helenus praised, furthermore, consists largely in winning by trickery what you cannot gain by force of arms, as his "tragedy" makes very clear. The treacherous ambush of Hector by Achilles and his Myrmidons is a good example of such "wisdom" and is in marked contrast to other accounts of the Trojan War. The "policy" in the fraudulent lottery by which Ajax becomes the Greek champion (unique to Shakespeare) is also quite in accord with Greene's "wisdom."

The last remarks have probably pushed conjecture too far. But another conjecture is both more to the point and more important. If the evidence makes it probable that Shakespeare knew Greene's work and derived from it themes that he developed in the Trojan council scene (II.ii), and I think it does, then a more important possibility develops—namely, that Greene may actually have suggested the cynical, not to say scurrilous, treatment of the Trojan War itself. Source studies are more likely to be concerned with substance than with point of view. Yet the Elizabethans clearly thought of imitation as involving both material and method of treatment. Roger Ascham sententiously defines two kinds of imitation, "dissimilis materiei similis tractatio" and "similis materiei dissimilis tractatio." [6] The love story in *Troilus and Cressida* would be a good example of the second kind, matter derived largely from Chaucer having been treated dramatically in accordance with a far more cynical view of Cressida derived largely from Robert Henryson. But the similar treatment of dissimilar matter immediately becomes involved in that the familiar material is recast in imitation of examples of the new literary genres involved—namely, comedy and satire to form satiric comedy. We therefore have two principles at work somewhat like the medieval dichotomy of form and substance, the form being imitated and the substance borrowed or adapted. But the "form" in Shakespeare's handling of the love story also involves the different, satiric point of view, which is much clearer, in fact, than the literary genre of the play. Needing a cynical or satiric point of view of the war—that is, a "form"—to match the handling of the love story, Shakespeare may have derived from Greene suggestions for the kind of devastating ethical analysis to which he subjects the Trojan War; if we may push conjecture to even more daring lengths, he may even have derived from Greene the idea of a double treatment of war as well as love in equally cynical terms. His main source, Chaucer's *Troilus and Criseyde*, mentions the war only incidentally. Any such hints from Greene, on the other hand, would have extended only to the war, for in Greene Cressida is a member of the Greek party and first encounters Troilus at Agamemnon's entertainment.

A final parallel between Greene's prose and Shakespeare's play should be mentioned, namely the entertainment of the Trojans by Agamemnon and the Greeks in *Troilus and Cressida* IV.v and V.i. Hector's challenge, which leads to the meeting, is derived from *Iliad* VII, although Shakespeare adds the trappings of chivalric romance; the lot falling to Ajax is bona fide in Homer but rigged in Shakespeare; and the combat is broken off by night in Homer but avoided by Hector in Shakespeare. In Caxton's *Recuyell of the Hystoryes of Troye*, Hector goes to the Greek camp alone and has an exchange with Achilles somewhat like that in Shakespeare (IV.v.233–70). They make an agreement to settle the war by single combat, but their bargain is overruled by the Greek leaders.[7] A general entertainment of Trojans by Greeks is necessary if Troilus is actually to see the falsity of Cressida rather than, as in Chaucer, merely finding in Diomedes' captured armor a brooch that he had given her (V, 1660–66). This has no parallel in the obvious sources. On the other hand, in Greene Achilles is chosen to meet the Trojans and guide them to Agamemnon's tent; in Shakespeare we see only the beginning and end of the entertainment which provides half of Greene's narrative, and Achilles appears only at the end. So one can only speculate that Greene may have suggested to Shakespeare a way to get Troilus into the Greek camp and to provide a much stronger conclusion to the love story than in Chaucer.

To summarize, the evidence that Shakespeare knew Greene is less than definitive. But the possibility that *Euphues His Censure to Philautus* provided material for the Trojan council scene seems to me to amount to strong probability. The other influences that have been suggested are only possibilities, and one's assessment of the possibility must depend largely upon one's evaluation of the evidence for influence upon the Trojan council scene.

GEOFFREY BULLOUGH

Another Analogue of
Measure for Measure

I PRESENT below a story from the Italian, not as a certain "source" for Shakespeare's *Measure for Measure* (though it may be one), but as providing interesting parallels to aspects of the plot and characterization, and as an additional illustration of the popularity of the play's motifs in Renaissance story.

It is generally agreed that in writing *Othello* and *Measure for Measure* (1603–4) Shakespeare drew directly or indirectly on the *Hecatommithi* of G. Giraldi Cinthio, published in 1565 and translated into French by Gabriel Chappuys (1584). For *Measure for Measure* he may also have used Cinthio's tragicomedy *Epitia* which provides a happier ending by restoring the "executed" brother than that in Cinthio's short story (Decade VIII, Novella V). He certainly knew George Whetstone's *Promos and Cassandra* (1578), a two-part play possibly based on Claude Rouillet's Latin *Philanira*, and took from it the general idea of his low-life comic scenes.

Many versions of the "unjust judge" and "monstrous ransom" theme have been listed and discussed by F. E. Budd and other writers on Shakespeare's play.[1] The man who abuses his authority may be the governor of a city, a judge, a deputy, the captain of a garrison. Always there is an overlord, a king or duke who hears the woman's complaint and apportions justice at the end. The condemned man is a husband or a brother. The degree of his criminality varies greatly. In Rouillet's *Philanira*, Hippolytus has been condemned for robbing the Piedmontese people entrusted to his care; in Thomas Lupton's *The Second Part of . . . Too Good To Be True* (1581) he has killed his friend in a fit of jealousy. Cinthio's Vico has ravished a virgin but is willing to marry her and she him. Whetstone's Andrugio, like Shakespeare's Claudio, has committed fornication with his sweetheart; so the death penalty seems harsh at the outset; the laws of the city are ultrasevere.

The woman is usually the wife of the condemned man, but occasionally (Cinthio, Whetstone, Shakespeare) his sister. Invariably she receives the judge's infamous proposal with incredulity turning to abhorrence, but in most instances she agrees, sometimes (as in Lupton) after long persuasion by the tempter, sometimes after consultation with the condemned man, who, terrified of death, urges her to save him by surrendering herself. Whetstone's Andrugio declares, "Justice wyll say thou dost no crime commit,/For in forst faultes is no intent of yll" (III.4). A similar argument is used by René in Belleforest's *Histoires Tragiques* (*Tome* 6, 1582), in a story which may have suggested to Shakespeare Iago's use of Roderigo to involve Cassio in a guardroom quarrel. Shakespeare's Claudio begs,

> Sweet sister, let me live!
> What sin you do to save a brother's life,
> Nature dispenses with the deed so far
> That it becomes a virtue.

(III.i.133–36)

In Cinthio's story Epitia

did not leave her brother until, overcome by his tears, she had been persuaded to promise that she would give herself to Juriste, provided that he were willing to save Vico's life and fulfil her hope of becoming his wife.

In Cinthio's play Juriste's sister Angela came to see Epitia and confirmed these promises. But here as in later versions the judge's respect for legality and his fear of discovery make him betray his word. The lady complains to the overlord, who arranges a scene which will test both her and the unjust judge.

Shakespeare did not need any "source" to make him create Isabella, and a desire to depart from the traditional plot in some striking way would be enough to explain why he conceived her as determined at all costs to preserve her honor. But he was always ready to take hints from his reading, and it is quite possible that in Cinthio or Chappuys he had come upon *Hecatommithi*, Dec. V, Nov. VI, which presents the same dilemma as that of Epitia, but in much more elementary form, so that it is just a simple story about a faithful wife who refuses to be blackmailed and saves her husband by appealing to the King. I give a translation[2] of the tale, which follows one in which a brave woman gets her husband out of prison disguised as a friar, and is ultimately pardoned by the King.

A tailor is about to be hanged. The Judge promises the wretch's wife to set him free if she will pleasure him. The woman makes this known to the Lord of the land. The tailor is forgiven and the Judge is punished.

When everybody had lavished praises on the loving-kindness of that good wife and on the graciousness of the King, Portia said, "It seems we might say that, just as Orpheus drew his wife back from Hades, so this gentle lady drew back her husband from the shadow of death." "But with a much happier outcome, one might add," said Sempronius.

Then Portia, having to follow next in the appointed order of stories, said, "I am about to show you that such is the fidelity of honest women toward their husbands that not only noble ladies but poor women also prove themselves their most earnest protectors; and although what I am about to relate occurred among people of lowly rank, I shall prove to you nonetheless that the justice of the Prince about whom I shall speak concerning it is no less to be commended than the clemency of the French monarch."

In the reign of Alfonso I, third Duke of Ferrara (whose virtue and wisdom through all the various vicissitudes of the world made his rule so just and defended him so well from the attacks and wiles of his enemies, however powerful, that whereas they grieved and almost consumed themselves with rage at not being able to overcome him and lay low the valor and wisdom of so sage and strong a Prince, he lived securely with his people and enjoyed the just vengeance wreaked by Heaven on those who wished to see him and his state destroyed) there was a Judge, certainly not one of the least notable in the arts of the law, but very much more sensual than befitted the rank he occupied.

This man had condemned a tailor to be hanged for a theft which he had committed, and the latter, knowing that he was to die within three days, appealed to the Judge that for the little time he had left he might have his wife to stay with him. The Judge answered that if she desired it he would gladly allow it; and having summoned the woman he asked her if perchance it would pleasure her to go and stay in the prison with her husband. She replied, yes, if he would permit it, and as she spoke she began to shed floods of tears.

The woman was eighteen years old and of most pleasing face and figure, sweet and gentle, with lively eyes, but modest, and her cheeks looked as if red roses and white lilies had been joined there by nature and a master's hand; to which were added two wonderfully beautiful lips like coral. And, not to go on recounting minute particulars, she so tendered herself to whoever gazed on her, that by what was to be seen of her it could be understood that she was most lovely in every part. In addition to this natural beauty were the tears which fell on the cheeks of the young woman, like drops of dew on morning roses, so charming that it was a marvel to behold.

The Judge, who had no wife and was by nature inclined to lechery, having looked upon Graziosa (for that was her name) burned with lustful desire, and knowing himself to be rich and powerful and the young woman poor and afraid of losing her husband, he fancied that, by dazzling her and giving her hope of freeing her husband he could without opposition ensnare the sweet and lovely girl. But before giving her hope of her husband's life he decided to see whether arousing in her dislike of the former would suffice to obtain from her that which he coveted. So, pretending to console her, he said that he was sorry for her bad fortune, to have tied herself to a man of such evil ways that he must come to a wretched and shameful end by being condemned to the gallows for robbery. But in this misfortune she should be happy because soon she would be freed from the bond that held her joined to such a shameful fellow. Then, restored to her freedom, she would have cause to choose a better husband next time.

"A better choice" (she replied) "I have no desire to make, I intend that he who first had the flower of my chastity shall have it always, both alive and dead. I do not wish in the least to suggest that it does not grieve me as much as it would any other loving wife, to see my dear husband brought into such a bad situation. But it lessens my grief somewhat to know that it was not a natural bent for crime, but the poverty into which he fell during the present hard time (for that year there was a great scarcity), that led him to steal what was another's; for no other reason than not to die of want. And this, Sir, should make him deserve some compassion from you and our Lord Duke; and I dare to believe that when you inform his Excellency about the need that drove him to theft, you will, through the kindness of that great Lord, relieve me from any anguish and my husband from the peril in which he now finds himself."

By these words the Judge realized how dear her husband was to her, and how much she longed to see him freed from peril of his life. Hence, seeing that any attempt to turn her against her husband would not change her attitude, he thought it certain that he could entrap her by giving her hopes of freeing him and of being freed from poverty. He said, "Whenever you please, lovely young lady, you can rescue your husband from death and make yourself happy, and ensure that poverty will never again be the reason why, to escape from want, he may steal and risk being hanged."

The young woman had never heard anything more pleasing than this, and she said that she would be eternally grateful if she could obtain such a boon. Then the Judge said, "If you will let me take my pleasure of you I shall free your husband and give you enough for you to live happily with him."

On hearing these words Graziosa blushed all red and answered, "Sir, if you have found me determined never, after my husband is dead, to link myself with any other man, I will not say shamefully, as you desire me, but as a wife, how can you suppose that, while he is still alive, I could lie with you as if I were a strumpet? You may sooner condemn me to be hanged with him than to save him by such base and dishonorable means. Although I was born poor, nature has not made me so vile in spirit, or so unapt to endure the poverty in which I exist, as to prefer the dishonest gain which you promise me to the honest poverty in which I have lived till now."

"But your husband will die!" he replied. "Then let him die!" said Graziosa, "since both his cruel fate and mine will have it so. He will take with him at least the happiness that the woman who was his alone while he lived will remain his after his death; and he will know that, although you have had the power to slay him, you will not have had the power to slay the honor of his wife." And here weeping put an end to her speech.

The shameless man, turning toward her arrogantly, "You are indeed cruel," said he; "this cruelty does not go well with such beauty"; and thus speaking, he stretched out his hand and tried to touch her chin. At once Graziosa repulsed him, and not knowing what more to say, she left the room in disdain and went to the Lord of the city, and being granted audience, she told him what the Judge had said to her, and how he had sought to deprive her of her honor. Then with that grace which nature had bestowed on her with liberal hand, she threw herself at the Duke's feet and said, weeping, "My Lord, since my misery has not been able to wring any pity from that scoundrel, I beg you, of your great goodness, to let me find it in you, and that you will save my husband by your clemency, showing that a benevolent Prince such as you are knows well how to practice clemency in a royal way in other people's wretchedness. And if perhaps my husband does not seem worthy of it, through having erred gravely, look favorably, Lord, on the grief I am about to suffer by his death, and the hope I have that through your kindness I may not be borne down by so much anguish; especially since my husband was driven by extreme poverty, and not by an evil nature or criminal habits, to commit the crime for which he is condemned to death." Here, not being able to speak any more because of her many tears and sighs, she fell silent.

The Duke stood there among his servants, a courteous and benevolent man, although in demeanor he showed himself severe rather than otherwise. (Indeed, in compassion for the afflicted he was the equal of any other benign Prince.) Wherefore Graziosa's tears and pleading weighed heavily on his mind, as well as the clarity with which she expressed her sorrows and described the Judge's lasciviousness. For he recognized by her speech what honorable love a faithful woman may possess.

So turning toward her with an amiable look he said, "Fair young woman, be of good cheer, for if matters stand in fact as you have described them to me in words, you shall have recompense for your fidelity and the lecherous Judge the reward of his lust." And having made her go into a room near his own, he sent for His Honor the Judge, who, thinking himself summoned by his Prince for any other reason than because of what Graziosa had said of him, went along very cheerfully.

When he arrived the Duke chatted lightly with him (as he knew very well how to do), moving from one topic to another, and let some opportunity arise to mention the tailor, asking what must be done with him. The Judge replied, "Nothing else but send him to the gallows." The Duke said, "Could no means be found to save the poor man? For besides hearing that he committed the theft out of extreme need, I am besought by many people not to let him die, and if I could do so without offending justice I should gladly reprieve him, to please those who insistently beg me to do so." "I cannot imagine any way of doing that which would not go against justice," replied the Judge. "How can it be," said the Duke, "that you who make the laws in your own way cannot at least discover some pretext, some specious reason, for saving this petty criminal?" "As far as the civil laws go," answered the Judge, "some allowance might be made, since they do not condemn anyone to death for theft. But there are also the statutes of the Cities, which prescribe death, and those of your own City declare it also. So if you do not wish to go against your own laws, no means can be found to save this man, once the theft has been proved and the thief convicted, after he has submitted his defense and brought no evidence whereby we could stay the execution."

"But suppose that the tailor's wife came to lie with you," said the Duke, "couldn't you save him?" And at these words, according to previous instructions, the young woman was sent out from the room in which she had hitherto been hidden. Addressing the Duke—"This is he, my Lord," she said, "who was willing to give me back my husband if I would let him dishonorably have his pleasure of my body. I demand mercy for my husband and justice against that man."

The Judge, who was accustomed to terrify others, stood altogether dumbfounded by the confrontation and the woman's words, and this gave the just Duke very good reason to believe that all that Graziosa had told him was true. Turning to her he said, "Modest young woman, because of the love and faithfulness you bear your husband and the care you have of your honor, I feel compassion for you, and for your sake I have it for your husband, although he does not himself deserve it. As for the outrage which this man wished to commit on justice by satisfying his lust and harming your honor, I shall punish him as he deserves. I grant you your husband's life, and I desire him to have as much of this man's wealth as will suffice to pay for the things which he stole. Furthermore I ordain that this fellow be hanged tomorrow instead of your husband."

No need to ask whether the Judge, who knew by experience how severely the Duke punished whosoever violated justice, was filled with shame and fear. All pale and trembling he threw himself on his knees at the Duke's feet and began most humbly to beg for mercy. But the Duke, showing himself more angry than before, made him stand up and took him into the room into which Graziosa had gone out, saying that he should be guarded there until the Sergeants came for him. The Judge went in most miserably, looking as though he might find there the ruffian who would knot the noose round his neck to strangle him.

The Judge's friends however went to the Duke and begged for clemency, excusing him both by the young woman's beauty and the frailty of his youth (for he was scarcely more than thirty years old) and they adduced other similar reasons which had some influence on the Duke's mind. Nevertheless he gave no sign that any of them had the least importance, saying that the hearts of those who are in the likeness of magistrates must not be contaminated by perverse and irrational appetites, and that the punishment of those who err thus must be the greater inasmuch as other men should take from them an example of good living.

Among the courtiers was a noble youth who was always gay. He addressed the Duke with a merry look and said, "My Lord, these white devils carry about with them temptations too great for us to resist, and often the most wise and ancient men are overcome by them, not only young men like the Judge. Hence he deserves to be pardoned if he was conquered by such a fierce assault as the beauty of this woman made on him. Maybe, if your Excellency were not angry, as she is, you also would have had some difficulty in defending yourself." There was laughter among the company at the young man's pleasant words, and the Duke could hardly restrain himself, although he showed great severity, saying that one should not jest so cynically. At this the Judge's friends began to hope, and they never ceased begging the Duke not to proceed further in punishing his lust other than by depriving him of his office and making him give so much of his wealth to the tailor as would pay for the thefts which (they had heard) he had committed out of dire need.

The tailor, being freed from imminent death, and being made of better mind by the peril in which he had stood, left off stealing, set himself to live by his craft, and happily rejoiced in the fidelity and goodness of his wife.

We are not told whether in fact the Judge's punishment was lightened. The next story begins, "Leaving the Judge in the state of terror which he ought to feel."

Some points of comparison between Cinthio's simple tale and Shakespeare's play are easily seen. In most versions of the plot the condemned man is scarcely worthy of the woman's devotion. Here, however, the husband has stolen only through poverty in a famine year; in natural law his crime should be lightly punished. In this he resembles Claudio, who has committed fornication with his betrothed, Julietta, rather than Vico, who has violated a virgin. The Judge has little resemblance to Angelo, for we are told at once that he is sensual, whereas Angelo has a reputation for cold austerity, and he himself does not realize his potentiality for passion until desire for Isabella awakes in him. Both, however, are legalists: during the first interview with Isabella Angelo's attitude is not unlike that of the Judge in our story when the Duke asks whether it is necessary for the tailor to die.

> *Isab.* Must he needs die?
> *Ang.*   Maiden, no remedy.
> . . . .
> He's sentenc'd; 'tis too late.
> . . . .
> Your brother is a forfeit of the law,
> And you but waste your words.
> . . . .
> It is the law, not I, condemn your brother.
>
> (II.ii.48–80)

Both Angelo and the unjust Judge stand on the letter of the law. In Shakespeare the new deputy is putting into force laws of Vienna which have lain dormant for many years (I.ii.169–75). Cinthio's Judge admits that civil law does not lay down the death penalty for theft, but invokes the local laws of the Italian cities. Both Duke Alfonso and Duke Vincentio regard the penalty as too severe for the crime.

Most likenesses are generic and to be found in other possible sources. Our story is distinguished from the rest by Graziosa's steadfast rejection of the Judge's demand even though it cost her husband his head. When told that he must die if she will not give way, "Then let him die!" (*E muoiasi*) says Graziosa, and when the lecherous Judge tries to touch her face she spurns him and goes. Isabella's outburst when Angelo leaves her (II.iv.171 ff.) —"Then Isabel, live chaste, and brother die,/More than our brother is our chastity"—is uttered in the assurance that he would sooner die than have her unchaste (177–87). Here she resembles Graziosa, who believes that her husband would die happy knowing that she was true to him. Graziosa does not put her husband to the test, but Isabella, like Epitia and Cassandra, does, and in her resultant disillusionment she curses Claudio in terms (III.i.136–47) which have brought down upon her the wrath of many critics with less rigid ideas about feminine honor.

It may be that, having read Cinthio's Dec. V, Nov. VI as well as the offspring of Dec. VIII, Nov. V, Shakespeare decided to combine the two conceptions, the woman who steadfastly refuses to surrender her virtue and the romantic plot by which Vico and Andrugio are saved. A major problem was to make it dramatically plausible for the sister to prefer her brother's death to her own loss of chastity while retaining the audience's sympathy. Shakespeare solves it by making her a devotee, about to enter the novitiate, eager for further austerities and willing henceforth not to "speak with men/But in the presence of the prioress" (I.iv.1–13), shocked at her brother's sensual slip but not ignorant of the world and its ways ("O, let him marry her!"). This is no simple uneducated woman like Graziosa, armed with nothing but love and honesty. Isabella is well-born, and though Claudio believes that "in her youth/There is a prone and speechless dialect,/Such as move men" (I.ii.187–89), in fact she proves as clever an advocate as Epitia (who had studied philosophy). Though lust is "a vice that most I do abhor," and her first approach to Angelo is so cold and reluctant that she accepts his statement of the "just but severe law" which condemned Claudio, and would withdraw, once Lucio has persuaded her to try again she pleads for mercy and counters Angelo's specious arguments, both theoretic and personal, with great skill. Professor J. W. Lever has shown (Introduction, Arden ed.) how subtly she is portrayed, yet it is wrong to see any psychic confusion in her attitudes to Angelo and her brother, to sin, shame, and honor. Neither Shakespeare nor the Elizabethan popular audience would accept Tyndale's crass comment on Lucrece's martyrdom: "She sought her own glory in her chastity and not God's" (Arden ed., p. lxxx). The Duke's praise of Isabella's vehemence is what we are meant to feel: "The hand that hath made you fair hath made you good" (III.i.184–85). Though Isabella is now back in the licentious world, away from the convent, she lives in the Christian tradition which extends from the early Christian virgins to the Lady and her Elder Brother in *Comus*. The religious tradition is enforced by a moral and social code which puts special emphasis on female chastity. So in the last resort for Isabella as for Cinthio's Graziosa the issue is quite simple: fornication or adultery, even if enforced, brings physical and spiritual pollution, mortal sin, lasting shame for the victim, dishonor for the family. No husband or brother should demand this sacrifice; being what she is, as strict in fact as Angelo was in seeming, she cannot offer it. This being admitted, the consequence is well stated by the Duke: "How will you do to content this substitute and to save your brother?" (III.i.191–93). And this occupies the rest of the play, at the end of which the puritan Isabella is taught to put off her rigor and to seek mercy for the would-be violator and murderer.

The story introduces another feature of *Measure for Measure* not found in *Promos and Cassandra* or *Epitia*, namely, the young spark Lucio. Cinthio's "noble youth who was always gay" pleads for the Judge on the grounds that he was young and open to temptation, that it is natural for all men to desire fair women ("these white devils"), and that the Duke himself might have been tempted by Graziosa's beauty in normal circumstances. The court is amused by his daring, and the Duke too is amused, though he affects severity and reproves his cynicism. I suggest that Shakespeare found here the germ of his fantastic courtier whom he developed to exemplify (as Claudio must not) the moral corruption of a libertine society. Dissolute and conscious that he himself deserves arrest, he pleads for Claudio to Isabella and encourages her in her first interview with Angelo. But he is completely untrustworthy and irresponsible. When Pompey needs his help he mocks at him, and has apparently informed against Mistress Overdone although she has looked after the child he has had by a whore. The impertinent suggestion in Cinthio that Duke Alfonso might well have been tempted to seduce Graziosa is transformed into a whole series of slanders made by Lucio against Duke Vicentio. The Duke, Lucio tells the "friar," has been a lecher but is now impotent:

Ere he would have hang'd a man for the getting a hundred bastards, he would have paid for the nursing a thousand. He had some feeling of the sport; he knew the service, and that instructed him to mercy.

(III.ii.124–28)

At the trial he keeps interrupting with facetious remarks which go down badly. He accuses the "friar" of maligning the Duke, and it is he who unmasks the latter. In his contempt for such a rascal the Duke affects greater severity toward him than he feels, and finally forgives his slanders but makes him marry his punk.

It has been suggested that Shakespeare may have taken the idea of a slanderous courtier from Barnabe Riche's *The Adventures of Brusanus Prince of Hungaria* (1592) which contains a King (Leonarchus) wandering in disguise as a merchant to observe the manners and morals of his kingdom, and an extravagant braggart (Gloriosus) who mocks at the "counterfeit Merchant," boasts that he knows the King well, and accuses the merchant and his companions of treason. When Leonarchus, after a trial scene, reveals himself, Gloriosus is banished.

There are certainly some resemblances between *Brusanus* and *Measure for Measure* which suggest that Shakespeare knew the romance (as he knew other of Riche's works). Gloriosus, however, as his name indicates, is a pretentious Armado, "like a *Mallcontent* . . . a *Monarcho* . . . a counterfeite Souldier." Though, like Lucio, he mocks at his disguised overlord, and tries to curry favor by treachery, he entirely lacks Lucio's lively resourcefulness, eel-like slipperiness, and Rabelaisian humor.

In the light of this it seems probable that Cinthio's Dec. V, Nov. VI provided *données*, not only for Isabella's indomitable chastity, but also for the gay young courtier with his impertinent jests and permissive attitude to sex.

MAURICE CHARNEY

Webster vs. Middleton, or
the Shakespearean Yardstick
in Jacobean Tragedy

*J*N DAVID FROST'S recent book, *The School of Shakespeare*, Shakespeare is conceived as a schoolmaster trying— mostly in vain—to set high standards for his gifted but wayward pupils. This is a new twist to the old theme of bardolatry, and Frost lays about him mercilessly in the name of his Master: "All the dramatists with whom this study is concerned are minor, if our standard is to be anything but parochial or chauvinist; and we must guard against the vice of the specialist, who hails as a masterpiece anything that noses above the swamp." [1] This is a fighting metaphor, with its echo from "I Am a Fugitive from a Chain Gang." A bit further on Frost establishes his position with unmistakable clarity: "Yet, though his contemporaries must suffer, I shall use Shakespeare as a yardstick of excellence throughout; for it is on the ground that, fitfully, fragmentarily, they reached a comparable height that the Jacobeans lay claim to our attention." [2] As a perspective on Jacobean drama, this seems to me almost completely wrong. The very postulation of a Shakespearean yardstick encourages the comparative mood, in which Shakespeare always emerges as the untarnished representative of the good old days. Rather than invoking Shakespeare, we should be expending our energy on what is distinctive—and un-Shakespearean—in his fellow dramatists.

No critic has executed more grandiose gestures with the Shakespearean yardstick than Swinburne, "who gave us," as Archer maliciously observed, "the Lamb doctrine through a megaphone." [3] Shakespeare broods over Swinburne's *Age of Shakespeare*. He is the final criterion of all excellence, and his fellow dramatists are only occasionally allowed to approach his hallowed shrine. Nowhere is the Shakespearean yardstick more actively displayed than in the essay on John Webster, in whom Swinburne recognized striking resemblances to the Master:

Mere literary power, mere poetic beauty, mere charm of passionate or pathetic fancy, we find in varying degrees dispersed among them all [Shakespeare's fellow dramatists] alike; but the crowning gift of imagination, the power to make us realise that thus and not otherwise it was, that thus and not otherwise it must have been, was given—except by exceptional fits and starts—to none of the poets of their time but only to Shakespeare and to Webster.[4]

Swinburne is not one to back away from rhapsodic generalization, and he has a distinct predilection for superlatives and the enumeration of immutable characteristics:

In the deepest and highest and purest qualities of tragic poetry Webster stands nearer to Shakespeare than any other English poet stands to Webster; and so much nearer as to be a good second; while it is at least questionable whether even Shelley can reasonably be accepted as a good third. Not one among the predecessors, contemporaries, or successors of Shakespeare and Webster has given proof of this double faculty—this coequal mastery of terror and pity, undiscoloured and undistorted, but vivified and glorified, by the splendour of immediate and infallible imagination.[5]

As Archer was so ungentlemanly as to point out, nothing in Swinburne's criticism reveals that Shakespeare and his fellow dramatists were actually writing plays that were put on in theaters. Swinburne is not interested in theatrical performance, and the play is only one incidental form among many for the expression of grand poetic passions. Shakespeare and Webster are poets who happened to write plays, and the Shakespearean yardstick is invoked to measure the greatness of passages of lyric poetry that are more or less detachable from their context. Swinburne only echoes the orthodox Romantic view of Shakespeare and the Elizabethans when he assumes that drama has nothing special to contribute to dramatic criticism. Poetry is an undifferentiated mass, and the conditions of its origin do not much affect what appears on the printed page.

Swinburne owes an obvious and much acknowledged debt to Charles Lamb, whose *Specimens of English Dramatic Poets* (1808) was an extraordinary stimulus to the study of Elizabethan plays.[6] Lamb generally eschews "single passages and detached beauties," [7] but his "scenes of passion" are still only specimen scenes, and he tends to choose eloquent, climactic moments rather than quiet, understated, intensely dramatic ones which would depend more crucially on context. "Pray you undo this button" is not Lamb's idea of poetry. Shakespeare receives his expected tribute as the nonpareil of Elizabethan drama: "how much of Shakespeare shines in the great men his contemporaries, and how far in his divine mind and manners he surpassed them and all mankind." [8] In his perceptive notes, Lamb is constantly using Shakespeare as the yardstick of excellence. Of Cornelia's dirge for her son Marcello, Lamb writes, "I never saw anything like this Dirge, except the Ditty which reminds Ferdinand of his drowned Father in the *Tempest*. As that is of the water, watery: so this is of the earth, earthy. Both have that intenseness of feeling, which seems to resolve itself into the elements which it contemplates." [9] There are indeed verbal and stylistic similarities between the passages in *The White Devil* and *The Tempest*, yet the contexts are so radically different that I cannot feel any resemblance at all. In the broadest terms, one play is a romantic pastoral, the other a Machiavellian revenge tragedy.

Lamb and Swinburne are not alone in insisting on the comparison between Shakespeare and Webster; it is one of the clichés of nineteenth-century criticism. Hazlitt offers his own special version when he writes that *The White Devil* and *The Duchess of Malfi* not only "come the nearest to Shakspeare of any thing we have upon record," but that they are also "too like Shakspeare, and often direct imitations of him, both in general conception and individual expression." [10] Everywhere one turns in the literature on Webster one finds critics doing obeisance to the Shakespearean yardstick. Hereward T. Price, for example, concludes his essay on Webster's imagery with the inevitable link:

The only possible comparison is with Shakespeare. There can be no doubt that Webster profited by Shakespeare's example. But even Shakespeare could in his turn have learned something from Webster's skill in interlacing long chains of figure and action in order to express an irony so varied, so subtle, and so profound. [11]

I cannot understand why the "only possible comparison is with Shakespeare." What about Marston, Tourneur, Chapman, to all of whom Webster has an important affiliation? I am afraid that because Shakespeare's poetic style has been so fully studied, it offers an excessively convenient system for the examination of Webster.

Another aspect of the marriage of Shakespeare and Webster is the petulant and even unprincipled attack on Webster by critics associated with *Scrutiny*,[12] who score Webster for being not only a failed Shakespeare, but also a rather chuckleheaded pretender to maturity, or, in other words, a decadent. Ian Jack's statement of the case is typical.

Great tragedy can be written only by a man who has achieved—at least for the period of composition—a profound *and balanced* insight into life. Webster—his plays are our evidence—did not achieve such an insight. The imagery, verse-texture, themes, and "philosophy" of his plays all point to a fundamental flaw, which is ultimately a moral flaw. [13]

And further: "No moral order represented itself to his imagination as real. Consequently his plays contain brilliant passages of poetry—they appear whenever he touches on the small area which acted as his inspiration—but lack imaginative coherence." [14] Shakespeare, we are not surprised to learn, does not suffer from this profoundly dissociated sensibility. He is not "an interesting example of a very great literary and dramatic genius directed toward chaos," [15] as Eliot said of Webster, and Shakespeare is therefore capable of writing great tragedy, as Webster is not. This pejorative approach to Webster through invidious comparison with Shakespeare can only be a dead end, as the Hunters wisely note in their Penguin critical anthology of Webster: "The vein is virtually exhausted. . . . New insight into Webster is not likely to be derived from these premises." [16]

There are obvious echoes of Shakespeare in Webster's work, but there are also obvious echoes of just about every Elizabethan writer one can think of—and more from those who do not immediately come to mind, like Matthieu and Sir William Alexander. Alexander is, in fact, one of Webster's leading dramatic sources. If we are to believe the strong evidence of Robert Dent's researches into Webster's "borrowings," he wrote *The White Devil* and *The Duchess of Malfi* with his commonplace book at hand, and one single Websterian sentence may be compacted from bits and pieces out of three or more unrelated sources.[17]

I mention this embarrassing matter of sources only to discount in advance the ever-present echoes from Shakespeare we seem to hear in Webster. A casual look at *The White Devil*, for example, suggests that Camillo, the foolish cuckold, is modeled on Polonius and that Vittoria as courtesan reminds us of Cleopatra, just as Bracciano at his best recalls Antony. Monticelso's formal lecture to Bracciano about how lasciviousness is destroying his better nature (II.i.22 ff.) is very much in the manner of Caesar's rebuke of Antony, and Bracciano's wife Isabella has a formal resemblance to Antony's Octavia. The martial declarations of Bracciano's son Giovanni (II.i) are in the spirit both of Coriolanus and his son, the notorious mammocker of gilded butterflies. Cornelia in her madness is practically quoting from the flower-distributing Ophelia in *Hamlet*, and Bracciano in his madness indulges in a wild free-association reminiscent of King Lear. Perhaps the strongest link is between *The White Devil* and *Troilus and Cressida*, where the sardonic wit of Flamineo suggests Pandarus and Thersites. The mood of satire, disillusion, misdirected commitments, and even world-weariness establishes itself in both plays, and there is even a certain touch of romantic possibility in act I, scene ii, when Flamineo is pandering his sister Vittoria to the Troilus-like Duke of Bracciano. "I could wish," says the Duke wistfully, "time would stand still/And never end this interview, this hour,/But all delight doth itself soon'st devour." [18]

Despite these echoes—and one could easily extend the list by using Dent's book and the notes in the editions of F. L. Lucas and John Russell Brown—there is very little resemblance between the dramatic imagination of Webster and of Shakespeare. Even in *Troilus and Cressida*, which is closer to Webster than any other Shakespearean play (with the possible exception of parts of *Hamlet*), the differences are more significant than the similarities. In Shakespeare's play the satirical questioning of all values is set against the turmoiled debate of these values in the Greek and Trojan camps. Cressida is a creature of the wars, and it is Troilus's ultimate folly to believe that true love alone can exist when all other truths are being annihilated. Webster does not choose to debate ultimate values at all, and moral truth enters his plays primarily in the knobby, gnomic *sententiae* with which he embellishes his discourse. Flamineo is the spokesman for the world of *The White Devil*, with a confidential directness in dealing with the audience that Thersites and Pandarus are never allowed to assume. In *The Duchess of Malfi* Bosola is a profounder and more compassionate Malcontent-Machiavel, but he too speaks for the world of the play with a disquieting authority. It is as if Bosola were presiding over the end of the world rather than just over the death of the Duchess of Malfi and of everyone associated with her. To put the matter in a more positive way, Shakespeare was never able to create villain-heroes so bitter-sweet, so witty, so eloquent, so emotionally and metaphysically disturbing as Flamineo and Bosola.

There is no doubt that Webster is a satirist,[19] with a strong link to Marston and even to the mysterious Cyril Tourneur.[20] All three are self-conscious stylists, who indulge in bravura passages and brilliant set pieces without any uneasy feeling about the interrupted action. The sardonic, witty mood often *is* the action, which is an effect of tone, coloring, and general reflections rather than a complex tale that pushes ahead by its own momentum. These displays of pointed rhetoric are the tragic equivalent of the Vice-Clown solos in comedy. Flamineo, for example, is disturbingly at ease in *The White Devil*, with the clown's omnipotence in the face of moral perturbation. And though Bosola is a darker figure in *The Duchess of Malfi*, his guises and shapes and serviceably quick changes of mood and style also betoken his derivation from the Vice-Clown. Bosola and Flamineo are both so intensely histrionic that we are delighted to allow them to stop the play in order to present their satiric turns.

Nowhere is this interruption more startling than in Bosola's meditation on mortality in act II, scene i of *The Duchess of Malfi*. An Old Lady is suddenly introduced as the unwitting object of Bosola's diatribe against "painting":

your scurvy face-physic—to behold thee not painted inclines somewhat near a miracle: these, in thy face here, were deep ruts and foul sloughs the last progress. There was a lady in France, that having had the smallpox, flayed the skin off her face to make it more level; and whereas before she looked like a nutmeg-grater, after she resembled an abortive hedgehog.[21]

The Swiftian indignation is masked by Bosola's malcontent wit, and the misogynistic prose leads up to a formal passage in verse inveighing against the human condition:

> What thing is in this outward form of man
> To be belov'd? we account it ominous
> If nature do produce a colt, or lamb,
> A fawn, or goat, in any limb resembling
> A man; and fly from't as a prodigy.
> Man stands amaz'd to see his deformity
> In any other creature but himself.

(II.i.45–51)

This Juvenalian set piece, in the spirit of Rochester's "Satire Against Mankind," suggests that Webster could not resist the temptation to make Bosola the mouthpiece for the kind of generalized moral reflection usually attributed to the author.

This is definitely not in the Shakespearean vein. Shakespeare's remarkable impersonality above and beyond and behind his works guarantees the authenticity of his characters. In Hamlet's discourse to Ophelia, for example—"I have heard of your paintings too, well enough. God hath given you one face, and you make yourselves another" (III.i.148–50)—his passionate misogyny is integral to the meaning of the action. The bitter refrain of this passage is the exhortation to Ophelia to sequester herself from the world of breeders: "Get thee to a nunnery." Both in the word and in the context, there is Elizabethan ambiguity about "nunnery," as a devout place or as a house of prostitution. Webster would not have been able, temperamentally, to leave this passage in *Hamlet* so snugly embedded in its context, but would have tried to extract from it the sort of universal meanings that Shakespeare scrupulously avoids.

J. R. Mulryne very shrewdly compares Webster's use of language with that of the Metaphysical poets. The dramatist shows "a certain cerebral ingenuity, a reaching out for comparisons to areas of experience not at all obviously related, and by their very unrelatedness and their (often) 'unpoetic' associations bringing to the image a bizarre effect." [22] This kind of imagery has a centrifugal effect on the dramatic action, so that the audience is encouraged to respond to brilliant, witty moments rather than to the continuity of a more tempered dramatic style. Webster's "restless intelligence," in Mulryne's phrase, produces a corresponding restlessness in his auditors, and the pervasive irony in which his intellect works "rarely ceases to mock every serious value, every impressive situation or striking pose, every 'affirmation' that the tragedy has to offer us." [23] Webster's style is so self-conscious, so full of artifice and rhetorical ingenuity, that it tends to work against any sustained development of character and action. "In the phrase and in the single image Webster is often superb," as W. A. Edwards notes in his *Scrutiny* essay, "yet he scarcely ever succeeds in writing a successful *passage* of verse, still less a whole scene." [24] Edwards attributes this difficulty to Webster's preoccupation with the conceited style of the character writers—we remember that Webster probably contributed thirty-two sketches to the sixth edition of Overbury's *Characters* (1615).[25] Both Edwards and Mulryne are calling attention to the discontinuity of Webster's style, his preference for immediate and local effects over the larger movement of the dramatic action.

These comments on style have important structural implications. No one has ever been able to explain away the insouciant plotting of *The Duchess of Malfi*, and it looks as if Webster, like Marston, really did not perturb himself about which way the action was moving and where it would eventually arrive. This carelessness about structure might account for the melodrama in Webster and Marston and in Beaumont and Fletcher, too, since melodrama is much more concerned with effective scenes than with an action that is credible in its component parts. After *Romeo and Juliet* Shakespeare was careful to avoid plot devices that depended too exclusively on chance, since they almost inevitably seem melodramatic rather than tragic. Bosola's ingenious discovery of the paper with the nativity of the Duchess's newborn son would surely have offended Shakespeare's strong commitment to dramatic logic. And what would he have said about the Duchess's enthusiastic revelation to Bosola that Antonio is her husband, or about Bosola's accidental killing of Antonio at the end? If these examples are ironic, as some critics would argue, then Webster's irony is awfully crude and mechanical and works against the feeling so strong in Shakespeare that the characters themselves are producing their own tragedy.

Webster's characters are much more Senecan than has usually been thought. Ferdinand is the most obvious example of the inflamed, frenzied, and wildly imaginative persons that people the pages of Seneca. There is no overt hint of incest in the play, but the Duchess inspires her twin brother with lascivious thoughts that he very imperfectly tries to suppress. Her first scene with her brothers, which bears a type resemblance to Laertes's advice to Ophelia, goes far beyond *Hamlet* in the openly lewd images of Ferdinand. *Hamlet* would have had some trendy new complications if Laertes had said, with Ferdinand, "And women like that part which, like the lamprey,/Hath ne'er a bone in't" (I.i.336–37).

Ferdinand's lycanthropia allows for an animal imagery that might have delighted Seneca by its combination of psychological abnormality, physical loathsomeness, abstruse physiological speculation, and witty, startling turns of eloquence. His physician is no spiritual minister to a mind diseased, as Macbeth hopes for, but a more up-to-date alienist who is prepared to "buffet his madness out of him" (V.ii.26). The physician shows an unholy fascination with his patient's lurid exploits:

> two nights since
> One met the duke, 'bout midnight in a lane
> Behind Saint Mark's church, with the leg of a man
> Upon his shoulder; and he howl'd fearfully;
> Said he was a wolf, only the difference
> Was, a wolf's skin was hairy on the outside,
> His on the inside.
>
> (V.ii.12–18)

This is what an Elizabethan would call a "nice paradox," and in typically Senecan fashion the fury and disgust of the literal events are much mitigated by the flowers of rhetoric. I cannot imagine how Webster would have handled the blinding of Gloucester in *King Lear*, but I am sure the scene would have had more quotable lines. In its bare, unmitigated horror, Shakespeare's scene is not Senecan at all. It refuses the sort of frisson that Seneca is offering at every likely opportunity.

Nothing I have said should imply that Webster was a failed Shakespeare. My casual, running comparisons with Shakespeare are meant to indicate that Webster and Shakespeare do not belong together, and that the conventional pieties of the Shakespearean yardstick have distorted Webster's real genius, which is akin to dramatists like Marston and Tourneur. The Shakespearean yardstick has also tended to inflate Webster's status among his fellow dramatists. Once we get beyond the extraordinary achievement of *The White Devil* and *The Duchess of Malfi*, *The Devil's Law Case* is disappointingly undeveloped (or perhaps overdeveloped, at least in its plot), and none of the other plays in which Webster is supposed to have had a hand (or only a finger) is at all Websterian—if one takes his two great tragedies as the criterion of excellence. Lucas's four-volume edition of Webster's *Works* is deceptively unrelated to the Webster we think we know, and Lucas is busy heaping scorn on the very plays he chooses to include. In sum, if we look at Webster as a literary figure who devoted his career to writing, he is the most spectacular under-achiever among Elizabethan dramatists.

I do not intend to set Middleton against Webster in equal combat, but I believe Middleton is important to this discussion because, unlike Webster, he is very close to Shakespeare in his approach to tragedy. The Shakespearean yardstick has never really touched Middleton. He is not overtly lyrical like Webster, nor does he write the kind of highly wrought passage that is usually called "poetic" (and therefore Shakespearean, by popular definition). Middleton specializes in quiet, underwritten, trenchantly ironic effects that are sometimes underscored by gesture and staging. When Beatrice in *The Changeling* touches the loathed De Flores, the gesture is the symbolic beginning of her involvement in evil, as well as the first overt expression of her overpowering sensuality. She handles De Flores as if he were so much meat: "Come hither; nearer, man!"; "Turn, let me see;/Faugh, 'tis but the heat of the liver, I perceiv't./I thought it had been worse." [26] To her gross and casual colloquial immediacy, De Flores responds with an aside that is intensely poetic in its dramatic context: "Her fingers touch'd me!/She smells all amber" (II.ii.81–82). Like Shakespeare at his best, Middleton rejects an obvious occasion for poetic expansion in favor of a more telling and more immediate effect of inarticulate wonder. The conception of the role and the speaking of the lines are inseparable here, and I think of the comparably "unpoetic poetry" [27] of Lear's recognition of the once-rejected Cordelia:

> *Lear.*   Do not laugh at me;
> For (as I am a man) I think this lady
> To be my child Cordelia.
> *Cor.*   And so I am! I am!
> (IV.vii.68–70)

Unlike Webster, Shakespeare and Middleton are both underplaying their poetic effects. The poetry is in the dramatic context, and it cannot be separated from that context without great loss.

Middleton has recently been attracting the kind of critical attention that Webster has always had. [28] T. B. Tomlinson, for example, sees Shakespeare, Middleton, and Tourneur as the main line in Jacobean drama. He admires

Middleton particularly for his "almost aggressively flat" and "uncompromisingly naturalistic" blank verse. Middleton has the kind of dramatic intelligence that Webster lacks, and "*The Changeling* is, outside Shakespeare, the most obviously *intelligent* play in English. Others deal intelligently with comparatively simple material, or sporadically with complicated material, but Middleton in *The Changeling* deals with complex ideas and feelings in such a way that the whole structure appears to rely on a sustained sureness and quickness of mind." [29] It is in "the whole structure" that Webster is most disappointing, if one understands by structure something more than plot or the unfolding of events. There is a moral thrust and propulsion in Middleton's *Changeling* and *Women Beware Women* that cannot be matched in Webster's more brilliant and atomistic *White Devil* and *Duchess of Malfi*.

It should be apparent from the exhortations of this essay that the Shakespearean yardstick can no longer be used as a measure of lyric intensity. Shakespeare is a playwright, whose aim is not to produce verses on a printed page, but dramatic poetry enacted in a theater. If the Shakespearean yardstick is to have any validity at all in the study of Shakespeare's fellow dramatists, we need to understand how his influence was felt in the whole dramatic experience and not just in the writing of poetic speeches. It seems particularly pointless to speak of a "school of Shakespeare," as if all dramatic effort depended on some central energy. Jacobean drama was much richer and more various than this formulation suggests. Although Shakespeare was a dominant figure (as were Jonson and Beaumont and Fletcher), a great deal of theatrical creativity has no reference to Shakespeare at all, and there are distinctive achievements entirely outside the Shakespearean range. It is a tired idolatry to insist at this late date that only Shakespeare is worthy of attention. In the new study of Jacobean drama that is even now proceeding at a feverish pace, Shakespeare will be understood in a truer relation to his own progenitors, such as Marlowe and Kyd, as well as to his contemporaries and his successors. This new alignment will clarify Shakespeare's own remarkable virtuosity, and it will rescue him, I hope, from the inanities associated with universal genius.

ROBERT ORNSTEIN

Bourgeois Morality and Dramatic Convention in *A Woman Killed with Kindness*

A *Woman Killed with Kindness* is not the kind of play that invites or seems to require detailed analysis. Its characterizations are shallow and apparently lack psychological complexity or nuance; its didactic lesson is conventional and explicit. It holds for a reader none of the puzzles or perplexities that make the interpretation of other Jacobean plays difficult and fascinating. If Heywood had the ironic, disillusioned perspective of a Tourneur or a Webster, one might have some doubts about the nobility of John Frankford, a paragon of familial devotion and Christian charity who, forgoing a savage vengeance on his faithless wife, decides to torment her soul with kindness. But who could imagine that Heywood, the earnest homilist and sentimentalist, would deliberately create a sardonic ambiguity about the motives of the character who seems to embody and express the fundamental bourgeois sanctities of the play?

It is hard to avoid critical clichés in dealing with Heywood because they are so appropriate to the vast bulk of his oeuvres, which, unlike the plays of Jonson or Webster, are fairly consistent in subject matter, artistic quality, and point of view. In the best of Heywood as in the worst, there is the same facile plotting and poetic style, the same middle-class pieties and stock characterizations. But Heywood's most interesting plays, *A Woman Killed with Kindness* and *The English Traveller*, stand apart somewhat from the others because they are more sophisticated in conception than first appears, and because they approach the edge of subtle irony even as they profess a frank unambiguous moralism. Remembering only the sentimentality and earnestness of *A Woman Killed with Kindness*, I was surprised on rereading it to find it different and more disturbing than I had recalled. Unable to smile patronizingly at Frankford's noble posturings, I found him smug in his self-congratulations, devious in the ferreting out of his wife's adultery, sanctimonious in his condemnation of her, and perhaps a trifle sadistic in his "renunciation" of a conventional revenge. Equally bad, Frankford's demeaning assumptions about the way that wives should behave are clearly the view that the play endorses, for it is a view shared by other characters, who applaud the Christian forbearance with which he treats his guilty wife. Or, more accurately, everyone (including Anne, who calls her husband's treatment of her a "mild sentence") applauds Frankford except his good friend Cranwell, who tries to speak when Frankford passes sentence on Anne. We do not know, however, if Cranwell found Frankford's killing kindness dreadful, even a travesty of Christian mercy, because Frankford prevents him from expressing his objection.[1]

It would not be just, of course, to blame Heywood for expressing moral sentiments commonplace in his age. If there is an obtuseness in the judgment of Anne, it is an obtuseness inherent in the double standard of sexual morality, which has been so firmly entrenched in our mores and so long native to our thinking that it has not been seriously questioned until very recent times. The ideal of female docility and submissiveness, which is elaborated in the opening scene of *A Woman Killed with Kindness*, is an ancient one, at least as old as the archetype of patient Griselda. And to modern minds the gratuitous, inhuman trials imposed on the innocent Griselda by her husband seem far worse than Frankford's sanctimonious response to his wife's adultery. We shake our heads, not only at Griselda's supine acceptance of the loss of her children and her humiliating rejection as a wife, but at the lack of any condemnation of her husband's unconscionable acts. For though his testing of her is seen as cruel, willful, and even evil, it is not treated as a flaw of character or a shameful wrong that must be expiated before he can enjoy a lifetime of happiness with his matchless wife.[2] Chaucer's tale is too remote from us, however, to stir feelings of outrage; it is the relic of a distant age that could cherish the sweet pathos and rare miraculous humility of Griselda's Pietà. It is not so easy to make a museum specimen of Heywood's play despite its Elizabethan "quaintness," because it does not purport to deal with a miraculous instance but rather with ordinary people, passions, and situations. It seems to uphold familiar and still cogent moral standards in a firm yet compassionate way. And there's the rub, because despite the sentimental treatment of the dying Anne, and despite all the tears and exclamations of sympathy by those who watch her die, *A Woman Killed with Kindness* limns the kind of implacable moral universe which is imagined in *Measure for Measure* by Isabella, who thinks that a single horrified submission to Angelo's lust must damn her forever. Although Heywood leaves no doubt that Anne was a true, loving wife until seduced by her husband's friend, and although she was tormented by guilt even before her adultery was uncovered, there is not the slightest intimation that any fate other than her wretched, lingering end was possible, because her sin was beyond forgiveness and her miserable death an appropriate retribution.

We could say with reference to the demeaning view of women in the writings of Church fathers, medieval satirists, and Renaissance moralists that Heywood's view of Anne Frankford is "traditional," but Anne is far from a typical or conventional Renaissance portrait of a woman. Whatever homilists said about the frailty and waywardness of women, Shakespeare, Greene, Dekker, Chapman, Middleton—and Heywood himself—depicted robust, strong-minded, and independent women who are unwilling to suffer any indignity at the command of their lords and masters. Although such dramatic portraits were idealized, there were many women of like spirit in Elizabethan society who refused to accept the dependent, submissive roles which were conventionally prescribed for their sex. Anyone as thoughtful as Shakespeare understood that women were trained from childhood to docility. There is great sympathy, therefore, in his portrayal of Mariana, who will accept any indignity from Angelo so long as she can be his wife, and Hero, who, utterly helpless in her innocence, seems to lack a sense of the injustice done her by Claudio. It is no accident, however, that readers prefer the cheeky Beatrice to the passive Hero, and that many find the enforced marriage of Angelo to Mariana a mockery of the conventional happy ending of romantic comedy.

Compared to Shakespeare, Heywood seems hopelessly lacking in human insight, when perhaps he is only hopelessly commonplace—of the same mentality as those who can smile complacently at the marriages that conclude *Measure for Measure* or weep complacently at the heartbreaking and edifying conclusion of *A Woman Killed with Kindness*. It would be a mistake, however, to exaggerate Heywood's ordinariness or to approach his dramatic portraits as if they were Elizabethan "primitives." Although in some respects Frankford is a cartoon figure, he is also a subtly equivocal character, one who is all benevolence except for a trace of cunning and a tincture of sophisticated cruelty. Yet who can accuse Frankford of hardness when it is Anne, not he, who insists that her adultery is beyond pardon? It is she who proclaims that she cannot be basely forgiven and that it would be shameless of her even to ask forgiveness. The strict condemnation of adultery in a play as conventionally moralistic as *A Woman Killed* is not surprising; what is odd is the absence of a like severity in the judgment of the other characters in the play. While Anne sinks to a well-merited death, the far more despicable Wendoll, who abused her husband's friendship and hospitality in seducing her, escapes the heavy burden of remorse that kills her. Indeed, while the seduced woman is viewed, not so much as a victim but as a heinous sinner, her seducer is neither punished nor apparently destined to a miserable end. Wendoll feels very guilty for a while and even speaks of himself as wearing the brand of Cain; but he plans to travel abroad to escape his infamy, and he expects to improve his skill in languages and find advancement on his return. Whereas Anne is not permitted to remain in the same room with her children lest she morally infect them, the young aristocrats Sir Charles Mountford and Sir Francis Acton can gamble, quarrel, kill men, and plan fiendish vengeances that include the corruption of an innocent virgin without facing moral condemnation. The romantic melodrama of the subplot should warn us not to ascribe a simple moralism to Heywood. Indeed, his didactic purpose is subordinate to the more primary goal of emotional effect even in the main plot of *A Woman Killed*, which allows an audience to rejoice in its charitable, tenderhearted sentiments while it spends its emotional rage at a faithless woman.

Although the moral sentiments of *A Woman Killed with Kindness* bear every hallmark of platitude, the treatment of an unfaithful wife as a moral leper is not conventional in Elizabethan literature. Sexual passion provides a basic motive in tragedy from Kyd to Ford, but adultery is not a common tragic theme before *A Woman Killed*, and the sinning heroines of later Jacobean plays are not shrinking, weak-willed creatures who meekly accept their guilt, but magnificently defiant figures like Webster's Vittoria and Middleton's Beatrice-Joanna. When Heywood's contemporaries treat adultery in drama, they are far less likely to portray the lingering death of a guilty wife than to depict the redemption of a fallen woman or the tearful return of an adulteress to the bosom of her forgiving husband. Few important dramatists other than Heywood undertake to demonstrate that infidelity is a cardinal sin, but many show, with varying degrees of sentimentality or cynicism, the redemption of hardened wantons.

I hesitate, however, to generalize about Elizabethan attitudes toward sexual conduct, because those attitudes are rarely consistent and logical, and there is a substantial disparity between officially sanctioned standards of sexual morality and the reality of human behavior and feeling. Although Elizabethan moral and religious condemnations of sexual license were severe, brothels prospered in London, and then as now young men were indulgently expected to sow their wild oats. For centuries the unwritten law had allowed a husband the right of private vengeance on his faithless wife; at the same time, however, a cuckold was a contemptible figure in literature and in life: a butt of a thousand jokes, an object of ridicule in jestbook tales, a gullible fool who could not satisfy or control his wife's sexual appetites. Despite a thousand admonitions against lewdness of thought, Heywood's contemporaries had a healthy appetite for bawdiness; they delighted in the raciness of Boccaccio and fabliau tales of sexual adventure and misadventure. Those with a taste for sophisticated literary eroticism could turn to Ovidian poetry past and present. Those who preferred coarser sexual humor could find endless comic tales about and references to punks and pimps, gallants and merchant's wives, in Elizabethan drama and prose fiction. The tension between moral denunciations of lewdness and the fairly universal interest in sex produced attitudes that were both moralistic and obliquely prurient. Elizabethan and Jacobean writers produced hundreds of uplifting tales about the licentiousness rampant in the hotter climes of Italy and Spain or in the luxury-corrupted courts of other countries. In these cautionary tales, puritanical instincts fused with pornographical impulses, especially when the writer's aim was to unmask the filthy vices of seemingly modest dames.

Moralistic and prurient interests intermingle, not only in cautionary tales about Italianate sensuality, but also in plays as contrary in temper as Tourneur's and Heywood's. Although some describe *The Revenger's Tragedy* as a decadent if not perverse work of art, it is deeply indebted to the themes and conventions of Morality plays as well as to medieval sermon and satire traditions. Fundamentally conservative in outlook, and capable in *The Atheist's Tragedy* of a literalistic moralism, Tourneur is obsessed by the sexual themes which Heywood repeatedly treats in his plays. For example, the vulnerability of an innocent woman to sexual coercion and corruption is a motif richly developed, not only in *The Revenger's Tragedy* and *The Atheist's Tragedy*, but also in *A Woman Killed with Kindness* and *The Rape of Lucrece*. Indeed, the sexual violation of a chaste woman, which is the central dramatic theme of *Lucrece*, is a crucial theme also in Tourneur's plays, in which rape or attempted rape provides a mainspring of plot. One cannot find in Heywood's plays anything like the cynicism that gives *The Revenger's Tragedy* its peculiar tonality, but one finds in *The English Traveller* the very kind of cunning, licentious, but apparently modest matron whom Vindice imagines in his most prurient moments.

At once cynical and enraged by vice, Tourneur creates in *The Revenger's Tragedy* a world almost totally depraved; he pictures a society so hypocritical and shallow in its morality and so corrupted by lust and greed that all innocence is suspect. His protagonist Vindice dwells sardonically on the clever wantonness of women, and yet he makes a fetish of virginity and dedicates himself to protecting it against harrying panders. Although morally and psychologically aberrant, Vindice can serve as a touchstone to normal bourgeois attitudes toward sex, because a certain skepticism, even a certain cynicism, about female honesty is the usual concomitant to middle-class demands for maidenly purity. For virginity would not have its high value and its almost magical aura if men did not customarily view women as sexual objects and make cynical distinctions between the purity of their wives, sisters, and mothers and the availability of other women.

The moral ambivalences of the greatest passages of *The Revenger's Tragedy* have their crude counterpart in the contradictions of tone that threaten the unity of *The Rape of Lucrece*. Heywood's play deals reverentially with the legend of Lucrece, but its high tragic seriousness is undercut continually by bawdy songs that celebrate the delights of promiscuity. The praise of Lucrece is never ironic, and there is not the slightest suggestion that she is less than she appears to be. As in Livy's tale, it is the rare beauty of her innocence that irresistibly attracts the cynical Tarquin, who earlier played the devil's advocate in a debate over the honesty of Roman women, a debate which Heywood invented.[3] Yet threading the scenes which unfold Lucrece's tragedy are the licentious songs of Valerius which describe the pleasures of wenching with fairly explicit and even obscene details about the delights of women's breasts, legs, downy bellies, and so forth. Most astonishing of all, after the rape occurs, Valerius recapitulates it in a bawdy catch that turns it into a lighthearted dirty joke by describing Tarquin's progress from her toe to her heel, from heel to shin, from shin to knee, to thigh, and so on.

A. W. Verity remarks that this catch, "which jokes in such a ribald fashion over Tarquin's crime, furnishes a pointed example of the way in which the dramatists of the period pandered to the tastes of the less refined among their audiences."[4] But it is difficult to blame the groundlings for Heywood's use of bawdy songs in *Lucrece*, when that use is so deliberate and continuing that it must be considered essential to his dramatic conception. In themselves Valerius's songs are no worse than most Elizabethan drinking songs. They are not sophisticated pleas for sexual surrender nor do they mock at innocence or chastity. Attacking no moral standards, they are hearty, frank expressions of the manly instinct for unconfined love; they voice the common masculine view of wenching that makes the innocence of Lucrece so admirable and legendary. Valerius's songs remind us that there is a little bit of Vindice (if not Iago) in all men, who make saints of Lucreces and Castizas,[5] precisely because their notion of most women is less worshipful.

Unable to imagine an artistic justification for the jarring incongruities of *The Rape of Lucrece*, one has to conclude that they exist only to titillate an audience—to create the kind of ambiguity of tone one ordinarily associates with the opportunistic dramaturgy of John Fletcher. That is to say, Heywood crudely juggles attitudes toward chastity and rape even as Fletcher cleverly toys in *Henry VIII* with the notion of the King's conscience, which is treated, on the one hand, as a providential force in English history and, on the other hand, as the butt of indecent jests.[6] *Lucrece*, which was printed in 1608, is probably too early a play to have been influenced by Fletcher, but his influence seems to me unmistakable in *The English Traveller*, which was written at least a decade later[7] and which resembles *A Woman Killed* in its middle-class domestic setting and its concern with adultery.

Any number of speeches in *The English Traveller* strike the didactic note of *A Woman Killed*, but its plot is more sophisticated in that the adulterous wife is not an innocent seduced but a wanton whose superb masquerade of modesty completely dupes her husband and his friend Geraldine, to whom she pretends an affectionate sisterly love. As in *A Woman Killed*, Heywood refuses to exploit the erotic possibilities of an adulterous love. But he does not hesitate to suggest a subtler, more ironic eroticism in the relationship between the Wife and Geraldine. Their first conversation reveals that people had once expected them to marry and that they probably would have, had not Geraldine's "unfortunate travel" prevented a wedding. Now, letting bygones be bygones, they have sublimated their youthful love into a matchless devotion to her elderly husband, Wincott. A situation of this kind would have posed emotional dangers for ordinary human beings, but Geraldine, who never abuses his freedom of the Wife's bedchamber day and night, asks only that they continue to love in a way that "the laws divine and human both/'Twixt brother and sister will approve." [8] When the Wife proclaims that he has in her bosom "a second place,/Next my dear husband," Geraldine begs but "to have a place next to him." When the Wife asks if he means "to stretch it further," he replies that he will be satisfied if she will confer her widowhood on him, to which the Wife replies that he asks "the thing I was about to beg."

If this earnest dialogue has its sexual overtones, it is because while the Wife and Geraldine protest too much their innocent love, the possibility of adultery is always on their minds. When he says that they are left alone, she says that no one should be jealous of them, for they have already spent hundreds of nights together in private. When Geraldine says that he would be a villain to deceive a husband as noble as Wincott, the Wife replies, "And she no less, whom either beauty, youth,/Time, place, or opportunity could tempt/To injure such a husband" (II.i, p. 181). Later in the play Geraldine, like Frankford, discovers his loved one in bed with a friend. Filled with a Hamlet-like rage at the Wife's betrayal, he thinks of killing her and her lover, but when he discovers that he providentially left his sword in another room, he decides to forgo revenge and leave England until he is an old man. His indignation has an ironic aspect, however, for he discovers the

Wife's lust only because he attempts to visit her bedchamber late at night. Left alone in Wincott's house and unable to sleep, he decides to spend the time in "sweet contemplation" of the Wife's beauty. The soul of courtesy, he fears that she would be very angry with him if he let slip this chance to visit her. Since "sweet opportunity" invites him to a "strange and unexpected meeting," he resolves to see her in her bedchamber, the place of their deep vows: "My fiery love this darkness makes seem bright,/And this the path that leads to my delight" (IV.iii, p. 223).

If one ignores the erotic overtones of Geraldine's platonic protestations and intentions, one can agree with A. W. Ward that Geraldine is "one of the truest gentlemen of Elizabethan comedy." [9] Otherwise Geraldine may seem a somewhat comic figure who is ignorant of his illicit desires and made an egregious ass by the Wife. Not accidentally, Heywood contrives it so that Geraldine rather than Wincott seems the cuckolded gull, because the Wife not only promises him a place in her bosom next to her husband but also insists that Geraldine swear an oath to keep himself, his house, and his name inviolate, and neither "converse nor company/With any woman, contract nor combine/With maid or widow," while he waits for Wincott to die. When he confirms his oath with a chaste kiss, the Wife announces: "You're now my brother;/But then, my second husband" (II.i, p. 183). Even without knowing that the Wife is a licentious hypocrite, one can savor the irony of this preposterous arrangement. Irony is more obvious in the later Closet scene (one of many reenactments of the Shakespearean moment in later Jacobean drama) where a disillusioned Geraldine confronts the still solicitous and seemingly innocent Wife. She continues her pose until the very moment when he names the day he overheard her and Delavil in her chamber. When she asks, "Who gave you this intelligence?" Geraldine, forgetting the "fiery love" that prompted him to her bedchamber, declares that God led him to the place "by miracle."

The scene in which Geraldine and the Wife first declare their chaste affection for each other reminds me of the scenes in Ford's *Love's Sacrifice* where Bianca declares her innocent love for her husband's trusted friend, Fernando, whom she converts from would-be seducer to platonic servant. Despite the sensationalism and confusion of its final scenes, Ford's tragedy portrays with great insight the inward strife and self-deceptions of a heroine who thinks that she can remain faithful to her husband while enjoying a passion just short of adultery for another man. Despite its many earnest speeches, *The English Traveller* is a less serious play, one which allows a perceptive listener to enjoy the comedy of Geraldine's noble sentiments but which finally presents the cliché of Geraldine's devotion to Wincott as if it were untouched by irony. At once high-minded and fatuous, Geraldine is not a revelation of emotional self-deception. Like Philaster and Amintor, he has the contradictory doubleness of Fletcherian characterizations: he is both heroic and inept, sublime and ridiculous. The Wife, who enjoys playing platonic charades with Geraldine, is perhaps a paler version of the cynical, lustful Evadne, who enjoys a similar mocking game with Amintor in *The Maid's Tragedy*.[10] But though the Wife seems as corrupt as Evadne, she never develops as a portrait of perversity and reverts instantaneously to a moral cliché when her adultery is discovered, for then she shrinks like Anne Frankford into life-devouring remorse.

The deadpan comedy of Geraldine's high-minded affection for Wincott's wife does not complicate the moral action of *The English Traveller* any more than Valerius's bawdy songs complicate the moral action of *Lucrece*. Such opportunistic devices merely add a spice of sophistication to plays that otherwise proclaim the perfection of bourgeois virtues. The main plot of *A Woman Killed with Kindness* is relatively untouched by that kind of opportunism, but the subplot seems to me almost prophetic of the techniques of Fletcherian tragicomedy. I am thinking of its continuing hyperboles of emotion and action, and its attitudinized explorations of the meaning of honor by aristocratic antagonists whose overrefined and overwrought sensibilities lead them to bizarre gestures and dedications. Like many of Fletcher's heroes, Sir Charles Mountford and Sir Francis Acton lack an emotional center of gravity and are therefore capable of sudden unpredictable rages and arrogances or sudden unpredictable generosities and humilities. Their descents into passion and their ascents into noble spirituality are a fantasizing of human behavior which sacrifices psychological credibility to theatrical effect.

At first Mountford and Acton seem mundane enough to belong in the bourgeois scenes of the main plot. When they discuss Anne's wifely virtues in the wedding scene, they sound for all the world like Frankford himself. In their very next appearance, however, they quickly veer into noble extravagances of passion, into the unchecked furies which befit those of aristocratic blood. An argument over a hawking wager sends Sir Charles into an insulting, murderous rage; he provokes a quarrel with Acton and slays two servants before he falls into a sudden profound repentance. First the seeming villain of the subplot, he next appears as the helpless victim of grasping moneylenders and callous relatives. Even as Mountford goes to debtor's prison with an almost Christ-like patience, Acton, who seemed before the more reasonable and self-controlled of the two, gloats like an Iago over the sadistic satisfaction of hearing his enemy plead from a prison gate. Suddenly devoid of all scruple, Acton plans a hideous revenge on his wretched enemy by bribing Mountford's sister "to shame herself by lewd, dishonest lust." The sight of her angelic beauty shakes that resolve, however, and when she refuses his gold, he is so rapt with admiration of her divine perfections that he seeks to win her by paying her brother's debts and releasing him from the law. But when Mountford learns of Acton's generosity, he is so obsessed with the need to free himself from any obligation to his foe that he decides to pander his sister to Acton. But when Susan hears of her brother's intention, . . . This zigzag course is not a credible development of plot; it is a succession of melodramatic crises and pathetic tableaus acted out by characters who apparently lack stability and have a predilection for emotional extremes.

The main plot of *A Woman Killed* has a far greater sobriety of characterization and dramatic action. It has a greater realism too, but not the factual realism of *Arden of Faversham* and *A Yorkshire Tragedy*, the plays most often linked with Heywood's as chief examples of Elizabethan domestic tragedy. Where these anonymous tragedies, based on accounts of notorious contemporary crimes, dramatize the coarser passions of ordinary life, *A Woman Killed with Kindness* creates a mundane provincial scene and unexceptional bourgeois characters who behave under duress in ways dictated by the conventions of Italianate revenge tragedy. For example, one would logically expect Frankford, who seems without guile or suspicion, to confront his wife openly when told by a servant of her infidelity. Instead, Frankford, like a sly Italianate intriguer, hides his suspicions, enjoys the ironic double entendres of the card game with Anne and Wendoll, and cunningly entraps them by giving them the opportunity to enjoy their lust. If this deviousness does not square with Frankford's personality,[11] it allows Heywood to fashion a suspenseful climactic scene (one used also by Marston, Tourneur, and Webster) in which adulterers are surprised in their illicit embraces.

In Jacobean tragedy, sinners like Vittoria and Beatrice-Joanna meet violent deaths. In Jacobean comedy, faithless wives are pardoned rather than punished; the realistic acceptances of the fabliaux and the jestbook tales prevail, and a shrug of the shoulders or a sentimental reconciliation substitutes for tragic fury. Heywood's treatment of adultery ingeniously joins the sentimental aura of comic reconciliation to the retributive impulse of revenge tragedy. Because his main characters are too mild-mannered and ordinary to play the violent roles revenge tragedy demands, Heywood uses the melodrama of the subplot to create an emotional atmosphere in which extremes of violent emotion and action seem normal. Thus, when Anne, caught in the act of adultery, faces her husband, she does not expect from him a rebuke commensurate with his mild manner and gentle heart. Rather she anticipates the half-mad savagery of an Italianate revenger. She asks,

When do you spurn me like a dog? When tread me
Under your feet? When drag me by the hair?
Though I deserve a thousand, thousandfold
More than you can inflict,
. . . .
                        mark not my face,
Nor hack me with your sword, but let me go
Perfect and undeformed to my tomb.

(IV.iv.90–98)

Anne's expectation that her husband will carve her with his sword seems preposterous, but it serves to make Frankford's treatment of her seem like a noble forbearance, even though Heywood leaves no doubt that Frankford's charity is in fact a calculated spiritual torment—a kind of mortification by degrees. "I'll not martyr thee," Frankford says to Anne,

Nor mark thee for a strumpet, but with usage
Of more humility torment thy soul,
And kill thee, even with kindness.

(IV.iv.151–54)

Showing not a trace of sympathy for his sister Anne, Sir Francis Acton remarks that Frankford showed too mild a spirit "in the revenge of such a loathed crime":

Less than he did no man of spirit could do.
I am so far from blaming his revenge
That I commend it. Had it been my case
Their souls at once had from their breasts been freed;
Death to such deeds of shame is the due meed.

(V.iv.16–20)

But in the final scene, where all join in shedding tears over the dying Anne, Acton shows that he understands the oblique effectiveness of Frankford's revenge:

Brother, had you with threats and usage bad
Punish'd her sin, the grief of her offence
Had not with such true sorrow touch'd her heart.

(V.iv.132–34)

Although the dying Anne is pardoned by her husband, who thinks her now honest again in soul, and is restored by him to the name of wife and mother, not one compassionate word is said in extenuation of her guilt. An explanation might be that Heywood, regarding chastity as a sacred and inviolable virtue, thinks Anne's behavior execrable. But then how shall we judge the behavior of Mountford, who demands that his sister prostitute herself to relieve him of a sense of obligation to Acton? By any reasonable standard of conduct, Mountford's demand would indicate a mental aberration caused by the shock of calamity and imprisonment. In Heywood's play, however, Mountford's desire to pander his sister, who holds her virginity as sacred as her immortal soul and who promises to kill herself after submitting to Acton, is simply a proof of his extraordinary noblesse. Of course, the bizarre variation of the sacrifice of Isaac which Mountford contemplates is never a serious possibility, and once the maximum theatrical advantage has been wrung from it, the characters withdraw from the edge of catastrophe into noble attitudes that demand our complete admiration. Few members of an audience are likely to note that the praise of Mountford's "honourable wrested courtesy" does not square with the anathematizing of Anne. What they will note, because Heywood underlines it, is the parallel between the seemingly perfect docility of Anne and the truly perfect docility of Susan Mountford, who is obedient to her brother's demand that she sacrifice her purity but who courageously prefers death to unchastity.

It would have been easy enough for Heywood to have posed serious moral questions about Anne's guilt and suffering and about Mountford's and Frankford's motives. He could have underlined the fact that while Frankford twice compares his pardoning of the dying Anne with divine mercy, the only true charity shown in the play is Acton's generosity to Mountford, which transcends the motives of sexual desire and revenge. But rather than make Acton an exemplar of true mercy, Heywood has him first criticize Frankford for his mild response to Anne's adultery and later appreciate the finesse of his revenge. There are no moral questions to be pondered in *A Woman Killed with Kindness*, even though Heywood deliberately creates the ambiguity of Frankford's mildness. There is bathos enough for the piously inclined and just enough irony to allow a sophisticate to smile at the tear-sodden conclusion.[12] It is worth pausing over the emotional design of *A Woman Killed*, however, to try to understand the psychology of the treatment of Anne, who receives everyone's sympathy, but only when she suffers the extreme anguish of a lingering death and only when she remains clearly labeled a "spotted strumpet." Why must Anne expiate her sin with such suffering when in so many Elizabethan plays and tales far more guilty wives and practiced whores can be redeemed and granted happy futures?

We cannot, of course, explain why Heywood wrote his play as he did, but, with the help of Shakespeare's insights, we can perhaps understand the implicit (and unconscious) premises of Heywood's play. Written just about the time of *A Woman Killed with Kindness*, and sometimes called a domestic tragedy, *Othello* illuminates conventional attitudes toward sex, and especially the conventional ways that men think about, respond to, and treat women. Its plot suggests the connection between the way that men adore an exquisite young woman like Desdemona and the way they joke about a trull like Bianca or keep a wife like Emilia in line. Although it is easy to despise Othello's gullibility, Shakespeare understood the masculine anxieties about sexual love that make Othello vulnerable. A. C. Bradley has wisely pointed out that any man would have been moved by Iago's filthy innuendoes and lies; I would add that Iago is convincing as a slanderer, not only because he is a brilliant poseur and intriguer who knows his victims' natures and weaknesses, but because his joking cynicism about women is absolutely plausible, cut apparently from the same cloth as Valerius's bawdy songs. After all, it is an Iago-like cynicism about female sexuality that licenses the contradictions of the double standard, that makes Desdemona's chastity a precious commodity while it permits young gallants their casual sexual pleasure with the Biancas of the world.

If we think of Anne, for a moment, as a Desdemona who was actually false, we can understand the emotional necessity for her death. For like Desdemona, Anne is apparently an ideal, a perfect wife: obedient, loving, gentle, and yielding to her husband. It is dreadful enough that such a woman should fall; it is unforgivable that when she falls, she shows no outward sign of her corruption. The "judgment" which Othello passes on Desdemona to vindicate her murder is that she must die because she remains so fair and seemingly innocent that she could cunningly betray many more men. Anne's unpardonable guilt is similar in kind. If she were obviously degraded by adultery or showed a coarseness of spirit that had been masked by an appearance of modesty, she might be forgiven and redeemed, because her fall would confirm conventional notions of sexual vice. But Anne threatens moral assumptions because she is not hardened or made brazen and contemptible by her fall. She cannot be forgiven her sin because she seems as decent and as morally sensitive after her fall as she did before. Can chastity and fidelity be cardinal virtues if a gentle woman can commit adultery and not be spiritually and physically degraded? Vindice, cynical guardian and avenger of virginity, could understand Othello's murderous fury at Desdemona's seeming innocence, because the cunning whore of Venice whom Othello imagines is almost identical with the wanton whom Vindice imagines slyly opening her chamber door for her lover. Like the coy dame Vindice imagines, Anne is a creature who justifies the prurient bent of the rigidly moralistic imagination. In her submissiveness, she is at once the perfectly obedient wife and the ideal victim of the aggressive masculine will, a woman trained to, and praised for, her yielding to man. A pliant innocent and a chaste-seeming strumpet, she is a scapegoat figure who embodies what men desire and fear in women, and whose death is a fitting sacrifice at the altar of the double standard.

Heywood's blurring of the antithesis between vengeance and mercy and his ingenious equivocation of the meaning of kindness indicate his ability to ring changes, not only on dramatic conventions, but also on moral clichés. Although his dramatic protraits are shallow and stilted, *A Woman Killed with Kindness* is nevertheless a fascinating revelation of the link between sentimentality and priggery in middle-class sexual morality. Because Heywood knew his audiences superbly well and gave them the edifying emotional satisfactions they expected and cherished, his plays remain important social documents whatever their limitations as dramatic art.

JONAS A. BARISH

The True and False Families of
The Revenger's Tragedy

*T*HE HISTORY of the criticism of *The Revenger's Tragedy* over the past two generations might be described as one of gradual disintoxication. The horror felt by critics at its "sewer-like windings," [1] its "cynicism, . . . loathing, and disgust," [2] its "distorted, bestial, infernal world of unspeakable depravity," [3] its "burning hatred of the vicious humanity [it] depicts," its "morbid passion," [4] has considerably abated. Eliot, who did so much to quench romantic subjectivism in his essays on the other Elizabethan dramatists, got Tourneur criticism off to a bad start by treating the characters as "spectres projected from the poet's inner world of nightmare, some horror beyond words," and the play itself as "a document on one human being, Tourneur," whose motive was "truly the death motive, for it is the loathing and horror of life itself." [5]

That this failed to take into account the highly conventional basis of much of the play's dramaturgy was lucidly shown in the late 1930s by L. G. Salingar, who located the play firmly within the tradition of English morality drama. Its characters are not realistic psychological portraits but "personified abstractions and moral or social types"; its actions are "symbolic, not realistic, and the incidents are related to each other logically, as parts of an allegory, or as illustrations of the argument." Salingar's analysis did much to cool the inflamed tone into which criticism had fallen in attempting to define the play's atmosphere. "The total impression," he correctly perceived, "is that of a hectic excitement. . . . But the satire is not hysterical; Tourneur maintains an alert sardonic irony which makes its objects grotesque as well as disgusting." [6]

"Not hysterical," "grotesque as well as disgusting": so much has for the most part been granted by subsequent commentary. Eliot's view of the play as a projection of its author's private obsessions no longer seems persuasive. Later critics have tended to confirm Salingar's thesis, linking the play more firmly to its morality antecedents, and viewing its details as part of a symbolic rather than a realistic design. One result has been the restoration to their due importance of the Castiza-Gratiana scenes,[7] even if these are still often felt to be too arbitrary, and lacking in the kind of single-minded conviction that lends the court scenes their power.[8]

With Vindice detached from his creator, however, new misunderstandings arose. Having first been pressed into service as an authorial spokesman, the protagonist was now converted into a target of authorial reprehension, a blackguard from whom we recoil as we do from the Duke and his repulsive brood, a "thorough-going villain" whose "smirking admissions" of his crime lead to his being "hustled off to prison" and (together with his brother) executed "like common criminals," to our entire satisfaction.[9] "By the end," declares one of the play's best critics, "little semblance of Vindice's moral purpose remains; he and Hippolito are hardly distinguishable from the men they slaughter." [10] In the words of another commentator, Vindice dies "as corrupted by sin as the others";[11] for still a third, the "parallel" between him and his victims becomes "virtual fusion" in the final moments.[12]

Now it is undeniable that Vindice and Hippolito do to some extent become creatures of their revenge. Revenge coarsens and hardens them; it seems after a time almost to take on a life of its own apart from their directive wills. But to equate them, even in their blackest moments, with the degenerates of the ducal court, is to substitute a reading of the play as prim and moralistic as the older one was literal-minded and high-strung. For on any impartial account the brothers remain sharply distinguishable from their enemies, right up to the very end. They embody something more than the self-corrupting spirit of revenge, or the self-corroding spirit of satire,[13] or the pessimism of contemptus mundi: they embody values lodged in the family to which they belong, which contrast at every point with the anti-values, as we might call them, of the false family, or pseudo-family, of the court. Nearly all the characters in the play's large cast belong to one of these two families, the opposing life-styles of which form one axis of the plot. On the one hand the family of the Duke, a snake pit of hatred and lust—brother plotting against brother, wife against husband, son against father—and on the other hand the family of the revengers, a community linked in affection and bonded together in virtue. Gratiana does, momentarily, yield to sinful temptation, and Vindice's vengeance does at last unsettle his moral balance, but this family, as a family, succeeds in repelling all attempts to undermine it, and preserves its unitary closeness to the end.

We may find it instructive to look for a moment at a secondary personage, Vindice's brother and lieutenant Hippolito. Hippolito has usually been ignored by commentators. This is on the face of it odd, since he figures so prominently in the action. He appears on stage in twelve out of the play's twenty scenes (using the scene divisions of R. A. Foakes's Revels edition), and for about 1400 of its approximately 2400 lines. He also engages in much picturesque and interesting stage action. Moreover he has about 250 lines of his own to speak, three or four times as many as are given to such lesser figures as old Antonio the courtier, or Spurio the bastard brother, or the lecherous Junior Brother. Yet these three, Antonio, Spurio, and the Junior Brother, have clearly been felt to be more striking and noteworthy, for they are nearly always accorded the courtesy of an honorable mention in critical discussions, while Hippolito is either entirely overlooked or else bracketed mechanically with Vindice.

At the same time, no reader of the play is likely to find this situation surprising. For, except for the scene in which he prompts a group of disaffected noblemen to plot revenge against the violator of Antonio's wife, Hippolito takes no action on his own, scarcely seems to have an existence of his own, but appears rather as a kind of extension of his more militant brother. Throughout he makes himself into a selfless instrument of Vindice's will, the perfect associate, accomplice, and confidant, who merges his ego totally in that of his partner.

The note of brotherly camaraderie between them is struck strongly at their first meeting, in the first scene, and vibrates clearly and resonantly until the final moments of the action. "Thy wrongs and mine are for one scabbard fit," [14] says Vindice to Hippolito when they greet each other, and it reflects the nature of the entente between them that though this claim is not strictly true—since although the father of them both has suffered at the Duke's hands, the wronged mistress belongs to Vindice alone—Hippolito behaves as if it were. He welcomes his share in the intrigue as if he himself were the injured party. The vengeance, throughout, is "our" vengeance. At no point is anything done by one seriously criticized or disapproved by the other. The closest thing to it would be such occasional moments of comradely expostulation as that in which Hippolito taxes Vindice for not confiding in him according to their agreement: "Why may not I partake with you? You vow'd once/To give me share to every tragic thought" (III.v.5–6). A pact of sorts exists between them, a pledge of candor, which Vindice has infringed by his silence. He acknowledges as much at once, and mends his lapse by briefing Hippolito intensively on the details of his projected plot. Again, reviewing their plan to introduce Vindice to Lussurioso under a second disguise—as himself—Hippolito points out the pitfalls of their scheme, the need for prudence: "If you be but once tripp'd, we fall for ever" (IV.ii.24). He thus identifies his own survival unreservedly, and unresentfully, with Vindice's. We catch a further hint of fraternal warning when Vindice's fantasied revenges begin to take flight from reality. "Brother," cautions Hippolito, "we lose ourselves" (IV.ii.200). But, as the continuing use of the first person plural in itself makes clear, Hippolito's mild admonition does not mean any breach in the united front. He does not dissociate himself from his brother's extravagant fancies, but takes them, with their consequences, on himself. More characteristic still would be his frequent admiring comments on Vindice's powers of observation ("Brother, y' have truly spoke him" [I.i.91], "Brother, y' have spoke that right" [III.v.66]), or on the felicity of his wit ("You flow well, brother" [II.ii.146]), or on his persistence and ingenuity ("Brother, I do applaud thy constant vengeance,/The quaintness of thy malice, above thought" [III.v.108–9]). The word "brother," we may notice, rings perpetually in our ears in the course of the play—nearly a hundred times, and usually in the vocative. In its echoing back and forth it helps to underscore the solidarity between these two, either of whom would qualify as the "loyal brother" of the alternate title that seems accidentally to have fastened itself onto the play late in the seventeenth century.[15] At other moments, on other lips, the same term reminds us forcibly of what brotherhood is not, as well as of what it is.

As a striking example of concerted action between the brothers, we may recall the episode in which they "conjure the devil" out of their mother, circling round her with drawn daggers (IV.iv), alternately berating her in a kind of chanting antiphony, and then, on her capitulation, clasping her to them. They form, indeed, a unique pair of dramatic accomplices, the concord between them being of a wholly different order from the uneasy alliance between Volpone and Mosca, or Face and Subtle, or Barabas and Ithamore, or Richard and Buckingham, all of which depend on self-interest and break up as soon as self-interest is no longer served by confederacy. Even such virtuous revengers as Hamlet and Malevole cannot maintain a comparable intimacy with their confidants, Horatio and Celso. For in these cases only one of the twain is the true revenger, and he is also the prince and the giver of orders; the other remains an underling and henchman rather than a full copartner.

When the reckoning at length arrives for Vindice and Hippolito, after Vindice has blurted out their identities as the Duke's killers, fraternal solidarity remains unimpaired. Hippolito must climb the scaffold along with his brother, yet it scarcely occurs to him to embark on recriminations. There is only the barest hint of a protest, only the sardonic interchange— "Is 't come about?" " 'Sfoot, brother, you begun" (V.iii.106)—which amounts to a stoical shrug of the shoulders as they prepare to pay the supreme penalty. Vindice's last words stress the mutuality of their doings, and there is no doubt that when he turns to Hippolito for confirmation, he does not turn in vain. One French adapter of the play has interpolated a reply for Tourneur's silent Hippolito that catches exactly the right note: *"Je te suivrai partout."* [16]

The brothers, however, form a subsidiary molecule within the larger unit of their family, which includes a sister and a mother. Bound by blood, all three children the offspring of a single (evidently happy) marriage, the four surviving members feel their group identity strongly, particularly as that identity is threatened by the recent death of the father, without whom Vindice feels his own life "unnaturall." It is "naturall" for a man to have a father, with whom he can share and by whom he can be guided. "A Familie," says William Perkins in his *Christian Oeconomie*, "is a naturall and simple Societie of certaine persons, hauing mutuall relation one to another, vnder the priuate gouernement of one." [17] So the subject that springs to their lips, when they meet at the outset of the play, is precisely the memory of their lost "governor." But the family here is more than a natural unit, its stability imperiled by the loss of its leader; it is also a moral unit, to which an individual member belongs only in so far as he adheres to shared ethical standards. When Gratiana succumbs to Vindice's blandishments and plays bawd to her daughter Castiza, Castiza, in horror, addresses her as if she were absent, or dispossessed by an invading devil. That is, she refuses to recognize her *as* her mother so long as she persists in such unnatural and unmotherly behavior. Similarly, when the two brothers assail their mother for the same trespass, they decline to allow her her technical status. "Am not I your mother?" she demands, as they approach her with naked swords. "Thou dost usurp that title now by fraud," replies Vindice, "For in that shell of mother breeds a bawd" (IV.iv.8–10). "Mother," then, is not merely a biological concept, but also a moral concept, the reestablishment of which at this juncture spells the rehabilitation of the family as a whole.

The family coming under attack as it does, Tourneur takes pains to make the attack dangerous by using Vindice as its spearhead. Critics may be right in finding excessive schematism in these scenes compared to the scenes of evil at court. And they may be right in thinking that Vindice tackles his unsavory assignment with "unholy glee," [18] eager to make his mother and sister conform to his cynical stereotypes of their sex. But his eagerness is needed to give the scenes their bite. Tourneur is seeking a way to dramatize virtue, as he dramatizes vice in the court scenes. This poses problems. Traits like chastity, modesty, and obedience tend to be less flamboyant than their corresponding vices, a matter of quiet perseverance rather than spectacular gestures, and hence more resistant to theatrical treatment. The dramatist who would effectively portray them must resort to special tactics, and even Shakespeare has sometimes been thought to have bungled the job with characters like Cordelia. Tourneur adopts the time-honored device of the formal test. Under proper conditions, virtue can be *goaded* into displaying itself, and the severity of the test can provide a measure of the tenacity of the virtue. So the Castiza-Gratiana scenes unfold in live action the qualities of the two women, illustrating their differing responses to the pressure of evil. One, though virtuous, proves shallow—easily undermined and in need of shoring up from without. The other exemplifies virtue poised, assured, and, so far as we can tell, impregnable. The whole sequence serves as a necessary if programmatic counterweight to the antic dance of vices at the ducal court. Except, perhaps, for the final supererogatory test devised by Castiza to try a mother she believes to be already possessed by the devil, nothing in these scenes is inherently more improbable than any of the events of the court scenes.

Further, if Vindice's testing is to have its full impact it must be carried out with all the force at his command. He must entice his mother with the same furious energy he pours into his castigations of evil. What is notable is that in the very moment in which he is playing the tempter's role, he is praying, in asides, for his own failure, and reacting with dismay to the swift crumbling of his mother's resistance. Critics who find the vigor of his onslaught "gratuitous," [19] or who wish to make it a black mark against his character, would have had more reason to complain if Tourneur had made him slack or unpersuasive in the job. For this would have been to make the entire episode meaningless. By the force of his attack he jolts his family at a time when it is already off balance from the loss of its steadying central figure, the father; by the answering vigor of his own and Hippolito's conjurations, he reconsolidates it on a firmer basis, welding it together in virtue once more. His mission, then, in his own home as in the outer world, is an emblematic one—to apply a kind of litmus test to all the characters, and to descant meaningfully on the variety and changes of their degradation. It cannot, plainly, be dismissed for its implausibility, or ascribed to a neurotic indulgence on the part of a diseased imagination.

Diametrically opposed to Vindice's family is the ducal clan, not a family so much as a fierce aggregate of competing appetites, held together by the hope of inheriting the dukedom. This is a family splintered in every direction. The Duchess is the second at least of that title; we know nothing of her predecessors. The children stem from three different unions, one from a cast-off mistress rather than a consort. Spurio, the bastard son of this union, hints at irregularities in the begetting of Lussurioso, the eldest son and official heir. We have no reason to credit Spurio's malevolence, but on the other hand, the Duke's nature being what it is, goatishly unfaithful, all legitimacy is cast in doubt; there exists no firm basis for status within the family. Even when most casually viewed, then, this family lacks cohesion. Unlike Vindice's family it is "unnatural" to start with, and the most uninstructed outsider can see it for the shattered hulk it is. Far more terrible is its inner disintegration, with brothers, half brothers, and stepbrothers locked in a lethal struggle that ends only with the deaths of all of them. Tourneur seems almost systematically to box the compass of the possible betrayals and infidelities among them. Spurio harbors murderous sentiments toward all his kin, but especially his brothers. Early in the action he announces his hope that the Junior Brother will die for his offense, and that the entire court will turn "into a corpse." Acting on information from his spies, he attempts to surprise and kill Lussurioso in the very moment when Lussurioso, acting on information from *his* spies, attempts to surprise and kill *him* in bed with the Duchess. This bizarre contretemps, in which each fails to do away with the other because the other is trying to do away with him, leads to a grotesque aftermath, in which the Duchess's two older sons, Ambitioso and Supervacuo, hypocritically plead for their stepbrother's life while covertly trying to incriminate him and bring him to the block.

When it is a question of half brothers and stepbrothers and a dispossessed bastard, the resemblance between such pseudo-siblings and Vindice and Hippolito may be allowed to be tenuous. But in Ambitioso and Supervacuo we have a pair of full brothers who act, as they profess, in full concord, for the execution of their stepbrother and the release of their own brother from jail. Secretly, however, they hate each other. Each is ready to plunge the knife into the other's back at the slightest prospect of self-advancement. As Ambitioso, the elder, naïvely expatiates on the glories of the ducal throne, Supervacuo mutters fierce asides in which he swears to "prick" the "bladder" of his brother's ambition when the time is ripe (III.i.14–15). Even on the superficial level these two compete boastfully with each other, clamorous in claiming credit for the plot against Lussurioso, and then eager to disavow authorship when the plot miscarries. The relations between them suggest a pair of curs who either snap at other dogs or snarl at each other. The one moment of total agreement comes when they learn how wildly their "plot" has misfired—how they have sent to execution not their hated stepbrother but their own younger brother. Nothing could exceed in grand-guignol grisliness the scene in which they brandish the bloody sack containing their brother's head, threatening to brain the hapless jailer with it. And nothing could form a more devastating contrast with Hippolito and Vindice than the spiteful sniping between them, the readiness with which they turn on each other when their ambitions collide. As for their Junior Brother, who goes to his death thinking they have deliberately doublecrossed him, he dies violently cursing them both.

In the final scene, brotherly hatred reaches frenzied proportions. Lussurioso, having inherited the dukedom, ponders the banishment of his stepmother and the elimination of the bastard and both other stepbrothers. Spurio, in turn, marks out Lussurioso for his sword's point, while Ambitioso and Supervacuo together conspire to murder Spurio. Finally, to complete the circle of equations, and to match the earlier moment in which Supervacuo resolved to kill Ambitioso should the latter attempt to seize the dukedom, Ambitioso now resolves to kill Supervacuo and seize the dukedom for himself.

The brothers hate not only each other but their father and mother, in some cases openly and rancorously (Spurio), in other cases covertly and fawningly (Lussurioso). All long to wield the ducal sceptre, and have no scruples about doing whatever they think will enable them to acquire it. Unlike Vindice and Hippolito, mourning a dead father, these sons are plotting to get rid of a live one. When the Duke is in fact discovered murdered, each of them in an aside confides his relief and satisfaction. No trace of filial feeling is to be found anywhere among them, and it seems to be assumed in the imagery of the play that the relations between fathers and sons will be poisonous. "O, she was able to ha' made a usurer's son/Melt all his patrimony in a kiss,/And what his father fifty years told,/To have consum'd, and yet his suit been cold" (I.i.26–29): it is expected that sons will squander their patrimonies to buy themselves pleasures, that they will maliciously undo in an instant the hard toil of a lifetime on the part of their sires, as though in deliberate repudiation of all that those sires valued. Similarly, it is assumed that second marriages will produce bad blood between parents and children and sour the children's fortunes, for we hear of Lussurioso's search for "some strange-digested fellow . . . /Of ill-contented nature, either disgrac'd/In former times, or by new grooms displac'd/Since his stepmother's nuptials" (I.i.76–79). Wherever we look, we find the generations at loggerheads.

One striking badge of the false family is incest, an excessively close form of union that paradoxically signifies disunion. The Duchess, who thinks herself "mild" and "calm" for not at once murdering her husband when he hesitates to free her son from arrest, decides to cuckold him instead: "I'll kill him in his forehead, hate there feed" (I.ii.94–95, 108). On the grounds of their shared hostility to the Duke she invites Spurio to couple carnally with her: the Duke, by begetting him irregularly, has wronged him, depriving him of status and fortune. Let Spurio take revenge in the foulest and most injurious way, by horning his father; let him even the score for being so uncanonically conceived by defiling the wedding bond between his father and stepmother. Spurio accedes to her proposition at once, on precisely her grounds: "I'll be reveng'd for all; now hate begin,/I'll call foul incest but a venial sin" (I.ii.170–71). What the Duchess does not know is that Spurio hates her, and her sons, as bitterly as he hates his father.

> Step-mother, I consent to thy desires,
> I love thy mischief well, but I hate thee,
> And those three cubs thy sons, wishing confusion,
> Death and disgrace may be their epitaphs.
>
> (I.ii.193–96)

Adultery, then, and incest, have nothing to do with love in this world, and little enough even with lust: they are weapons in a power struggle. Incest betokens not intimacy but its reverse, alienation, deadly destructiveness, an anarchy tearing the family apart. Society itself is torn apart by it, in Vindice's nightmare vision of lawless appetite gone wild.

> Some father dreads not (gone to bed in wine)
> To slide from the mother, and cling the daughter-in-law;
> Some uncles are adulterous with their nieces,
> Brothers with brothers' wives. O, hour of incest!
> Any kin now, next to the rim o' th' sister,
> Is man's meat in these days.
>
> (I.iii.58–63)

Not only wife against husband, brother against brother, son against father, but also son against mother. When the Duchess's two older boys learn of her liaison with Spurio, they stalk her with drawn rapiers, only staying their hands in order to choose a better time. A recent critic has rightly seen this as a parallel to the scene immediately following, in which Gratiana's sons drag her forth at dagger's point, and berate her savagely into virtue.[20] But the force of the parallel lies in the contrast. The two events, so similar in outward gesture, are totally opposed in inner meaning. The sons of the Duchess are truly bent on killing—either their mother, or Spurio, or both. What angers them is not the affront to virtue, about which they could not care less, nor that their mother has taken a paramour, nor even that the paramour is linked with her in incest, but that he is such a base fellow as Spurio. "O, our disgrace!" they cry, with gritted teeth (IV.iii.14). It is their own shame, as they imagine it, the slight to their social position, that outrages them, and which they are bent on punishing.

Gratiana's sons, however roughly they proceed, are bent on reclamation, on rousing their mother to a sense of her own fault. That that fault is known only to them does not, in their eyes, abate its vileness, nor cause them to soften their tactics, which, in the event, prove successful. Before Gratiana has taken any irretrievable step, they bring her to her senses and restore her to honesty. The incident ends with a loving reconciliation among all three, significantly seen as a marriage of the spirit: "kiss her, brother./Let's marry her to our souls, wherein's no lust,/And honourably love her" (IV.iv.56–58). Loving and virtuous relations between sons and mothers thus form a marriage of true minds, free of carnal connection and untainted by selfishness, whereas incestuous relations constitute a furious merger of brute appetite with deadly hatred.

Wherever we look we see domestic bonds to be a reality in one family and a mockery in the other. The most that can be said for any of the relationships in the ducal household is that the Duchess displays a fierce maternal protectiveness toward her youngest son, and that her two older sons manage to maintain, at moments, a brutal and self-serving camaraderie. The genuine and abiding fellowship between Vindice and Hippolito, who do nothing that does not spring from full mutual consent, and who accept each other without reservation, therefore lends their revenge a certain nobility, removing from it the blight of ego and sensual self-indulgence that hangs like a pall over the doings at court. Quite apart from the rights and wrongs of their cause, Vindice and Hippolito are plausible as "disinterested" revengers precisely because revenge is all they are after. They desire nothing in the way of tangible reward; they do not seek money, power, or pleasure. What they wish is justice, to right the wrong done them by visiting an exact equivalent of it on their enemy. Nor does their revenge require the services of underlings, who need to be bribed or blackmailed to commit subsidiary crimes, and then be rubbed out once they have served their turn. It engages no one but themselves, endangers no one but themselves.

Once, however, the revenge is complete, the situation changes. With the Duke dead, the brothers do not simply down tools and return to their old occupations, but look about for new worlds to conquer. Vindice has come to dote on himself in his role as justicer. He has become addicted to playing dangerous games of wit for desperate stakes, and cannot bear to leave off. "Strike one strain more," he urges the doubtful Hippolito, "and then we crown our wit" (V.i.170). Aesthetic motives have begun to supplant the personal ones. The taste for justice, in itself slightly abstract, has grown increasingly impersonal, while at the same time Vindice's wish to execute it has become a feverish craving to find new scope for his own cleverness. One last triumphant feat, he thinks, will make him the monarch of wit. He now believes, moreover, or thinks he believes, that he is heaven's scourge and minister, that it is his mission to right the wrongs of society: "Let our hid flames break out, as fire, as lightning,/To blast this villainous dukedom, vex'd with sin" (V.ii.5–6). He and his collaborators will bring a cleansing holocaust, devastating not private persons nor even single public figures, but the whole corrupt ruling class. A group of disaffected noblemen will join in striking down the rotten edifice of the state, along with "those few nobles that have long suppress'd" them (V.ii.11). The fact that, as we hear, five hundred stalwart gentlemen wait ready to "apply themselves, and not stand idle" at this juncture (V.ii.28) reinforces the suggestion that what is proposed is not the prosecution of a private grudge, but a moral rebellion against an insupportable tyranny. When Lussurioso is stabbed, the heavens themselves unleash their thunder, and the blazing star bursts overhead, portents of heaven's concern in the cataclysm, though not necessarily of its approval.

The final reckoning proceeds in two distinct phases, two masked dances climaxed by two fierce flurries of stabbing. In the first dance, Vindice, Hippolito, and two unnamed accomplices kill Lussurioso along with three of his toadies as they sit at table. The second dance is intended to produce the same result, but of course this time the masquers discover that they have been anticipated: their destined victim, already thrust through, lies dying under their eyes. Whereupon they proceed to fall on each other in a truly horrendous massacre. Supervacuo proclaims himself Duke; Ambitioso immediately stabs him to death; Spurio stabs Ambitioso; and an anonymous fourth member of the quartet stabs Spurio.[21] On this occasion as on others, even in a seemingly identical act of violence the two families are differentiated. One acts in disciplined unison against a common enemy, on behalf of social justice and the greater good of the state. The other, seeking to bring down the enemy solely in order to seize his powers and privileges, disintegrates at once into a raging chaos in which every man hacks bloodily at his fellow.

It is consonant with his growing self-delight as master intriguer that Vindice should reveal himself and Hippolito to be the Duke's killers. Since, in the nature of the case, no one else can credit him with that supreme stroke of artistry, he must claim the credit himself. His final speech, addressed to Hippolito and the assembled lords, explains how fitting it is that they now lose their lives:

> May not we set as well as the duke's son?
> Thou hast no conscience; are we not reveng'd?
> Is there one enemy left among those?

>Tis time to die, when we are ourselves our foes.

This contains a touch of the bravado of the trapped villain, but only a touch. Vindice welcomes death because he will allow no one to usurp the glory he has earned with his knavery, nor will he stoop to implicate others in order to mitigate his own misery.

> This work was ours, which else might have been slipp'd,
> And, if we list, we could have nobles clipp'd,
> And go for less than beggars; but we hate
> To bleed so cowardly.

If there is bravado in this, there is also solidity, and courage. Vindice refuses to cheapen his death by trying to drag others to the same fate. He concludes with a last expression of satisfaction in his and his brother's joint accomplishments.

> We have enough, i'faith;
> We're well, our mother turn'd, our sister true;
> We die after a nest of dukes. Adieu.

(V.iii.107–25)

In this summing up Vindice stresses the positive side of their achievement: they have soldered up the chink in their mother's armor; they have tested their sister's temper and found it "true"; they have stamped out a nest of viperous dukes. They have, in other terms, salvaged their family honor, bolstered the virtue of the weakest member of it, and purified the state of its most malignant elements. In their own minds they have *earned* the right to die. Death has a positive meaning for them; it is an act of affirmation, not a pointless accident. Without hesitation, then, or accusation, they march cheerfully off to their end.

It would seem, then, that the finale forbids us to say, with Ornstein, that "little sense of moral purpose remains." [22] If stanching the wounds of family honor, if verifying the chastity of their sister, if reinforcing the virtue of their mother, and wiping out a band of stinging scorpions do not constitute moral purpose, what does? Nor is it acceptable to say, with Ornstein, that "in Vindice's society the good die as horribly as the evil," [23] for we have ourselves witnessed the contrary. Unlike the Duke, cut down by his erstwhile victims, and forced to behold the incest between his wife and son in his dying moments, unlike Lussurioso, made to know as he dies that he is paying for his outrages, unlike the rest of the ducal scions, felled by each other in a furious carnage, Vindice and Hippolito die by their own choice, alertly, courageously, and high-spiritedly, so as to make of their deaths both a political and a moral action. They are not, in our eyes, "hustled off" to execution like common criminals; they are escorted from the scene like noblemen of the spirit, glad to pay with their lives for the good they have accomplished.

The question remains, what do we make of this? Is Vindice *not* tarnished by his revenge, by the outbreaks of perverse ingenuity to which it leads him, by the self-congratulatory wit that more and more possesses him? The answer is that certainly he is tarnished, as is Hippolito, but that there is something in their mode of operation that rubs out much of the tarnish: the brotherly covenant between them that never falters, even at the moment of death, the family loyalty that remains unshaken, the pride in old-fashioned virtue that amounts to a moral passion, even if it is weirdly coupled to a code of blood revenge. All this apart from the energy, courage, and resourcefulness which they share with scores of other tragic heroes and villains, and which none of the ducal family display in the slightest degree. The finale, therefore, despite its sardonic grimness, contains tragic feeling. For in it the best and the brightest, having tainted their luster in the pursuit of honor, having picked up some of the foulness of their environment, must go under. But they are no more to be lumped with their victims than Hamlet is to be lumped with Claudius because in the process of combating Claudius's wrongs he too dips his hands in blood. There are taints and taints; there is corruption and corruption. *The Revenger's Tragedy*, even before it is a tale of the good contaminated, is a tale of good versus evil.

EUGENE M. WAITH

Struggle for Calm:
The Dramatic Structure of
The Broken Heart

*A*T THE opening of the fifth act of John Ford's tragicomedy, *The Lover's Melancholy*, Corax, the physician who is working to end the epidemic of melancholy in Cyprus, announces imminent success to Cleophila:

> Tis well, tis well, the houre is at hand,
> Which must conclude the busines, that no Art
> Coo'd al this while make ripe for wisht content.
> O Lady, in the turmoyles of our liues,
> Men are like politike States, or troubled Seas,
> Tost vp and downe with seuerall stormes and tempests,
> Change, and varietie of wracks, and fortunes,
> Till labouring to the Hauens of our homes,
> We struggle for the Calme that crownes our ends.

"A happy end Heauen blesse vs with," Cleophila replies,[1] and her prayer is answered. A struggle for calm is discernible in a number of Ford's characters, both those who succeed and those who do not succeed in imposing this calm on their turbulent natures. *The Broken Heart*, which may have been written shortly after *The Lover's Melancholy*,[2] has particularly striking examples of such characters. One thinks first of Calantha continuing a state wedding celebration with no outward sign of disturbance when she hears in quick succession of the deaths of her father, her prospective sister-in-law, and her husband-to-be. But Nearchus, Calantha's princely suitor, also masters his feelings in another scene, renouncing her when he sees that she loves Ithocles; Ithocles attempts to redress the wrong he committed earlier by breaking the engagement of his sister Penthea to Orgilus; and these two lovers, in their different ways and with varying success, struggle to control the resentment they feel at their cruel treatment.

In the reassuring speech by Corax the struggle apparently leads toward a happy ending, but the overtones of his metaphor (how characteristic of Ford!) are decidedly pessimistic. The end of the voyage, the final haven, "Calme that crownes our ends," inevitably suggest death, even though that is not what Corax means. It *is* what Penthea means in *The Broken Heart* when she says, in somewhat similar terms, "In vain we labor in this course of life/To piece our journey out at length, or crave/Respite of breath. Our home is in the grave." [3] And a movement toward the calm of death, often hinted at in *The Broken Heart*, seems to be the result of Penthea's, as of Calantha's, effort to suppress her feelings. If the struggle for calm restores health in *The Lover's Melancholy*, it contributes to the tragedy of *The Broken Heart*.

The portrayal of this struggle on the part of several major characters results in an unusual structure. Ford was obviously familiar with many earlier tragedies in which the final violence was succeeded by a lofty serenity, as in the closing speeches of Horatio and Fortinbras in *Hamlet*, but *The Broken Heart* is strange in that violence is avoided except in one instance, where it is severely qualified. In other cases the tensions between characters are dissipated, largely through their own efforts, before the expected outbreak, substituting order for agon. This pattern of violence avoided gives the play its distinctive tone and a large share of its meaning. Since the pattern can only be apprehended as a temporal sequence, it will be necessary to give up the broad, spatial view of the literary analyst for the more limited immediate view of a playgoer, experiencing the play in the theater.[4] Only in retrospect will it be possible to see the successive ups and downs of this experience as features of a single landscape, as if one left the road one had been traveling and took off in a plane, from which the preceding hours of the trip could be seen in an instant.

Leonard Meyer's approach to musical meaning in *Emotion and Meaning in Music*[5] suggests a useful way of thinking about dramatic experience. Drawing on the psychological theory that "Emotion or affect is aroused when a tendency to respond is arrested or inhibited" (p. 14), Meyer explores the process by which music arouses certain expectations, and concludes that "Affect or emotion-felt is aroused when an expectation—a tendency to respond—activated by the musical stimulus situation, is temporarily inhibited or permanently blocked" (p. 31). If the experience is to be pleasing, however, a sense of completion must follow: "a dissonance or an ambiguous progression which might be unpleasant when heard in isolation may be beautiful within a piece of music where its relationship to past events and impending resolutions is understandable" (p. 92). The pattern must finally be perceived. Because he finds that the same musical processes which give rise to affect also arouse the intellectual responses of the listener with a technical understanding of music, Meyer is able to treat the intellectually formulated meaning of music as part of the experience which may be emotionally felt (pp. 39–40).

Different as verbal communication is from music, the processes by which poetic form makes itself felt are analogous to the processes of music, and the dramatist, in particular, creates many of his effects by the arousal of expectations and the manipulation of response. If the expectations aroused by the first part of a familiar cadence differ in many ways from those aroused by the development of a familiar situation, they are sufficiently similar to warrant consideration of the effects the dramatist may achieve by temporarily or permanently refusing to resolve the situation in the expected way. In drama emotion is not generated solely by the formal means which are the chief ones available to the musical composer, but it seems likely that the spectator's experiences of suspense, for example, or frustration or surprise, when his expectations are not immediately fulfilled, correspond to those of the musical listener. It may be said in anticipation of the results of the following analysis, that *The Broken Heart* repeatedly creates a certain uneasiness, if not bewilderment, by the postponement or cancellation of the consequences of what we see and hear. Not until several of these moments of frustrated expectation have been experienced can they be seen to constitute a pattern.

In the expository opening scene, in which Orgilus tells his father, Crotolon, why he wants to leave Sparta, the important motif of trouble followed by calm is briefly sketched. Referring to the feud between his family and Penthea's, Orgilus says,

> After so many quarrels as dissension,
> Fury, and rage had broach'd in blood
> . . . .
> Our present king, Amyclas, reconcil'd
> Your eager swords and seal'd a gentle peace.
>
> (17–18, 21–22)

The pledge of this peace had been the engagement of Orgilus and Penthea, soon broken by her brother Ithocles, in order to make a more socially advantageous match for her. In Orgilus's account Ithocles appears to be a type familiar in Jacobean drama, a proud malcontent, who nourished his sense of injury "to glory in revenge" (42). But now Orgilus is the one injured, and his "griefs are violent" (71). Obviously, he might be expected to seek revenge, but instead, he seems to seek escape from his griefs by going where he will not be reminded of his loss by the sight of Penthea. In the latter part of the scene he appears to be a fond, protective brother to Euphranea, whom he promises to see well matched, after she agrees not to marry without his consent. In the course of this rather short scene Ford prepares carefully for the ensuing action without giving any clear indications of what it will be. The history of injury outlasting reconciliation is ominous, but the present is represented by an apparently harmonious family. The most disquieting notes are the description of Ithocles and the slight oddity of Orgilus's behavior, puzzling to both his father and sister.

The second scene shifts our attention to Ithocles, who is now described by the king as Sparta's great warrior hero and by his friend Prophilus as one who accepts his success with "moderation,/Calmness of nature, measure, bounds, and limits/Of thankfulness and joy" (35–37). Crotolon says, "You describe/A miracle of man" (47–48). This is not the Ithocles we might have expected from Orgilus's comments—the vengeful and cruel brother, made to be the villain of a tragedy. To the extent that such an Ithocles exists he is part of the past, a discarded self which lingers only in embittered memories—his own and those of Orgilus and Penthea. The character who appears on stage in this scene seems altogether admirable. As Mark Stavig says, "We naturally wonder which account of Ithocles is correct." [6] The sense (partly erroneous, as it turns out) that Ithocles' disturbing ambition has given way to "moderation" and "calmness of nature" tends to dissipate tragic expectation.

The last scene of the first act, one of the longest in the play,[7] goes much further than the opening scene to suggest that Orgilus will, after all, take some sort of counteraction to assuage his violent griefs. The opening of the scene presents an emblem of concealment as Orgilus, now supposed to have left for Athens, appears in the disguise of a scholar. Tecnicus, the artist-philosopher, encourages him to order his life by accepting his fate, and even tells him that it is dangerous to deny himself the usual pleasures of youth, but Orgilus insists that he is undertaking no more than a brief retreat to settle his mind. Only when he is alone does he admit that his real purpose is to watch over Penthea and to test his sister's faith. Thus the emblem has two sides: it represents the moral cloak which Orgilus throws over his feelings, or even to smother them; but it is also the disguise of a revenger, and as such a possible means to a violent end. When Orgilus sees Euphranea walking with Ithocles' friend Prophilus in the palace garden, he leaps to the conclusion that "There is no faith in woman" (90), and is soon agreeing, in the manner of a Vindice, to act as a messenger between them. When he ends the act with a Machiavellian soliloquy, calling for darkness and deceit, it seems clearly indicated that he will prevent his sister's marriage to Prophilus as at least a partial revenge for what has happened to him.

Ford's strategy in these early scenes depends to an unusual degree upon the familiarity of his audience with earlier plays. It is the strategy of one who made a late "entrance" (to adopt George Kubler's useful term[8]) in the tradition of English Renaissance drama, when many of the possible options had already been exercised. But if the moment of his entrance did not allow him to be original in the ways available to Marlowe or Shakespeare, it opened up other possibilities. In *The Broken Heart* he uses the work of his predecessors as a kind of shorthand to give his spectators a false assurance that they know what is to follow. The tradition enables him to be brilliantly misleading and, in this way, original.

Juxtaposed with Orgilus's craving for revenge is the grotesque jealousy of Bassanes, the old man to whom Ithocles has married Penthea. In the first scene of act II he is torn between his compulsion to isolate her from the world and his desire to please her even by taking her to court. He is a comic stereotype whose presence in the play is surprising but not so incongruous as it may seem. His emotional instability is not altogether different from that of Orgilus, the man his marriage has wronged, and the similarity is suggested by their names, which Ford translates as "vexation" and "angry." The tantrums inspired by his jealous infatuation for Penthea, monstrous as they are made to appear, are perhaps no more irrational than Orgilus's determination to keep Euphranea from Prophilus.

What may be even more important for the experience of this scene in the theater is the increased sense of movement it conveys. The first two scenes of the play consist mainly in conversations, relieved only by the pageantry accompanying Ithocles' return in the second. The third scene is again mostly talk, though the sight of Orgilus spying on his sister provides two centers of interest on stage, and both his asides and his soliloquy foreshadow action to come. But the scene with Bassanes translates his vexatious spirit into stage movement in a series of encounters. First Bassanes instructs a servant about guarding Penthea, displaying his absurd and tragic obsession in speeches which any actor would render with the fussy, extravagant mannerisms traditionally associated with the jealous old husband. Bassanes is a basically uneasy, and hence fidgety, sort of person. When Penthea, all melancholy docility, enters with the old woman who looks after her, Bassanes tries to ingratiate himself by seeming to offer his young bride more worldly pleasures while at the same time angrily rebuking old Grausis for not being more strict. Between his infatuation and his anxiety he bounces himself back and forth like a ping-pong ball. Then "a herd of lords," as the servant says, and "a flock of ladies" (128) arrive to pay a visit. Despite his hope of pleasing Penthea, the last thing Bassanes wants is much public attention paid to her. His distraction is intensified as he sees all these people hovering about his wife: "How they flutter,/Wagtails and jays together!" (135–36). The incursion is brief, but since the visitors take Penthea with them to see Ithocles, Bassanes is left, more uneasy than ever, to come to terms with Penthea's "overseer." Physical movement in this scene and the emotional turmoil it reflects augment the anticipations of critical action raised by Orgilus's behavior in the preceding scene.

Now, just when the machinery of the play seems to have been set in motion, come three scenes which unexpectedly put on the brakes. In act II, scene ii Ithocles soliloquizes on the evils of ambition, which are compared to "squibs and crackers," flying into the air, exploding, and then vanishing "in stench and smoke" (6–8). He is fully aware of the way to prevent such futile explosions:

> Morality applied
> To timely practice keeps the soul in tune,
> At whose sweet music all our actions dance.
>
> (8–10)

Both the ideal and the metaphor in which it is expressed are centrally important in *The Broken Heart*, but it is not immediately clear what Ithocles is talking about. We are apt to assume that he is regretting his ambitious plans for Penthea, and he soon reveals that this matter is not far from the surface of his mind. The conclusion of his speech, however, points to some other, unexplained, primary concern: whatever books may teach us about morality, "It physics not the sickness of a mind/Broken with griefs" (12–13). Only "means, speedy means" will do. From the vantage-point of later events we can see that he is thinking of his ambitious love for the Princess Calantha.

Despite this strong hint that Ithocles may once again be a disordering force, his behavior in the remainder of the scene is exemplary, as it was at his first appearance. He urges Crotolon to allow Euphranea to marry Prophilus by way of strengthening his own ties with Crotolon's family, and when he is forcefully reminded that he disrupted the marriage of his sister to Orgilus, he blames his conduct on the folly of youth. The discussion of Euphranea's love is continued when she arrives with the princess, Penthea, Bassanes, and others. Orgilus is to be sent for so that, with his consent, the marriage may take place.

Good manners prevail even when the sensitive topic of Ithocles' treatment of Penthea is brought up, as if the various characters were headed toward reconciliation. Ithocles addresses his accuser as "gentle sir"; Crotolon gives way gracefully; Bassanes extols "The joys of marriage" and the constant woman (though, in an aside, wondering if she exists). The subordination of doubts to apparent harmony, as in this speech by Bassanes, is the pattern of the scene. On the surface are the plans for the wedding of Prophilus and Euphranea; below are Bassanes' jealousy, Ithocles' ambitions, and the likelihood that Orgilus will refuse his consent.

In the following scene (II.iii), Orgilus is restrained by Penthea when he finds her waiting for her brother in the garden. Removing his disguise, he urges the consummation of their love, only to meet a stern rebuke. Again a possible complication is avoided, emotion suppressed, action inhibited. When Bassanes comes into the garden, prey to his usual anxieties, he too is calmed by Penthea. It is in this scene that she expounds her despairing philosophy of life as a journey to the grave. According to the psychological theory on which Meyer bases his explanation of response to music, it is just such blocking of instinctive reaction which results in affect. For the characters in the play restraint may lead, as Tecnicus has warned, to a dangerous intensification of feeling. For the audience the suddenly reduced likelihood of an outbreak may also be frustrating—a letdown but also the occasion of increased concernment.

The brief first scene of act III presents the avoidance of "giddy rashness" and "some violent design" (2, 6) in the form of a homily on the nature of true honor by Tecnicus to Orgilus. In this same scene the king sends to Tecnicus for an interpretation of the Delphic oracle. Thus to the order of philosophy is added the suggestion of a fatal design which may mysteriously order the lives of everyone at the Spartan court.

In act III, scene ii, a crucial scene, placed close to the center of the play, Ford contrives two surprises, which almost resolve the major tensions built up in the first act and then slightly relaxed in the preceding three scenes. As if to herald this development, music opens the scene—a song in praise of indescribable beauty. As it is being sung Penthea, who has been summoned to her brother's chamber, is led across the stage by Prophilus to enter what is imagined to be an inner part of the room. Bassanes and Grausis follow them, but reenter so that both may listen at a curtain for the creaking of the bed. Before Bassanes can indulge his suspicions further Prophilus brings word that everyone is to leave, whereupon the curtain is drawn, revealing Ithocles and Penthea seated next to each other in chairs.[9] He speaks to her affectionately, while she at first is bitter and accusatory, insisting that because of him she is living in spiritual adultery with Bassanes. As his apologies are followed by professions of despair, however, she suddenly relents, extracts the secret of his love for Calantha, and promises help. Brother and sister are reconciled.

Disturbing the calm of this scene, Bassanes bursts in again like a madman, poniard in hand, his mind bursting with thoughts of incest. Penthea says,

> My lord, what slackness
> In my obedience hath deserv'd this rage?
> Except humility and silent duty
> Have drawn on your unquiet, my simplicity
> Ne'er studied your vexation
>
> (157–61)

and suddenly his rage is at an end—not only the crazed suspicions of this moment but the jealous humor that has possessed him from the first. In the musical idiom already heard several times he says, "O, my senses/Are charm'd with sounds celestial" (173–74). Again calm triumphs over violence.

In its place in the sequence this scene goes a step beyond any that precede it in canceling out the threats to order and stability, while containing within itself striking instances of those threats in Penthea's bitter chiding of her brother and in the ravings of Bassanes. The tableau of Ithocles and Penthea seated together is a visual equivalent of the calm brought about by the end of the scene.

Up to this midpoint in the play Penthea is responsible for the most striking instances of violence avoided. She dissuades Orgilus from adulterous love, overcomes her own rancor toward her brother, and makes Bassanes see reason. Yet the calm she represents is the melancholy calm of resignation if not of death. If the expectations of tragic conflict are materially reduced by her actions, the tone of the play is confirmed as anything but happy. Hope of reconciliation is tempered by the sadness of irreparable injury.

The focus of attention now shifts somewhat toward Orgilus, who reappears in his own garb. In act III, scene iii Ithocles presents him to the king, the princess, and the Prince of Argos, of whom Ithocles is jealous, since he is a suitor to Calantha. Ithocles' sudden cordiality, now that he wants to arrange his friend's marriage to Euphranea, annoys Orgilus, as he reveals to his father in the following scene, and he seems ready to refuse his consent. His father cautions him about the dangers of the "wolf of hatred snarling in [his] breast" (III.iv.33), and urges him to go along with the wishes of all the court, lest he ruin the fortunes of the family. Once again we see the sudden collapse of hostility as Orgilus gives his consent, bringing to nothing his entire stratagem of disguise and surveillance. But if his maneuvers seem to have been futile, Ford's have been most successful, for by this time it can be seen that the contrivance of a revenge which is not taken fits perfectly into the characteristic pattern of the play's action.

In the fifth scene of the act Penthea, suppressing her resentment, pleads with Calantha to look with favor on Ithocles, and the opening scene of act IV rapidly develops his rivalry with Nearchus, the Prince of Argos. Though there is an important piece of action when Ithocles picks up Calantha's ring, which Nearchus has begged of her, the main emphasis of this scene is not on what happens but on what may happen. Ithocles' uncle is alarmed by his daring to be a rival to the prince. Orgilus, with how much sincerity it is difficult to tell, defends Ithocles to Nearchus and later to his uncle, saying, "Griefs will have their vent" (116). The irony of his applying this observation to Ithocles is striking. The scene ends ominously as Tecnicus brings a sealed interpretation of the oracle for the king, prophesies to Ithocles, "The lifeless trunk shall wed the broken heart" (134), and to Orgilus, "Let craft with courtesy a while confer,/Revenge proves its own executioner" (138–39). Then, like the Friar in *'Tis Pity She's a Whore*, he leaves the city, as if unable to bear any more. Despite the reconciliations of act III, trouble, if not disaster, again threatens.

Act IV, scene ii, the longest in the play, presents the first tragic occurrence, the madness of Penthea, which revives Orgilus's resentment of Ithocles and his thoughts of revenge. When he bursts out against Bassanes, now contrite and controlled, it is Ithocles, of all people, who counsels forbearance. The scene does not end with the threat of violence, however. Nearchus, having decided not to force himself on Calantha, abandons his quarrel with Ithocles and brings him a message from the princess. Thus the scene arouses two very different expectations: one that Orgilus will seek revenge, and the other that Ithocles' love for Calantha may no longer be opposed.

Between this important scene and the climactic one which ends the act occurs the quiet episode of Calantha's engagement to Ithocles, where hopes are again balanced with premonitions of trouble: the long-awaited oracle prophesies the king's death and seems to relate the continued life of the kingdom to a neighboring prince; Orgilus, amidst congratulations to Ithocles, reveals his jealousy; and "sad music" from Penthea's lodging hints that she is dying. With this musical signal the scene ends.

The act of revenge seemingly called for at the opening of the play, then made to seem less likely in the third act, only to become more so in the fourth, finally occurs in the last scene of the act. The body of Penthea is borne onstage in a chair and is set down between two other chairs as Orgilus and Ithocles enter. A servant whispers to Orgilus about one of the chairs. A few moments later, when the two men have been left with the body, Orgilus induces Ithocles to sit in a mechanical chair, a *machine infernale*, so to speak, where the proud hero is trapped and then killed by his enemy. It is a piece of stage horror bizarre enough to be dismissed as Ford's effort to outdo his predecessors in revenge tragedy, but we may be kept from this sort of judgment by the striking appropriateness of the device.[10] From the beginning of the play Ithocles, Orgilus, and Penthea have been trapped in a situation from which no repentance, no courage, no goodwill can extricate them. And the visual emphasis on immobility here, as in the scene with Ithocles and Penthea, is clearly fitting in a play where calm is a major ideal. Even this one violent act is so carried out that violence is not its chief effect. Not only is Ithocles immobile, but he accepts death with a quiet resolution which inspires Orgilus's admiration. Their two last speeches, filled with compliment and forgiveness, suggest the parting of friends more than the triumph of a revenger. Orgilus's words, "I will be gentle even in blood" (IV.iv.61) set the tone of this ritual killing.

A series of avoided crises in the first three acts is followed in the fourth act by the madness and death of Penthea and the murder of Ithocles, as if no effort could indefinitely postpone the tragic consequences of a past error. Penthea's tragedy permits the speculation that they may sometimes be hastened by the struggle to accept misfortune and impose a stoical order. But whether the outcome is a sort of self-destruction, due to rigorous repression, or murder, due to the release of long-contained impulses, it occurs in this play in an atmosphere of surprising calm. The effect is comparable to the unexpected resolution of a false cadence.

Though the murder of Ithocles ends one cycle of injury and suffering, it begins another. Orgilus, in repaying Ithocles for a gratuitous blow, injures the innocent Calantha in precisely the way that he and Penthea were injured. Thus, at the opening of the fifth act, Orgilus has moved into the position of Ithocles, as one against whom we may expect retributive action, while Calantha's response to the offense becomes the major unknown quantity. In the brief first scene of the act Orgilus at last offers friendship to Bassanes as he prepares to reveal to him the deaths of Penthea and Ithocles. Here jealousy is replaced by a "league of amity" (23), but the facts of the murder are not yet known.

The second scene, thanks largely to Lamb's commentary, is the best known in the play. Calantha amazes the guests at the celebration of Euphranea's wedding by her seemingly unruffled bearing as she orders the dance to continue after hearing the news of her father's death. She repeats her performance when Bassanes announces Penthea's death and again when Orgilus tells of the murder of Ithocles. The formal movements of the dance, resumed after each interruption, perfectly express the order to which Calantha sacrifices the expression of her loss and injury. Her conduct is the showpiece of the play, the surprise of surprises, the supreme example of feeling subordinated to the achievement of harmony. It is more spectacular than Penthea's self-denial and infinitely more effectual than Orgilus's sporadic attempts at overcoming his bitterness.

The story of Orgilus is not complete, however. In the second half of this scene, which is less often remembered than the first half, he also gives a spectacular display of self-control. Allowed to pick the means of his execution, he chooses to bleed to death. Like a perfect Stoic he opens one vein himself, persuades Bassanes to open another, and dies commenting on the prophecy of Tecnicus, "Revenge proves its own executioner." The image of order in movement given in the wedding dance is balanced here by another of the many images of order as stasis.

The final image in this series is reserved for the ceremonial scene which concludes the play. In front of an altar, beside which the body of Ithocles has been placed *"on a hearse, or in a chair,"* [11] Calantha instructs Nearchus in the government of Sparta, places a wedding ring on Ithocles' finger, and dies of a broken heart. Her explanation of her behavior at the dance, "When one news straight came huddling on another/Of death, and death, and death" (V.iii.69–70), leads to the contrast between the "shrieks and outcries" produced by shallow emotion and the "silent griefs which cut the heartstrings." If her action virtually epitomizes the several "struggles for calm" in the play, her comment on it brings out the tragic cost of an effort which is also a measure of greatness.

Calantha dies to the strains of a song which she "fitted for [her] end" (81–94), furnishing one last instance of the importance of music in the play. Ithocles spoke of morality "At whose sweet music all our actions dance." In the two final scenes, to which his words apply so perfectly, it is a dance of death.

In retrospect the strange pattern of violence avoided can be seen to constitute the chief meaning of the tragedy. The play obliges its spectators to experience repeatedly the building up of tensions and then their unexpected relaxation as a revenge is abandoned or deferred, a quarrel ended, a betrayal refused, a conversion accomplished, or a murder followed by reconciliation. In each instance the frustration of a prepared response is, in a general way, comparable to the musical composer's strategy for arousing emotion and serves to interest, surprise, or puzzle the spectator. Cumulatively, these repeated examples of action arrested call attention to the blocking force—the constant effort of Ford's characters to deflect the usual consequences of certain acts through self-mastery. Admiration and pity for this struggle are the specific emotions which the dramatic structure of *The Broken Heart* is calculated to arouse.

Notes / Bibliographies / Index

Notes

All quotations from the works of William Shakespeare are from *The Complete Works of Shakespeare*, ed. George Lyman Kittredge (Boston and New York: Ginn, 1936).

Harbage / Copper into Gold

1. "A precept for no playes to be played from the last day of May 1569, vntill the last day of September then next following," in E. K. Chambers, ed., *The Elizabethan Stage* (Oxford, 1923), IV, 267. (All the historical documents quoted below are printed in whole or in part in Chambers's matchless collection.)
2. Charles T. Prouty, "An Early English Stage," *ShS*, 6 (1953), 64–74.
3. *An Acte for the punishement of Vacabondes, Elizabethan Stage*, IV, 269–70.
4. *Elizabethan Stage*, II, 86.
5. Chamber Accounts, *Elizabethan Stage*, IV, 146–47.
6. "pro Iacobo Burbage & aliis de licencia speciali," *Elizabethan Stage*, II, 87, 88.
7. *Elizabethan Stage*, IV, 287–88.
8. Ibid., IV, 289–90.
9. Ibid., IV, 278 (emphasis added).
10. *A Sermon Preached at Paules Crosse* (1578), *Elizabethan Stage*, IV, 200.
11. *Playes Confuted in fiue Actions* (1582), *Elizabethan Stage*, IV, 216.
12. *Elizabethan Stage*, IV, 214.
13. *The Schoole of Abuse* (1579), *Elizabethan Stage*, IV, 204.
14. *Elizabethan Stage*, IV, 204.
15. *Greenes Groatsworth of Wit* (1596), *Elizabethan Stage*, IV, 241.
16. *Elizabethan Stage*, IV, 240.
17. Ibid., II, 4–5.
18. Ibid., III, 416.
19. John Maynard Keynes, *A Treatise on Money* (London, 1930), II, 154.

Hunter / Were There Act-Pauses on Shakespeare's Stage?

1. "Act and scene division in the plays of Shakespeare," *RES*, 3 (1927), 390.

2. It may be worth reciting the actual facts of the First Folio: of the thirty-six plays, six have neither act nor scene divisions (*TrC, RJ, Tim, AC, 2H6, 3H6*); eleven have acts marked, but not scenes (*Cor, TA, JC, H5, CE, Ado, LLL, MND, MV, AWW, TSh*); three are in various ways anomalous (*Ham, 1H4, KJ*); the remaining sixteen have both acts and scenes marked.

3. G. E. Bentley, *The Profession of Dramatist in Shakespeare's Time, 1590–1642* (Princeton, 1971), pp. 227–34. Cf. W. W. Greg, *The Shakespeare First Folio* (Oxford, 1955), pp. 144–45.

4. *Keep the Widow Waking*, written by Dekker, Ford, Rowley, and Webster in 1624. See C. J. Sisson, *Lost Plays of Shakespeare's Age* (Cambridge, 1936), p. 112.

5. *Dramatic Documents from the Elizabethan Playhouse* (Oxford, 1931), p. 110. Seven genuine plots are known. The only complete one, apart from the four I have described, is *Frederick and Basilea*. This shows no sign of act-division. Two others, *Fortune's Tennis* and *Troilus and Cressida* are mere fragments, but nothing in the pieces that survive suggests act-division. See, however, the fuller discussion in Greg, *Dramatic Documents*, p. 123 ff., and T. W. Baldwin, *On Act and Scene Division in the Shakspere First Folio* (Carbondale, 1965), pp. 27, 39.

6. "Act and scene division," p. 391.

7. See my edition of *The Malcontent*, Revels Plays.

8. William Prynne, *Histriomastix* (1633), cited in *The Shakspere Allusion-book*, ed. C. M. Ingleby et al., re-ed. John Munro (London, 1909), I, 369.

9. There is one exception to this statement, the 1622 quarto of *Othello*, which is exceptional in a number of ways, being by far the latest of the new printings in quarto. This has been supposed to be derived from a transcript of foul paper material, made for a private patron (see Greg, *First Folio*, p. 362). As such, it might be expected to have the fashionable characteristics of reading texts in its period.

10. Good evidence that the precise placing of scene endings was obscure, even for Elizabethans, is provided by the 1597 quarto of *Romeo and Juliet*. In the second half of this text the printer has been obliged to spread out his type to fill an uncomfortably large number of pages (see H. R. Hoppe, *The Bad Quarto of Romeo and Juliet: A Bibliographical and Textual Study* [Ithaca, 1948]). One way of doing this is to insert rows of type ornaments at breaks in the action (usually moments when the stage is cleared). But of the eleven breaks thus created in the 1597 text, only eight are allowed by modern editors.

11. See Greg, *First Folio*, p. 144, for examples.

12. See Greg, *Dramatic Documents*, p. 293 ff.

13. Cf. Harley Granville-Barker, *Prefaces to Shakespeare: Second Series* (London, 1930), pp. 34–35: "What value is there in an act pause after Capulet's supper, between Romeo's first meeting with Juliet and the balcony scene? There is no interval of time to account for, nor has the action reached any juncture that asks for the emphasis of a pause."

14. Jonson's *Sejanus* provides, as so often in structural matters, the clearest example—Sejanus is totally absent from act IV. In *Volpone* there is a similar effect:

Volpone is absent from all but 37 lines of act IV, and even then he is quasi-dead on a stretcher, unable to speak. Hamlet's only prolonged absence from the stage is throughout the second half of act IV (scenes v, vi, vii), and Macbeth follows the same pattern (IV.ii, iii). Leontes and Hermione are absent from *Winter's Tale*, act IV, and in act IV of *Twelfth Night*, neither Viola nor Orsino appear.

15. *Sejanus* again provides a model of exemplary clarity. Chapman's *Caesar and Pompey* offers an interesting parallel. *Volpone* act V opens with the protagonist's determination to overgo Mosca's success in act IV. *Othello* opens act V with the separate confidences of Othello and Iago that all is going forward swimmingly. In both *Julius Caesar* and *Coriolanus* we hear of the hybris of the protagonists, but with typically Shakespearean indirection, so that we do not know quite what to make of it. In comedy, the opening of act V sometimes is used to establish a heroic self-confidence which the happy ending fully justifies. Of this kind is Theseus's opening to act V of *A Midsummer Night's Dream*, and Prospero's at the same point in *The Tempest*.

16. *Scenic Form in Shakespeare* (Oxford, 1971).

Beckerman / Shakespeare and the Life of the Scene

1. Madeleine Doran, *Endeavors of Art* (Madison, 1954); Wolfgang Clemen, *Shakespeare's Dramatic Art: Collected Essays* (London, 1972).

2. The term *scenic unit* designates a subdivision of a formal scene. It is akin to the term *beat* popularized by the followers of Constantin Stanislavski, the director of the Moscow Art Theatre, and also to the term *segment* which I employ in *Dynamics of Drama* (New York, 1970).

3. The beginning and end of V.iii have minor scenic units that set off the central action. They deal with Coriolanus's relationship to Aufidius and the Volscians and thus serve to frame the mother-son encounter much in the way Mark Rose describes the triptych form in *Shakespearean Design* (Cambridge, Mass., 1972).

4. So numerous are the examples of this pattern that only a few can be cited here. See Electra's speech over the urn supposedly containing Orestes' ashes (Sophocles' *Electra*), Lopahin's recital of his purchase of the orchard (Chekhov's *The Cherry Orchard*), and Clov's final speech (Beckett's *Endgame*).

Akrigg / Shakespeare the King-Maker

1. Cal. S.P. (*Venetian*) (*1623–1625*), p. 309.

2. *The Cease of Majesty: A Study of Shakespeare's History Plays* (London, 1961), p. 109.

3. *Basilicon Doron*, ed. James Craigie (London, 1944), p. 163.

4. *R3*, III.vii.167; *3H6*, V.ii.11; *Ant.*, IV.xii.23–24.

5. "The Pity of It," *Sunday Times*, 11 June 1972, p. 37.

6. "The Status and Person of Majesty," *SJ*, 90 (1954), 286.

7. G. P. V. Akrigg, "*Henry V*: The Epic Hero as Dramatic Protagonist," in *Stratford Papers*, ed. B. A. W. Jackson (Ontario, 1969), pp. 186–207.

8. "His majesties speach in this last session of Parliament" (1605), *STC* 14393, sig. B1.

9. "An Homily Against Disobedience and Wilful Rebellion, First Part," *Certain Sermons or Homilies Appointed to be Read in Churches in the Time of Queen Elizabeth of Famous Memory* (London, 1899), pp. 594–95.

10. *The Court of King James the First* (London, 1839), I, 268–70.

11. *The Letters of John Chamberlain*, ed. N. E. McClure (Philadelphia, 1939), I, 301.

12. "The Status and Person of Majesty," p. 286.

13. E. K. Chambers, *William Shakespeare: A Study of Facts and Problems* (Oxford, 1930), II, 214.

14. Ibid., II, 212.

15. *Shakespeare's Imagery and What It Tells Us* (Cambridge, 1935), p. 190.

Leech / The Moral Tragedy of *Romeo and Juliet*

1. See Nicholas Brooke, "Marlowe as Provocative Agent in Shakespeare's Early Plays," *ShS*, 14 (1961), 34–44.

2. See my "Marlowe's Humor," in *Essays on Shakespeare and Elizabethan Drama in Honor of Hardin Craig*, ed. Richard Hosley (Columbia, 1962), pp. 69–81. For a contrary view see J. B. Steane, *Marlowe: A Critical Study* (Cambridge, 1964), ch. II.

3. See F. P. Wilson, *The English Drama 1485–1585* (Oxford, 1969), pp. 146–47.

4. See F. P. Wilson, *Marlowe and the Early Shakespeare* (Oxford, 1953), p. 108.

5. See *The Poetics*, ch. XVII: "Poetry demands a man with a special gift for it, or else one with a touch of madness in him; the former can easily assume the required mood, and the latter may be naturally beside himself with emotion" (Bywater's translation). In his note on this passage Bywater refers to relevant comments in Aristotle's other writings. See *Aristotle on the Art of Poetry* (Oxford, 1909), pp. 244–45.

6. For a major scholarly discussion of love-melancholy, see Lawrence Babb, *The Elizabethan Malady* (East Lansing, 1951).

7. *Not Wisely but Too Well: Shakespeare's Love Tragedies* (San Marino, 1957), esp. pp. 116–17.

8. *Marlowe's Tamburlaine: A Study in Renaissance Moral Philosophy* (1941; rpt. Nashville, 1964).

9. *Shakespeare's Early Tragedies* (London, 1968), esp. pp. 102–3.

10. *TGV* V.iv.7–10. See my new Arden edition of *TGV* (London, 1969), p. 112.

11. The act-divisions derive of course only from the Folio, but in this play they seem to have high authority. Cf. G. K. Hunter's essay in this volume.

12. "The Structure of *Richard the Third*," *DUJ*, 31 (Dec., 1938), 63.

13. *The Essayes of Michael Lord of Montaigne translated by John Florio* (London, 1897), II, 149.

14. On this matter see "Le dénouement par le suicide dans la tragédie élisabethaine et jacobéenne," in *Le Théâtre tragique*, ed. Jean Jacquot (Paris, 1962), pp. 179–89.

15. On the curious ambivalence in the fact that the statues are golden, see my British Academy lecture, *Shakespeare's Tragic Fiction* (London, 1973), p. 7.

16. (London, 1967), p. 135.

17. *Shakespearean Tragedy* (1904; rpt. London, 1951), pp. 38–39.

18. *Tragedy* (London, 1969), pp. 53–54.

Webber / *Hamlet* and the Freeing of the Mind

1. The same point, with additional examples, is made by Julian Markels in *The Pillar of the World: Antony and Cleopatra in Shakespeare's Development* (Columbus, 1968), pp. 89–90.

2. Willard Farnham, *The Medieval Heritage of Elizabethan Tragedy* (1936; rpt. New York, 1963); Donald R. Howard, "Hamlet and the Contempt of the World," *SAQ*, 58 (1959), 167–75, and *The Three Temptations: Medieval Man in Search of the World* (Princeton, 1966).

3. See Farnham, *Medieval Heritage*, and Howard, "Renaissance World-Alienation," in *The Darker Vision of the Renaissance*, ed. Robert Kinsman (Berkeley, 1974). Among the many *de contemptu* commonplaces in this play are the use of the human skull for meditation; references to fortune and the fall of the mighty; paradoxes concerning the illusory glory and real unworthiness of man and his world; imagery of corruption and death.

4. Any educated person of the period would probably have read Pope Innocent III's *De Miseria Humanae Conditionis* and some of the *ars moriendi* literature, and would also have been encouraged to find a *de contemptu* moral in some classical authors like Vergil and Seneca. It was also usual to remind princes of the limitations and dangers of glory and power; as scholar and prince, Hamlet would have been schooled to disdain Fortune. Also, of course, contempt is akin to Stoicism, which it encourages. Shakespeare's audiences need not have done the reading in order to have absorbed what was in the atmosphere of the age.

5. Or simply as another contempt *topos*, which it is.

6. Most readers do not realize that Ophelia stops her relationship with Hamlet, on Polonius's instructions (II.i.107–10), especially since Ophelia herself behaves as though things had gone the other way around. Dramatic interpretations often show Hamlet discovering the hidden presence of Polonius and Claudius in III.i, and realizing that Ophelia has been set out as bait, but whether or not this rendering is valid, the original betrayal is in the text. It is important to understand that Hamlet responds with rejection to rejection, but has not initiated the break in any way. This is the only one of Hamlet's bereavements for which Claudius is not directly responsible.

7. I do not mean to belittle the friendship of Horatio, which is essential to Hamlet, yet Horatio is another outsider, metaphorically and perhaps literally (he has to have Danish drinking customs explained to him), who seems to exist solely for Hamlet's benefit without providing any bridge to or defense against the rest of the world. Horatio is the exception who proves the rule.

8. The theme of coming naked into the world (Job 1:21) is a contempt *topos* of which Hamlet makes himself an illustration, signifying both the easier feeling that he now has toward contempt, and his awareness that this moment is a kind of rebirth.

9. Some of this language was first pointed out to me by James Stewart at Ohio State University. See also Harry Levin, *The Question of Hamlet* (New York, 1959), for discussion of questioning and doubt in the play.

10. Hamlet Senior is also asking Hamlet to take on a role for which he is not ready and which early in the play is as impossible for him as the role of loyal son to Claudius and Gertrude.

11. The humor of *Hamlet*, while often seeming more desperate in its context and less accountable, is very like that in *The Winter's Tale*, especially in the juxtaposition of life and death, comedy and tragedy in III.iii, where the ship sinks, Antigonus is eaten by a bear, and Perdita is discovered. In many ways, *Hamlet* anticipates Shakespeare's whole subsequent development.

Whitaker / Still Another Source for *Troilus and Cressida*

1. It has been briefly treated in Robert Kimbrough, *Shakespeare's Troilus and Cressida and Its Setting* (Cambridge, Mass., 1964), pp. 34–36.

2. Quotations are from *The Life and Complete Works in Prose and Verse of Robert Greene, M.A.* (The Huth Library), ed. Alexander B. Grosart, 15 vols. (1881–86; rpt. New York, 1964), Vol. VI.

3. Cf. Geoffrey Bullough, ed., *Narrative and Dramatic Sources of Shakespeare*, Vol. VI: *Other 'Classical' Plays* (London and New York, 1966), pp. 101–2, 113–23.

4. Ibid., Vol. V: *The Roman Plays* (London and New York, 1964), pp. 97, 102–3.

5. Cf. Virgil K. Whitaker, *Shakespeare's Use of Learning* (San Marino, 1953), pp. 199–201.

6. Roger Ascham, *English Works*, ed. William Aldis Wright (Cambridge, 1904), p. 267. Apparently the great humanist made a slip, since classical usage allows *materia* in all cases in the first declension but only the nominative and accusative *materies* and *materiem* in the fifth declension. Cf. Charlton T. Lewis and Charles Short, *A Latin Dictionary* (Oxford, 1879), s.v. "materia"; Charles E. Bennett, *A Latin Grammar* (Boston, 1895), 59, 2a.

7. Bullough, VI, 201–2.

Bullough / Another Analogue of *Measure for Measure*

1. Budd, "Material for a Study of the Sources of Shakespeare's *Measure for Measure*," *RLC*, 11 (1931), 711–36; Kenneth Muir, *Shakespeare's Sources I: Comedies and Tragedies* (London, 1957), pp. 101–9; Mary Lascelles, *Shakespeare's "Measure for Measure"* (London, 1953), pp. 6–42; Madeleine Doran, *Endeavors of Art* (Madison, 1954), pp. 385–89; J. W. Lever, ed., *Measure for Measure*, Arden edition (London and Cambridge, Mass., 1965), pp. xxxv–liv; Geoffrey Bullough, *Narrative and Dramatic Sources of Shakespeare*, Vol. II: *The Comedies, 1596–1603* (London and New York, 1958), pp. 399–417. The last of these includes Cinthio's

Decade VIII, Novella V, a summary of *Epitia, Promos and Cassandra* (entire), and selections from T. Lupton and B. Riche.
2. Translation from the 1583 edition of *Hecatommithi*.

Charney / Webster vs. Middleton, or the Shakespearean Yardstick in Jacobean Tragedy

1. David L. Frost, *The School of Shakespeare: The Influence of Shakespeare on English Drama 1600–1642* (Cambridge, 1968), p. 24.
2. Ibid., p. 25.
3. William Archer, *The Old Drama and the New* (Boston, 1923), p. 29.
4. Algernon Charles Swinburne, *The Age of Shakespeare* (London, 1908), p. 15.
5. Ibid., p. 45.
6. See T. J. B. Spencer, "Shakespeare *v.* The Rest: The Old Controversy," *ShS*, 14 (1961), 76–89.
7. *Charles Lamb's Specimens of English Dramatic Poets*, ed. Israel Gollancz (London, 1893), I, xix.
8. Ibid., I, xx.
9. Ibid., II, 30.
10. William Hazlitt, *Lectures on the Literature of the Age of Elizabeth* (London, 1907), p. 95.
11. Hereward T. Price, "The Function of Imagery in Webster," *PMLA*, 70 (1955), rpt. in *John Webster: A Critical Anthology*, ed. G. K. and S. K. Hunter (Baltimore, 1969), p. 202.
12. See Don D. Moore, *John Webster and His Critics 1617–1964* (Baton Rouge, 1966), esp. ch. 5: "Eliot, Leavis, and *Scrutiny*."
13. Ian Jack, "The Case of John Webster," *Scrutiny*, 16 (1949), rpt. in Hunter, *John Webster*, p. 158.
14. Ibid., p. 159.
15. T. S. Eliot, *Selected Essays 1917–1932* (New York, 1932), p. 98.
16. Hunter, *John Webster*, p. 106.
17. See R. W. Dent, *John Webster's Borrowing* (Berkeley, 1960), esp. Introduction.
18. John Russell Brown, ed., *The White Devil*, Revels Plays (London, 1960), I.ii.202–4. All quotations and line references are from this edition.
19. See Travis Bogard, *The Tragic Satire of John Webster* (Berkeley, 1955). See also Jane Marie Luecke, O.S.B., "*The Duchess of Malfi*: Comic and Satiric Confusion in a Tragedy," *SEL*, 4 (1964), 275–90, and George F. Sensabaugh, "Tragic Effect in Webster's *The White Devil*," *SEL*, 5 (1965), 345–61.
20. See Bogard, *Tragic Satire*, and Frederic Ives Carpenter, *Metaphor and Simile in the Minor Elizabethan Drama* (Chicago, 1895). Carpenter makes a running parallel between Webster and Tourneur.
21. John Russell Brown, ed., *The Duchess of Malfi*, Revels Plays (London, 1964), II.i.23–29. All quotations and line references are from this edition.
22. J. R. Mulryne, " 'The White Devil' and 'The Duchess of Malfi,' " in *Jacobean Theatre*, ed. John Russell Brown and Bernard Harris (London, 1960), p. 202. Carpenter also notes this similarity under the rubric of "hyperbolical conceits."

23. Ibid., p. 206.

24. W. A. Edwards, "Revaluations (1): John Webster," *Scrutiny*, 2 (1933), 17.

25. See G. E. Bentley, *The Jacobean and Caroline Stage* (Oxford, 1956), V, 1241.

26. N. W. Bawcutt, ed., *The Changeling*, Revels Plays (London, 1958), II.ii.78, 79–81.

27. See Maurice Charney, "Shakespeare's Unpoetic Poetry," *SEL*, 13 (1973), 199–207.

28. See, among others, Inga-Stina Ewbank, "Realism and Morality in 'Women Beware Women,'" *E&S*, 22 (1969), 57–70; Dorothy M. Farr, *"The Changeling,"* *MLR*, 62 (1967), 586–97; and Richard Levin, *The Multiple Plot in English Renaissance Drama* (Chicago, 1971). Levin's book puts a very strong emphasis on Middleton.

29. T. B. Tomlinson, *A Study of Elizabethan and Jacobean Tragedy* (Cambridge, 1964), pp. 168 and 171.

NOTE: This paper is a revised version of a talk given at the Modern Language Association on December 28, 1972.

Ornstein / Bourgeois Morality and Dramatic Convention in *A Woman Killed with Kindness*

1. When Frankford announces his intention to kill his wife with kindness (IV.iv.154), Cranwell attempts to intervene but never states his thought and seems later to accept without murmur Frankford's treatment of his wife. All references to *A Woman Killed with Kindness* are to the Penguin edition of the play in *Three Elizabethan Domestic Tragedies*, ed. Keith Sturgess (Baltimore, 1969).

2. All in all, Walter's behavior is viewed as one of the unfortunate quirks to which husbands may be subject. The envoy of *The Clerk's Tale* warns other husbands against testing their wives in similar fashion, not because it would be immoral, but because their wives would not prove to be Griseldas.

3. In Heywood's source, the debate in the Roman camp is simply over who has the most admirable wife. In Heywood's play, the debate is over the honesty of wives, and the question of whether women are capable of genuine chastity is raised by Tarquin in an Iago-like manner (III.iii, p. 373). All references to *The Rape of Lucrece* are to the Mermaid edition of *Thomas Heywood*, ed. A. Wilson Verity (London, 1888).

4. *Thomas Heywood*, p. 401*n*.

5. Castiza is Vindice's sister, the beleaguered virgin of *The Revenger's Tragedy*.

6. See my argument for the Fletcherian qualities of *Henry VIII* in *A Kingdom for a Stage* (Cambridge, Mass., 1972), pp. 203–20.

7. Most scholars date *The English Traveller* in the 1620s, a period when Fletcher's influence on the English stage was supreme.

8. Act II, scene i, p. 182. All quotations from *The English Traveller* are from the Mermaid edition of *Thomas Heywood.*

9. Quoted in *Thomas Heywood*, p. 152.

10. See my discussion of Fletcherian characterizations in *The Moral Vision of Jacobean Tragedy* (Madison, 1960), pp. 173–79.

11. Frankford's very name seems to describe the openness and directness of his character.

12. In the midst of all the tearful sentimentality of the last scene, there is one wry if not jarring note. When Frankford in pardoning Anne says that "in mere pity/Of thy weak state, I'll wish to die with thee" (V.iv.96–97), the others chorus, "So do we all." But the servant Nicholas declares in an aside, "So will not I,/I'll sigh and sob, but, by my faith, not die." Since this comic aside threatens to expose all the tearful sympathizing as sentimental cant, one cannot imagine Heywood risking it unless he thought that some in the audience would appreciate its honesty.

Barish / The True and False Families of *The Revenger's Tragedy*

1. Adolphus William Ward, *A History of English Dramatic Literature*, 2nd ed. (London, 1899), III, 69, 70.

2. T. S. Eliot, *Selected Essays 1917–1932* (New York, 1932), pp. 189–90.

3. Lacy Lockert, "The Greatest of Elizabethan Melodramas," in *Essays in Dramatic Literature: The Parrott Presentation Volume*, ed. Hardin Craig (Princeton, 1935), p. 122.

4. Harold Jenkins, "Cyril Tourneur," *RES*, 17 (1941), 21.

5. Eliot, *Selected Essays*, p. 190. The present discussion is in no way affected by the attribution of the play to Tourneur or to anyone else. However, to my mind the case against Tourneur's authorship remains unproved. In defense of Tourneur see R. A. Foakes, "On the authorship of *The Revenger's Tragedy*," *MLR*, 48 (1953), 129–38; Robert Ornstein, "The Ethical Design of *The Revenger's Tragedy*," *ELH*, 21 (1954), 81–93; Inga-Stina Ekeblad, "An Approach to Tourneur's Imagery," *MLR*, 54 (1959), 489–98, and "On the Authorship of *The Revenger's Tragedy*," *ES*, 41 (1960), 225–40; T. B. Tomlinson, *A Study of Elizabethan and Jacobean Tragedy* (Cambridge, 1964), pp. 97–131.

6. "'The Revenger's Tragedy' and the Morality Tradition," *Scrutiny*, 6 (1938), 403–4, 415.

7. E.g., John Peter, *Complaint and Satire in Early English Literature* (Oxford, 1956), p. 259; Irving Ribner, *Jacobean Tragedy: The Quest for Moral Order* (New York, 1962), pp. 79, 83–84; Lawrence J. Ross, ed., *The Revenger's Tragedy*, Regents Renaissance Drama (Lincoln, Neb. 1966), pp. xxiv, xxviii.

8. E.g., T. B. Tomlinson, "The Morality of Revenge: Tourneur's Critics," *EIC*, 10 (1960), 134.

9. Fredson T. Bowers, *Elizabethan Revenge Tragedy: 1587–1642* (Princeton, 1940), pp. 132, 134.

10. Robert Ornstein, *The Moral Vision of Jacobean Tragedy* (Madison, 1960), p. 87.

11. Ribner, *Jacobean Tragedy*, p. 80.

12. Peter B. Murray, *A Study of Cyril Tourneur* (Philadelphia, 1964), p. 203.

13. See Alvin Kernan, *The Cankered Muse* (New Haven, 1959), pp. 229–30.

14. R. A. Foakes, ed., *The Revenger's Tragedy*, Revels Plays (London, 1966), I.i.57. All quotations and line references are from this edition.

15. Cyril Tourneur, *Works*, ed. Allardyce Nicoll (London, 1930), p. 18, n. 4.

16. Léon Ruth, trans., *La tragédie de la vengeance*, in *L'avant-scène du théâtre*, nos. 386–87 (1967), p. 105.

17. Trans. Thomas Pickering (London, 1609), sig. B1ᵛ.

18. L. G. Salingar, "Tourneur and the Tragedy of Revenge," in *The Age of Shakespeare*, ed. Boris Ford (London, 1955), p. 327.

19. Charles Osborne McDonald, *The Rhetoric of Tragedy: Form in Stuart Drama* (Amherst, 1966), p. 241.

20. Murray, *Cyril Tourneur*, p. 203.

21. I follow Fluchère, Foakes, and other editors in assigning line 53 to Supervacuo rather than (as in the quarto) to Spurio.

22. Ornstein, *Moral Vision*, p. 111.

23. Ibid., p. 112.

Waith / Struggle for Calm

1. In the absence of a reliable modern edition the quotation is taken from the 1629 quarto, sig. K3ᵛ.

2. See H. J. Oliver, *The Problem of John Ford* (Melbourne, 1955), pp. 47–48; G. E. Bentley, *The Jacobean and Caroline Stage* (Oxford, 1956), III, 441–42.

3. Donald K. Anderson, ed., *The Broken Heart*, Regents Renaissance Drama (Lincoln, Neb., 1968), II.iii.146–48. All quotations and line references are from this edition.

4. See Bernard Beckerman, "Dramatic Analysis and Literary Interpretation," *NLH*, 2 (1971), 391–406.

5. Chicago, 1956. My attention was first called to this book by Paula Johnson, who makes excellent use of the method in *Form and Transformation in Music and Poetry of the English Renaissance* (New Haven, 1972).

6. *John Ford and the Traditional Moral Order* (Madison, 1968), p. 150.

7. Only acts I and II are fully divided into scenes. Acts III and IV have no scene division, and act V is divided into two (instead of three) scenes. Modern editors mark scenes at every clearing of the stage, as the printers did in the first two acts of the play, though they then failed to carry the plan out consistently.

8. *The Shape of Time* (New Haven, 1962), p. 6.

9. Or possibly in a single large chair. The stage direction is not explicit.

10. On Ford's use of the chairs see Donald K. Anderson, *John Ford* (New York, 1972), p. 75.

11. As Donald Anderson says, "We wish that Ford had left no choice other than the sedentary posture" (*John Ford*, p. 75).

A Selected Bibliography of Works by Madeleine Doran

Books

Endeavors of Art: A Study of Form in the Elizabethan Drama. 1954; rpt. 1963; rpt. (paperback), Madison, 1964.
Something about Swans. Madison, 1973.
Time's Foot. Los Angeles, 1974.
Shakespeare's Dramatic Language. Madison, 1976.

Monographs

"Henry VI, Parts II and III": Their Relation to the "Contention" and the "True Tragedy." University of Iowa Humanistic Studies, vol. 4, no. 4. Iowa City, 1928.
The Text of King Lear. Stanford Studies in Language and Literature, vol. 4, no. 2. Palo Alto, 1931.

Editions

If You Know Not Me, You Know Nobody. Parts I and II. 2 vols. Oxford: The Malone Society Publications, 1934 (1935).
A Midsummer Night's Dream. Baltimore, 1959. Revised in *The Complete Pelican Shakespeare.* Gen. ed. Alfred Harbage. Baltimore, 1969.

Articles

"Actors Names in the *Contention* and *2 Henry VI*." *Philological Quarterly*, 7 (1928), 399–400.
"Elements in the Composition of *King Lear*." *Studies in Philology*, 30 (1933), 34–58.
"The Quarto of *King Lear* and Bright's Shorthand." *Modern Philology*, 33 (1935), 139–57.

"Manuscript Notes in the Bodleian Copy of Bright's *Characterie.*" *The Library*, 16 (1936), 418–24.

"On Elizabethan Credulity: With some questions concerning the use of the marvelous in literature." *Journal of the History of Ideas*, 1 (1940), 151–76. Rpt. in *The Elizabethan Age.* Ed. David L. Stevenson. New York, 1968.

"That Undiscovered Country: A problem concerning the use of the supernatural in *Hamlet* and *Macbeth.*" *Philological Quarterly*, 20 (1941), 221–35.

"Imagery in *Richard II* and in *Henry IV.*" *Modern Language Review*, 37 (1942), 113–22. Rpt. in *Henry IV, Part I.* Ed. James L. Sanderson. New York, 1962.

"An Evaluation of Evidence in Shakespearean Textual Criticism." *English Institute Annual, 1941.* New York, 1942. Pp. 95–114.

"*A Midsummer Night's Dream*: A Metamorphosis." *Rice Institute Pamphlet*, 46 (1960), 113–33.

"Pyramus and Thisbe Once More." In *Essays on Shakespeare and the Elizabethan Drama in Honor of Hardin Craig.* Ed. Richard Hosley. Columbia, 1962. Pp. 149–62.

"The Language of *Hamlet.*" *Huntington Library Quarterly*, 27 (1964), 259–78.

"'Yet am I inland bred.'" *Shakespeare 400: Essays by American Scholars on the Anniversary of the Poet's Birth.* Ed. James G. McManaway. New York, 1964. Pp. 99–114. (*Shakespeare Quarterly*, 15, No. 2.)

"Some Renaissance 'Ovids.'" In *Literature and Society.* Ed. Bernice Slote. Lincoln, 1964. Pp. 44–62.

"'High events as these': The Language of Hyperbole in *Antony and Cleopatra.*" *Queen's Quarterly*, 62 (1965), 26–51.

"Shakespeare as an Experimental Dramatist." In *Shakespeare Celebrated: Anniversary Lectures Delivered at the Folger Library.* Ed. Louis B. Wright. Ithaca, N.Y., 1966. Pp. 61–88.

"Good Name in *Othello.*" *Studies in English Literature*, 7 (1967), 195–217.

"A Tribute to Hardin Craig." *Shakespearean Research Opportunities*, 4 (1968/69), 92–97.

"Iago's 'If—': An Essay on the Syntax of *Othello.*" In *The Drama of the Renaissance: Essays for Leicester Bradner.* Ed. Elmer W. Blistein. Providence, 1970. Pp. 69–99.

"Command, Question, and Assertion in *King Lear.*" *Shakespeare's Art: Seven Essays.* Ed. Milton Crane. Chicago, 1973. Pp. 53–78.

"Titania's Wood." *Rice University Studies* (*Renaissance Studies in Honor of Carroll Camden*), 55 (1974), 55–70.

"The Idea of Excellence in Shakespeare." *Shakespeare Quarterly*, 27 (1976), 133–49.

A Selected Bibliography of Works by Mark Eccles

Books

Christopher Marlowe in London. Cambridge, Mass., 1934.
Shakespeare in Warwickshire. 1961; rpt. (paperback), Madison, 1963

Monographs

"Barnabe Barnes" and "Sir George Buc, Master of the Revels." In *Thomas Lodge and Other Elizabethans.* Ed. C. J. Sisson. Cambridge, Mass., 1933, Pp. 165–241, 409–506.
King Lear. An Outline Guide to the Play. New York, 1965.

Editions

Othello. Crofts Classics. New York, 1946.
Twelfth Night. Crofts Classics. New York, 1948.
Richard III. New York and London, 1964. Rpt. in *The Complete Signet Classic Shakespeare.* Gen. ed. Sylvan Barnet. New York, 1972.
The Macro Plays. Oxford: Early English Text Society, 1969.

Articles

"Middleton's Birth and Education." *Review of English Studies,* 7 (1931), 431–41.
"Arthur Massinger." *Times Literary Supplement,* 16 July 1931, p. 564.
"Whetstone's Death." *Times Literary Supplement,* 27 August 1931, p. 648.
"Spenser's First Marriage." *Times Literary Supplement,* 31 December 1931, p. 1053.
"The 'Mortal Moon' Sonnet." *Times Literary Supplement,* 15 February 1934, p. 108.
"Marlowe in Newgate." *Times Literary Supplement,* 6 September 1934, p. 604.
"Marlowe in Kentish Tradition." *Notes and Queries,* 169 (1935), 20–23, 39–41, 58–61.

"Jonson's Marriage." *Review of English Studies*, 12 (1936), 257–72.

"'Memorandums of the Immortal Ben.'" *Modern Language Notes*, 51 (1936), 520–23.

"Jonson and the Spies." *Review of English Studies*, 13 (1937), 385–97.

"Samuel Daniel in France and Italy." *Studies in Philology*, 34 (1937), 148–67.

"Thomas Dekker: Burial-place." *Notes and Queries*, 177 (1939), 157.

"Francis Beaumont's *Grammar Lecture*." *Review of English Studies*, 16 (1940), 402–14.

"A Biographical Dictionary of Elizabethan Authors." *Huntington Library Quarterly*, 5 (1942), 281–302.

"Shakespeare's Use of *Look How* and Similar Idioms." *Journal of English and Germanic Philology*, 42 (1943), 396–400.

"Elizabethan Edmund Spensers." *Modern Language Quarterly*, 5 (1944), 413–27.

"Chapman's Early Years." *Studies in Philology*, 43 (1946), 176–93.

"'Thomas Middleton a Poett.'" *Studies in Philology*, 54 (1957), 516–36.

"Bynneman's Books." *The Library*, 12 (1957), 81–92.

"Martin Peerson and the Blackfriars." *Shakespeare Survey*, 11 (1958), 100–106.

"Anthony Munday." In *Studies in the English Renaissance Drama*. Ed. Josephine W. Bennett, Oscar Cargill, and Vernon Hall. New York, 1959. Pp. 95–105.

"Sir John Beaumont," "Jeremy Collier," "John Heywood," "Henry Howard Earl of Surrey." In *Collier's Encyclopedia*, 1960.

"Sir John Beaumont," "Samuel Daniel," "Barnabe Googe," "Thomas Middleton," "George Turberville." In *Encyclopaedia Britannica*, 1960–.

"Ludus Coventriae: Lincoln or Norfolk?" *Medium AEvum*, 40 (1971), 135–41.

"Emendations in Whetstone's 'Promos and Cassandra.'" *Notes and Queries*, 216 (1971), 12–13.

"Research in the Humanities." In *The University of Wisconsin: 125 years*. Ed. Allan G. Bogue and Robert Taylor. Madison, 1975. Pp. 228–36.

"Words and Proverbs from Thomas Whythorne." *Notes and Queries*, 219 (1974), 405–7.

Index

Lodge, Thomas, 13, 18
London and its environs: Aldgate, 3; Islington, 3; Middlesex, 3; Westminster, 3; Surrey, 3; Fleet Street, 4; London Bridge, 4; Newington, 4; Stepney, 4; Whitechapel Road, 4; Shoreditch, 4, 9, 10; Gracechurch-Bishopsgate Street, 4, 129; mentioned, 2–13 passim
Lope de Vega: *Castelvines y Monteses*, 60
Lorca, Federico García, 74
Lord Chamberlain, 7
Lord Mayor of London, 7, 8, 9
Lorris, Guillaume de, 60
Lucas, F. L., 122, 126
Luecke, Jane Marie, O.S.B., 175n*19*
Lupton, Thomas: *The Second Part of . . . Too Good To Be True*, 108, 109
Lyly, John: *Campaspe*, 12; *The Woman in the Moon*, 12; mentioned, 2, 13, 46

McClure, N.E., 172n*11*
McDonald, Charles Osborne, 178n*19*
Machiavelli, Niccolo, 53
Manningham, John, 58
Markels, Julian, 173n*1*
Marlowe, Christopher: *Doctor Faustus*, 14, 73; *Tamburlaine*, 61, 73; *Edward II*, 73; *The Jew of Malta*, 145; mentioned, 13, 19, 46, 47, 59, 105, 127, 159
Marlowe and Nashe: *Dido Queen of Carthage*, 59
Marston, John: *The Malcontent*, 19, 145; mentioned, 21, 120, 122, 124, 125, 137
Massinger, Philip: *Believe As You List*, 23, 24
Master of the Revels, 7
Matthieu de Vendôme, 121
Meun, Jean de, 60
Merchant, W. Moelwyn, 50, 55
Meyer, Leonard, 156–57, 161
Middleton, Thomas: *The Changeling*, 126, 127, 131, 137; *Women Beware Women*, 127; mentioned, 21, 126–27, 130, 176
Milton, John: *Comus*, 116
Montaigne, Michel de, 68
Moore, Don D., 175n*1*
Muir, Kenneth, 174n*1*
Mulryne, J. R., 123, 124, 175n*22*
Munday, Anthony, 9, 24
Munro, John, 170n*8*
Murray, Peter B., 177n*12*

Nashe, Thomas, 13
Nicoll, Allardyce, 178n*15*
Northbrooke, John, 9
Norwich, 3, 13

Oliver, H. J., 178n*2*
Ornstein, Robert, 153, 177n*10*
Overbury, Sir Thomas: *Characters*, 124

Ovid, 59, 71, 102
Oxford University, 12, 13, 59

Paul's Children of, 2, 4, 8
Peele, George: *Endymion*, 12; mentioned, 13, 18, 19, 46. *See also The Battle of Alcazar*
Perkins, William, 146
Peter, John, 177n*7*
Pickering, Thomas, 178n*17*
Plato, 60, 95
Plautus, 60
Plays of Plays and Pastimes, 13
Plutarch: *Lives*, 103
Poel, William, 16
Preston, Thomas: *Cambises*, 4, 5, 11
Price, Hereward T., 120, 175n*11*
Privy Council, 6, 7, 8
Prouty, Charles T., 169n*2*
Prynne, William: *Histriomastix*, 170n*8*
Ptolome, 11

Queen's Men, 7, 12
Quintus Fabius, 59

Racine, Jean: *Phèdre*, 74
Red Lion Inn (Stepney), 4, 10
Reese, M. M., 47
Revels Office, 6
Ribner, Irving, 177n*7*
Rich's Men, 12
Richard II/Thomas of Woodstock, 23, 24
Riche, Barnabe: *The Adventures of Brusanus Prince of Hungaria*, 117, 174–75n*1*
Rochester, John Wilmot, Earl of, 123
Rose, Mark, 171n*3*
Rose playhouse, 10
Ross, Lawrence J., 177n*7*
Rossiter, A. P., 66
Rouillet, Claude: *Philanira*, 108
Rowley, William, 18, 170n*4*
Royden, Mathew, 12, 13
Ruth, Léon, 178n*16*

St. Botolph's Church (Aldgate), 3
St. Paul's, 9
Salingar, L. G., 142, 178n*18*
Saracen's Head Inn (Islington), 3
Schücking, L. L., 36
The Second Shepherds' Play, 61
Seneca, 59, 71, 124, 125, 173n*4*
Sensabaugh, George F., 175n*19*
Seven Deadly Sins, 19
Shakespeare, William: *All's Well that Ends Well*, 25, 32, 34, 46, 170n*2*; *Antony and Cleopatra*, 42–44, 47, 49, 52, 57, 71, 73, 80, 121, 170n*2*; *As You Like It*, 25, 79, 80; *The Comedy of Errors*, 32, 60, 170n*2*; *Coriolanus*, 39–40, 41, 121, 170n*2*, 171n*15*; *Hamlet*, 16, 28, 31, 40–41, 42, 53, 57, 69, 70,